A HISTORY OF
DELANO
PENNSYLVANIA

1861–1931

by

H. O. Moser

HERITAGE BOOKS
2019

HERITAGE BOOKS
AN IMPRINT OF HERITAGE BOOKS, INC.

Books, CDs, and more—Worldwide

For our listing of thousands of titles see our website
at
www.HeritageBooks.com

A Facsimile Reprint
Published 2019 by
HERITAGE BOOKS, INC.
Publishing Division
5810 Ruatan Street
Berwyn Heights, Md. 20740

Originally published 1931

— Publisher's Notice —
In reprints such as this, it is often not possible to remove blemishes from the original. We feel the contents of this book warrant its reissue despite these blemishes and hope you will agree and read it with pleasure.

International Standard Book Numbers
Paperbound: 978-0-7884-2837-1
Clothbound: 978-0-7884-9272-3

Mrs. George Folweiler

To

MRS. GEORGE FOLWEILER

whose life of fifty years in Delano has been a constant influence for good and who has directed the footsteps of several generations of young people in the ways of righteousness, this book is affectionately dedicated by the writer, who was one of her "boys" in years long past.

FOREWORD

A PREFACE to a history may be as pointless as an index to a dictionary, but the compiler of these chronicles has in his heart a desire to speak a personal word to his readers before venturing upon the arduous, but pleasant, task of falling into step with the march of events moving down through the years that have encompassed life in old Delano from its beginning to this day.

Youth has a spiritual quality that is lost to maturer years. It invests the days of childhood with a glory that transcends all things material. The tears that flow at childish griefs melt quickly and easily into laughter and when youth is gone and adult responsibilities press hard on every hand, memories of its happy days still remain to compensate for the most trying hours the world can offer.

These reflections come to the mind of the writer as he approaches this work, induced by precious recollections of childhood's enchanted hours spent with friends beloved in the little railroad town on the mountain-top. Out of the joy of the reunions of 1930 and 1931 came the idea of this history, which grew rapidly into a settled purpose as awakening thoughts retraced the almost forgotten paths to days long gone.

The historian spent nine years of his boyhood in Delano—not many years, perhaps, in the span of life, but those years that contain this spiritual essence; when each day holds within itself a complete romance, when adventure lurks behind each rock and tree. The years that never die, but live always, and spring into new life at memory's least behest.

And what a delightful undertaking this old-timer has set for himself. For months past he has been reaching out in every direction, touching friends here, there and everywhere; reading delightful letters, collecting from many sources bits of information, facts hitherto unknown to him, personal reminiscences, court records, old documents and pictures—everything most intensely interesting. And above all, receiving the finest sort of co-operation and encouragement from the old-time friends; confirming his own conviction that a permanent record of the events woven into three-score years and ten of life in Delano would be wholly worthwhile.

Acknowledgment is due to many friends for needed help in the way of information, pictures and local color. It is not possible to mention all by name, but the writer is particularly indebted for valuable material and unremitting co-operation to these former and present Delano people: William McCarroll, Robert Swank, Esq., William Campbell, William C. Keiber, Professor J. M. Schrope, Professor Maurice Singley, Mrs. Anna Swank Bailey, Mrs. Miriam Moore, Charles Collum, Robert Martin, Miss Annie Bretz, Mrs. George Folweiler, Mrs. Ruth Engle, Garfield James, Llewellyn Bannan, Albert Werner, Esq., F. Clare Bickle, George Hofmann, John J. Neifert, Harry Shafer, John Houser, Al Zimmerman, Miss Florence Richards; and to K. C. Hopper, Division Passenger Agent for the Lehigh Valley Railroad at Bethlehem, Pa.; Frederic A. Delano, a son of Warren Delano, in whose honor the town was named, and Mr. H. Sillcox, District Land Agent for the Lehigh Valley Railroad at Wilkes-Barre, Pa. To these kind friends, and all others who shared in the work, his sincere appreciation goes out.

In this first excursion into the field of extended literary effort, the writer covets the sympathetic understanding of his readers, believing that the story which follows will infuse new life into hallowed memories and that across the pages of this book will move again the dreams and hopes, the joys and griefs of bygone days, mellowed now by the gentle touch of time, but still potent to stir the heart and move the soul.

BOOK ONE

Delano, Pennsylvania

CHAPTER I

Delano

THIS book is meant to be more than an historical fact-finding report. The history of any place cannot, of course, be true to its purpose without setting forth accurately and in orderly fashion the outstanding events and incidents that through the years have been woven into the fabric which we call community life. And that those who read this book might have the assurance that it is more than just a story and has genuine historical value, the most careful and painstaking efforts have been made to verify the data out of which it has been constructed. Thorough searching of records, checking, re-checking and comparing information received from those who dipped into the store-houses of memory, tracing down every lead that promised valuable material—all these consumed months of time and hour upon hour of arduous toil. As the events here related unfold themselves to the reader, let him be confident that they are as true to the facts as the most conscientious effort could make them.

But if we should content ourselves with a mere recital of facts, however necessary they are to any serious historical record, the result would be as tasteless and dull to the reader as the perusal of life expectancy tables to a centenarian. A wise man long ago wisely said that the real history of a nation is written in the biographies of its great men. Epochs, dates, records—all these have their part in the orderly presentation of historical truth; but they are, after all, only the means by which the truth is preserved and the instruments employed in revealing it. The heart of the truth itself is in the achievements of men; the hopes and ambitions and strivings, the joys and sorrows, the courage and unbending purpose to reach set goals, the pride of accomplishment and satisfied contemplation of work well-done and ends attained; these are some of the threads that are caught up into Life's looms and woven into the many-hued patterns we call History.

With these things in mind, the compiler of this record approaches his difficult task—the setting down in order of the momentous facts and human relationships that have made up the life of the little mountain town of Delano, in the County of Schuylkill and State of Pennsylvania, over its Biblical span of three-score years and ten, from the date of its founding in 1861 to the day of this record.

The question may be raised as to this compiler's right to set himself up as the historian of a town from which he has been separated for thirty-five years. The answer to that pertinent question is, that he has long felt that his own abiding affection for the old town is shared by all those who at one time or another knew it as home and that a permanent record of its history would be welcomed eagerly by the hundreds of former residents who have long since been sojourning in other places. It is true that this story might more appropriately have been written by some present resident of Delano, and certainly there are such who are eminently qualified for the task, but as a prophet is not without honor save in his own country, so seemingly a town is not without due appreciation save among its own people. Apparently, the factors of time and distance are needed to furnish the perspective necessary to a correct appraisal of the worth of a community, even as in the case of humankind.

Looking back from this distance, it has seemed good to this writer to gather up the threads of achievement that in many respects have elevated Delano to a place of importance out of all proportion to its size, and to give permanence to those things in its history that approach uniqueness. That this undertaking is most timely has been impressed upon him forcibly in his quest for facts. Only a few of those whose memories go back to pioneer days are left. And it is fortunate for the success of this work that they have marvelous memories as well as a lasting affection for the home of their childhood, and that they gave glad co-operation to the historian.

This story, then, shall seek to record personal achievements, bits of biography, perhaps some little autobiography, matters of industrial importance, social and religious life, educational and fraternal interests, as they relate to Delano; all so permeated with warmth and color that the reader may live again the happy days of the long ago, or, if now residing there, that he may look upon his residence with a new pride as befits one who has a place in the life of a community of no mean reputation.

Geographically, Delano is located in the northeastern portion of Schuylkill County, in the eastern part of Pennsylvania, being the principal community in the township bearing the same name. Originally it was a part of the old township of Rush, but was made an independent political subdivision in 1882, of which more detailed information is given later in this book. It occupies a strategic place in the heart of that portion of the rich anthracite region known as the Lower Anthracite Field; this location, indeed, being directly responsible for the existence of the town and its importance as a railroad center.

Topographically, it occupies an elevated plateau almost on the top of the Mahanoy Mountain, some distance northeast of its juncture with the Broad Mountain. This plateau is flanked to the northeast and north by the sweeping curve of the higher portions of the Mahanoy Mountain, these higher points being among the highest elevations in the State. The town site itself is about 1,200 feet above sea level. Westward and southwestward the plateau stretches for several miles almost on a level, furnishing a straightaway course for the strong winter gales that sweep down from the high places and lash the old town with the Arctic fury that has made Delano winters traditional. Eastward and southward the plateau falls away abruptly into the valleys below, a narrow pass to the east breaking through the mountains and making an outlet for railroad traffic into the Quakake Valley, which gateway was a deciding factor in selecting this place for the town's location.

Delano, as everyone knows, is a railroad town. More especially, it is a Lehigh Valley Railroad town; a statement which carries more meaning than the uninitiated reader may suspect. The town was built for the Lehigh Valley Railroad, controlled by the Lehigh Valley Railroad, derived and derives its total sustenance from the Lehigh Valley Railroad, and, until very recent years, was owned in toto by the Lehigh Valley Railroad.

To the youngster who grew up in the town years ago, the words "railroad" and "Lehigh Valley" were two ways of saying the same thing. In later years came vague reports of the existence of other railroads, and when maturer years enabled him to loosen home ties and travel abroad, he came back to boast to stay-at-homes that he had traveled on the Pennsy, or Reading, or other foreign roads. These stories made little impression on the minds of Delano youth. Big folks might admit that there were other roads with their good points. The youngsters could accept the idea of other roads, but, in the matter of points, there was only one Lehigh Valley. Didn't their dads build the engines that ran on the Lehigh? Or, if they didn't build them, they ran them. Answer that, if you can. When this story has all been told, it will be found that this youthful conviction arose not only from the enthusiasms of youth, but rested as well upon solid bases of fact.

The population of Delano probably never much exceeded 1,200 souls, and for the greater part of its existence it has varied little numerically. This has been due to limitations of expansion in a physical way, and not to industrial reasons. The area of the site upon which the town is built, which was owned formerly by the Delano Land Company and later by the Lehigh Valley Railroad Company, is 255 acres. Within this restricted area were constructed necessary shop buildings, round houses, offices, freight and railroad stations, railroad yards and residences. At no time in Delano's history was such a thing as a vacant house heard of. There always has been a waiting list of applicants for homes there.

Westward, southward and eastward of the town was ample space for building sites, but whether the company considered it unwise to expand the town beyond its present limits, or whether the additional acreage could not be acquired, the historian is not able to say. It is likely, though, that mining operations made it impracticable to use these outlying sections for building developments. It is known to all Delano people that mining activities made it necessary years ago to remove a whole street from its original location to other parts of the town. Also that mine breaches opened up within a hundred yards or less of the school building and that a change in the location of the highway leading westward to Mahanoy City had to be made for that reason.

Had the growth of Delano kept pace with its industrial development, the population might well have reached 4,000 or more. At one time over three hundred fifty men were employed in the shops alone and probably many more than that on the railroad. The

WARREN DELANO IN 1866
AT AGE OF 57
Text Page 16

WARREN DELANO IN 1857
(AT AGE OF 48) WITH SARA, AGED 3 (NOW MRS.
JAMES ROOSEVELT) AND WARREN, JR., AGED 5
(1852-1920)
Text Page 16

greater portion of the employees, of necessity, lived in surrounding towns and country.

Although the town never attained prominence in the matter of size, it boasted, from the beginning, an unusual class of citizens. Many of the first settlers came direct from the English Isles and Germany. English, Irish, Welsh and Germans, with a large proportion of native-born, made up the population, and nearly all of them skilled workers in the mechanical trades. This gave the town, from the beginning, a select type of citizens, who have maintained to this day an enviable reputation in many spheres of human endeavor. It is the recollection of these outstanding qualities in town and people that has kept warm in the hearts of the little town's wandering sons and daughters an abiding affection and interest.

With this brief general survey, let us turn our attention to a more specific view of the varied phases of life in Delano.

CHAPTER II

Before the Beginning

NO ATTEMPT is here being made to trace back to early Pennsylvania history land titles or records as they relate to the Delano tract. It is necessary, however, to any intelligent consideration of the reasons for founding the town, that we review the part played by the natural resources of the region in attracting the attention of those who came before the founders.

Turn back the hands of Time seventy-five or eighty years and beyond, and let us traverse the plateau on which the town now stands and the sloping hills surrounding it; if, indeed, we can penetrate the dense growth of great stately trees then found here. "This is the forest primeval," might well be our cry, in the words of the poet who wrote so glowingly of his New England wilderness. Here were magnificent specimens of virgin pine, hemlock and hardwoods, standing rank upon rank, stretching in silent and unbroken grandeur over mile after mile of majestic woodlands. The sound of the axe and the saw had not yet been heard and the despoiling hand of man was yet withheld. The deep, cool depths of this mighty forest heard little of the tread of human footsteps, save those of an occasional white hunter, or, perhaps, an Indian who passed this way. Wild life was abundant—deer, bear, wild-cat, panther, with smaller game animals—these lived here almost unmolested. Passenger pigeons came in clouds to alight on the giant gum trees, and myriads of other birds added color and life to the primitive picture.

At the time that Delano was founded, no roads had yet been built through the place upon which it is located. The nearest highway was an old turnpike connecting Tamaqua and other towns to the south with Catawissa and towns to the north and west. This turnpike ran quartering along the Quakake side of the mountain and passed near the location of the present Lehigh Valley Railroad arch to the crest of the mountain just north of Delano, thence across this table-land westwardly and through and over a rugged terrain of valley and mountain into the Catawissa Valley. Traces of this road are still to be found and any Delano youngster who picked huckleberries along the Lofty road some distance north of Bunker Hill will remember the old cross roads there, this being a landmark of the Catawissa turnpike. Over this pike a stage coach plied its way between Tamaqua and Catawissa, driven by Isaac Mason, father of Ollie Mason, both of whom were later residents of Delano.

From this old highway, at a point near the railroad arch, a rough path was cut over the hill and down the other side across the Delano plain and on to Mahanoy City. This was cut by Joseph Neifert, of Quakake, then supervisor of Rush Township, and father of the Neifert boys who have had an important part in the operation of the Lehigh Valley Railroad for the past fifty years. This path at the time the town was established constituted the sole means of ingress and regress to and from the place.

There are still some of the pioneers of the early days in Delano who speak of the thick forests which surrounded the first buildings erected there and the wilderness-like conditions in which they dwelt. William McCarroll, affectionately known to his many friends as "Major," who came to Delano at the age of eight, just four years after the first house was built, and who now resides in Philadelphia, tells of having seen deer and bear within sight of the little settlement, and, on one or two occasions, Indians passing through. Mrs. Jonathan Bretz, one of Delano's oldest residents, and still enjoying life in the little town, tells of traveling when a girl with her father from Mahanoy City to Quakake over the path just described, and that frequently on these trips her father would shoot at deer and bear which roamed over the mountain between Delano and Quakake.

The writer himself can recall the great grove of trees that stood back of his home in Swamppoodle in the 80's and reached back to the reservoirs and over the mountains to the north. What a wonderful playground it provided for the children of that day! And who among the middle-aged former or present Delanoites does not recall the great pine forest just "over the hill" that provided a splendid recreation center for a whole region. The Picnic Ground! For years it was the mecca of picnickers for twenty miles around, coming in great excursions to make merry there.

But the gifts of a beneficent Providence to this region were not all visible to the eye of man. Deep beneath the surface, ages before, had been stored billions of tons of heat and power in the form of anthracite, and the discovery and development of this great natural resource provided the stimulus to the enterprise of man which in turn set in motion the forces of commerce that brought into existence the "big" little village that is the subject of this work.

In the early 50's, the development of the anthracite business in the Lower Field had reached large proportions and had attracted the attention of wealthy men in the great cities of the East. The year 1854 was one of the prosperous years in the early history of the industry and many city capitalists were led to seek investments in this field. Already annual shipments of anthracite to sea-board were running into millions of tons and railroads were being extended into the region to facilitate the carrying of the product to market.

It was early in this decade that Warren Delano, a prominent New York capitalist, together with his brother, Franklin H. Delano, John Forbes and Peter Brooks, of Boston, with others, including Judge Asa Packer, of Mauch Chunk, Pa., was attracted to the anthracite country by the promise of profitable industrial development of virgin coal territory. Several thousands of acres of land were acquired, the titles to these tracts being traceable to various original warrants from the Commonwealth of Pennsylvania. Included in these tracts was the 255-acre tract which makes up the town-plot of Delano.

Warren Delano, before becoming interested in coal lands in Schuylkill County, had been in the mercantile business in China, and, in 1859, during the panic which started in 1857, he returned to China where he resumed and continued his business for a number of years, leaving his Pennsylvania affairs in the hands of his brother, Franklin. These facts have been furnished the writer by Frederic A. Delano, youngest son of Warren Delano, who is a prominent engineer of Washington, D. C. By courtesy of Mr. Delano, two photographs of his father, Warren Delano, have been made available for this book and it is a privilege to reproduce them here in recognition of his important connection with the industrial development of the region.

The one picture of Mr. Delano was taken in Paris in 1866 and the other, taken in 1857 when he was forty-eight years old, includes two of his children: Sara, at the age of three, who was later to become the wife of James Roosevelt and the mother of the present Governor of New York, Franklin Roosevelt; and Warren, Jr., at the age of five, who was for many years connected with anthracite mining at New Boston, having died in 1920. Mrs. Roosevelt is still living at her home in New York. These pictures of Mr. Delano were taken at the time he was actively interested in mining lands surrounding the town of Delano.

It is quite obvious that the town received its name from this prominent family, whose activities in promoting the resources of that section resulted directly in bringing Delano into being. Warren Delano, as the head of this enterprise, is recognized here as the one most entitled to credit for giving the town a place on the map.

In 1857 occurred a severe business panic which almost paralyzed the anthracite business for the time. Many of the men who had invested their capital in this section hastened to dispose of their holdings, getting out at great financial sacrifice. Warren Delano, his brother, Franklin, and a few others, among them Judge Packer, refused to let go of their interests and later organized several mining corporations for developing their tracts. Among these was the New Boston Land Company, which is still in existence. This company gave its name to the little mining village of New Boston and promoted extensive mining operations.

In the year 1872 the interests of Warren Delano and his associates in the 255-acre plot comprising the town of Delano were conveyed to the Delano Land Company, a corporation made up of Philadelphia capitalists and a number from Mauch Chunk, Pa. The Delano Land Company held title to the ground until 1891, when it was conveyed to the Lehigh Valley Railroad Company, which had for many years leased it from the Land Company.

It will be noticed that Warren Delano and his associates were the owners in fee of the site of Delano during the first twelve years of its existence.

With this glance at the conditions antedating the establishing of the town, we pass to an examination of the industrial considerations that were the immediate factors that brought Delano into being.

CHAPTER III

The Beginning

THE rapid development of the anthracite industry in the Mahanoy region and westward to Shenandoah and Mount Carmel, with the ever increasing markets in eastern cities, and the growing rivalry among the various transportation companies for this rich business, formed the combination that resulted directly in the founding of Delano in 1861.

The Philadelphia and Reading Railway, with its connections with other lines and with the Schuylkill Canal, was making great strides in annexing the coal transportation business in this section. Judge Asa Packer and other capitalists, who had invested heavily in coal lands in the Mahanoy area, realized that great advantage would accrue to their coal interests and large profits could be gained in the transportation field if a direct route could be opened to the canal at East Mauch Chunk, which was already receiving large shipments of anthracite from the Hazleton and Beaver Meadows territory. Judge Packer was heavily interested in the Lehigh Valley Railroad and in the canal at Mauch Chunk. Already a single-track line had been built from Black Creek Junction up through the Quakake Valley to connect with the Catawissa and Reading Railroads at Quakake. This road was built by a contractor named John H. Osborn, of Morrisville, Pa., who boarded at the home of Michael Reynolds in the Quakake Valley while he had the work under way.

The junction of the line from Black Creek with the Catawissa at Quakake was only two miles from the Delano coal tracts and a way was soon made to carry it to the desired goal. The Quakake Valley line had been built by the Lehigh and Mahanoy Railroad, chartered in 1857, and on March 22, 1859, a supplement to this charter was granted which authorized the extension westwardly of this road to the headwaters of and down the Mahanoy Creek 'as far as expedient'; with authority to make connection with any railroad in the valley and to construct branches.

The extension of this line presented no insurmountable engineering difficulties, in spite of the formidable Mahanoy Mountain which raised its bulk to the west of the Quakake terminus. The engineers for the railway were familiar with mountain problems in this section and their lines for the new route carried the road on a rather stiff grade along the side of old Mahanoy and swung around the shoulder of the mountain well toward the summit through what is now known as "Haak's Cut," thence along the southeast side of the mountain through the pass or ravine to which reference was made in a previous chapter, and on to the site where the town was soon to be.

The building of this extension was begun in 1861 and was under the direct charge of Michael Reynolds, later assistant road foreman of the Lehigh Valley Railroad, and to be the first permanent resident of Delano, who had had years of experience in railroad construction. The contract for building the line was held by Peter and James Collins, of Ebensburg, Pa., for whom Mr. Reynolds acted as construction superintendent. The Collins brothers were located in Delano during the continuance of the contract, boarding at one of the temporary boarding houses erected to accommodate the men employed at this work. The part of Delano that was later to be known as "The Patch" was in the beginning called Collinsville. Mrs. Miriam Moore furnished the writer with a photograph of Mr. Peter Collins, whom she describes as a fine gentleman. This picture is made a part of the record.

By the early part of 1863 the road had been completed as far as Mahanoy City, Pa., the first passenger train to operate from Delano to Mahanoy City being run on June 19th, 1863. Mount Carmel was reached in 1865, where the new line connected with the Northern Central Railway. This road was at first single track. The portion from Quakake to Delano was double-tracked in 1876.

An interesting personal incident touching the building of the road from Quakake to Delano is related by Mrs. George Folweiler, who still resides in Delano. Her parents, Mr. and Mrs. Stephen Mowery, at that time had their home in the country near Haak's, just at the foot of the mountain, and quite a number of the men working on the construction gangs found board and lodging in this home. Mrs. Folweiler still has most vivid recollections of standing on a chair by her mother's side drying the interminable number of dishes needed to serve the largely-increased family.

As the new railroad approached the goal set, it became evident to the builders that a permanent place would be needed to locate the operating forces and power equipment, as well as the classification yards necessary for handling the traffic that they knew would develop rapidly out of the new venture. The natural advantages of the Delano plateau made it the logical place for the new railroad center. Here was the needed space for yards, engine houses, shops, stations, homes, and other appurtenances thereunto belonging.

Here, too, Nature had provided the ideal topography for handling business of this kind. The grades from the mines to the proposed yards would be moderately ascending, making it an easy matter to bring the coal from the mines in small trains, the output of each mine to be handled by a single train crew, as is still the custom; while the grade to the canal boats which carried the coal to tidewater was a steadily descending one, so that one crew could handle a large train made up in the yards from the smaller ones brought from the mines. The return of the cars to the yards would be easily accomplished, since their burden of six tons per car would be left in the coal pockets at the head of the canal.

So it was, that in the early part of 1861 the ambition and enterprise of man began clearing this unbroken wilderness for a new center of industrial activity, bringing into existence a town never destined to become mighty in numbers, but of wide importance because of the things wrought within its confines and because of the men and women whose lives were molded in the atmosphere of this little railroad center and who carried to far places of our land the skill of hand, the keenness of mind and the fineness of character that developed naturally in this wholesome American community.

CHAPTER IV

The Pioneers

EVERY age has its pioneers. We are wont to associate the term with the years of long ago. The schoolboy of fifty years ago could not conceive of a pioneering age that bore a date mark later than the time of the Pilgrim Fathers, or, mayhap, the days of sturdy Daniel Boone and those other early Americans who pushed westward the frontiers of our great land. And yet, his age was a pioneering age, as is every age. The latest age is always the greatest pioneering age. To consider the achievements of this day is to prove it. Pioneers in aviation, in automotive fields, in radio, in the advance of electrical science and the countless advances in scientific discoveries generally, as well as in all other places of human activity, have opened new vistas, beaten new paths and enlarged horizons beyond the wildest dreams of the old-time pioneers.

The first settlers of our little community were pioneers in the true sense of the word. The things they wrought here stamped upon them the hall-mark of genuine pioneering accomplishment. They came much in the manner and spirit of the old heroes of the schoolboy; for it was into a veritable wilderness that they set foot and, by virtue of stout hearts and sturdy souls, combined with strong determination and dogged purpose, they wrested from the forest a place to make their homes and to make their industrial dreams come true.

During the construction period of the new railroad, many temporary buildings had been erected at the present location of Delano to accommodate the working forces. Among others, a boarding house was operated by a family named Paddick, who had come from Ebensburg, Pa., with the Collins'. They remained in Delano for some time after the completion of the contract, and it was in their family that the first death in the new town occurred, a daughter of about twenty years of age dying very shortly after the town was permanently established. These temporary buildings were erected along the right-of-way of the railroad, in the general vicinity of the old station building which was later to be erected.

The first permanent resident of the new town was Michael Reynolds, who came with his family about 1861. He had charge of the construction of the railroad from Quakake and later became assistant road master for the Mahanoy Division. Mr. Reynolds came from Ireland as a boy, having been born there in 1831. He was still a young man when he made his home in Delano. He learned railroad construction work with the Richmond and Danville Railroad in 1851, helped build the Camden-Atlantic City Railroad in 1854 and worked at similar work in Lebanon and Schuylkill Counties prior to his location in Delano. He is credited with having laid the first rail on the Camden-Atlantic City Railroad. He remained a resident of Delano until his death in 1881, when he was killed in a wreck on the Mahanoy City branch near Park Place.

The first house to be permanently occupied in Delano was that which housed the family of Mr. Reynolds. When first built, it stood almost on the spot of the house later occupied by David Fletcher and family, just in the rear of the brick office building. Later it was moved across the railroad east of the station building, where it remained for many years. It was a small single, frame structure.

In this little home was born the first baby in Delano—Margaret Reynolds, who is now Mrs. Clinton Engle, and who has had a continuous residence in Delano since that time. Mrs. Engle was born on October 28th, 1864, and she still resides within a few yards of the spot where she was born. She can boast of a continuous residence in Delano of over sixty-seven years and to her and her four sisters belongs the proud distinction of being Delano's First Family. Three of these sisters were also born in Delano and one of them, Mrs. Irvin Gouldner, has continued her residence there until this time. A photograph of Mrs. Engle, Delano's first-born, is shown here.

The second child born in Delano was Julia Le Van, daughter of Henry Le Van, the first train dispatcher employed at Delano. She was born in February, 1866. Mrs. Julia Le Van Person is now residing in Allentown, Pa. Mary Fegley, daughter of Jesse and Mrs. Fegley, and later to become the wife of Willis Fegley, was the

Peter Collins
Text Page 19

Mrs. Margaret Reynolds Engle
First Child Born in Delano
Text Page 22

Samuel Depew
Text Page 23

Levi Artz
Text Page 23

third child born in the town, in May, 1866. Mrs. Fegley died in Lehighton several years ago.

The erection of homes for the accommodation of the men who were employed in the pioneering work went along apace, and these were occupied as fast as completed. The first homes were built in the vicinity of the one occupied by Mr. Reynolds, being generally along the railroad right-of-way. Samuel Depew, Sr., who became a permanent resident of Delano in 1866, had charge of the construction of nearly all the houses built in Delano. He was the father of J. A. Depew and his brothers and sisters, all of whom were prominent in Delano history for many years. An excellent picture of Mr. Depew appears in this book, with one of another pioneer, Levi Artz, father of Mrs. J. A. Depew.

The population of the town was limited to just a few families until about 1865, when the total number of residences was sixteen, including boarding houses. From that date a very rapid increase in the number of homes and residents began.

The historian is pleased to quote here from material furnished him by William McCarroll, touching upon life in Delano in these early days. Says Mr. McCarroll:

"My father came to Delano in the latter part of 1864 at the request of Mr. A. A. Mitchell, the first master mechanic. He had been recommended by Mr. R. W. Wilder, superintendent of the Mine Hill Railroad. My father and mother and I, and a dog, arrived in Delano on Sunday afternoon, May 5th, 1865. I remember distinctly it was a beautiful day. The first night in town I slept on the floor of a large living room behind a stove in the house of Newton Sheriff, an engineer on the road.

"There was no house for us at Delano at that time and my father secured accommodations for us in Quakake in the home of Mrs. Shuler. The following day, on Monday, we went there to live for several months, until a house could be built for us. Mrs. Shuler was a dear old German lady who was better known as "Mammy." Here I had the time of my life chasing the chickens, ducks and geese. There was a creek close to the door full of fish and with all these new features for entertainment and the green apples, I had plenty to do.

"They started to build the house we were to occupy and in the Fall we moved to Delano. This house was built down the railroad and opposite the coal dump. It was the regulation style of Delano double house. There were two small single houses on each side of our house and on the opposite side of the tracks there was one small shanty. Farther north there was one large single house built for Mr. Le Van, who was the train dispatcher, and farther north and near the wagon road was another small single house (the Reynolds home), a building for a station, office and supply house. Across the wagon road was a small water tank and directly back of it, where the freight house now stands, was a building used for all wares and supplies. Northeast and on the right side of the wagon road were two small single houses. These were all the homes and buildings on the northeast side of the town.

"On the southwest side and back of the present brick station, were two double houses and south of the station was one very long single-story boarding house that would accommodate sixty to seventy-five men of the construction gangs. Then south in the Patch were two large and one smaller boarding houses for the construction gangs. Here were also two small two-story houses. This accounted for all the buildings in town except for a number of small shanties used by one or two men who had bachelor quarters there. Sixteen dwellings and boarding houses and two service buildings was the total number.

"Delano was built right in the thick woods. Trees had to be cut down to build. The hills and land were heavily timbered with pine, oak, chestnut and maple. Where Swamppoodle is built there was a very thick laurel and bushy swamp and big gum trees. All the way down to the wagon road and north for a distance were thick laurels and forest lands. These woods were full of pheasants. There were also a number of deer, bear, fox and wild cats, and the streams had many fine trout in them. On two occasions I saw Indians in town.

"Quite a number of houses of the regulation type were built from 1866 to 1869. In 1870 they built a large, three-story building on the northeast side of the tracks opposite the present brick station. This building was used for a boarding house, freight and passenger station, telegraph office and train dispatcher's quarters, and had one large room on the second floor with a well-stocked library."

This interesting sketch gives a graphic picture of those first days. The completion of the railroad into the mining fields and the consequent shipping of coal to market through this new outlet made necessary the increase in road equipment and crews to man it. This, in turn, raised questions of storage and maintenance for the equipment and homes for the crews. The first decade of the town's development saw the erection of many homes, station and office buildings, engine house and the first shop buildings. These shops, built in the first place to make necessary repairs to the engines, were destined to acquire world fame for the new ideas in engine construction that originated in the fertile mind of Alexander Mitchell, their first master mechanic. Later chapters will be devoted to the story of these shops.

It seems timely here to mention the names of a few of the first families to take residence in Delano in this first decade of its history. These include: Michael Reynolds in 1861, Michael Neary very shortly thereafter, David Fletcher in 1862, William Luckenbill (said to be the third family in the town) in 1864, Joshua Butler in 1864, Henry Le Van in 1864, Mrs. Cushing, Jerry Ryan and James Kelly in 1864, Jesse Fegley and Jacob Messersmith about 1864, William Opp in 1865, John McCarroll in 1865, Dennis Lynch in 1865, Charles Whitehead in 1866, Samuel Depew in 1866, Josiah Swank in 1867, Henry Barclay, Theodore Howell and Roland Correll in 1867, Thomas Donnelly very early in the 60's, Charles Mills in 1867, John McMullen in 1868, George Crossan in 1869; with others whose names the historian was not able to learn. These were the people who laid the foundations for the civic and industrial life of Delano seventy years ago.

We turn now to consider for awhile the industry upon which the town was founded, as it developed in this early period.

CHAPTER V

Early Railroading

UP TO the year 1866 the Lehigh and Mahanoy Railroad, chartered in 1857, operated the railroad through Delano, but in that year it was merged with the Lehigh Valley Railroad, by which it has since been operated.

The first equipment on the new line consisted of three Mogul engines and five ten-wheelers, all second-hand engines. The first engine actually to run into Delano was delivered at Quakake over the Catawissa Railroad and was taken to Delano under its own steam in 1863. It was a second-hand locomotive and was built by the Taunton Locomotive Works. It had two driving wheels on each side and a double truck in front and weighed twenty-eight tons. This will give the readers an idea of the size of the first locomotives as compared with the powerful monsters now used.

Other locomotives and cars were delivered at Quakake and some at Mahanoy City over the Reading Railway. Many supplies were at first hauled from Mahanoy City to Delano by teams. By the spring of 1865 a total of nine locomotives had been delivered for use at Delano.

The first superintendent of the Mahanoy Division was James I. Blakslee, who, with Judge Asa Packer, was one of the organizers of the Lehigh and Mahanoy Railroad. He was located at Mauch Chunk, which in the beginning was headquarters for the division. During the early part of this decade, Alonzo P. Blakslee, a son of James I. Blakslee, and who was later to take his place as superintendent, was employed on the engineering corps and came to Rush Township in 1863 and to Delano proper in 1871. He acted as assistant superintendent under his father, being in active charge of the division until his father's death, upon which he was made superintendent.

Delano was made division headquarters in 1865. The first train-dispatcher was Henry Le Van, who came to Delano with his family from Easton, Pa., late in 1863 or early in 1864. Mr. Le Van first boarded with the family of Mrs. Boughner at Tamanend and

Henry A. Le Van
First Train Dispatcher
Text Page 27

William McCarroll
Text Page 34

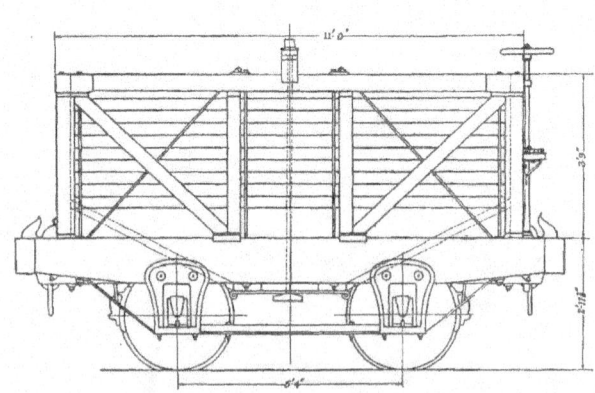

Old-Time Coal Car. Plate VIII
Text Page 30

brought his family to Delano when a house was ready for him. This house stood near the coal dump, facing west, immediately adjoining the Campbell home that was built later, and it was the same house later to be occupied by Frank Packer and his family.

Mr. Le Van later was instrumental in bringing to Delano Aaron Lattig, who was his assistant and later succeeded him as train dispatcher. Mr. Lattig also for a time conducted the boarding house. A photograph of Mr. Le Van was furnished for this volume by courtesy of Mrs. Miriam Moore, a daughter, and it is here shown. The first coal shipped over the new line out of this new division center went out in 1864 and the same year the building of the shops commenced, this work being completed in 1866. The first engine house was built in 1866. These dates indicate that real activity in operating the railroad at Delano began about 1865, as did the rapid increase in the operating forces and in the population of the town.

In these early days each train crew had its own engine, and the word "own" is used advisedly, for the engineer and fireman of one of the old-time consolidation engines could not have coddled their pet more had it actually been paid for out of their own hard-earned money. The most meticulous care was taken in keeping the engines entrusted to them in the finest state of mechanical perfection, as well as scrupulously clean. Woe unto the wiper boy who overlooked a speck of grease on rod, cross-head or guide. "Pools" and "bituminous" were two enemies to engine-pride that had not yet reared their ugly heads. And the old-time fireman had more to do in those twelve-hour days than to crack big lumps of anthracite and to feed his iron horse. Oil and lamp-black, with brass polish and plenty of elbow-grease, were as much a part of his everyday equipment as scoop, fire-hook and coal hammer. These were the days when the front brakeman was a sort of assistant fireman, whose duty it was to swing the fire-door as well as the hammer, and to serve his apprenticeship in other ways. The lot of the flagman was considerably different then than now. There was no warm, comfortable caboose furnished for easy riding and cold winter days. He rode the last little "hopper" in the train, and sometimes on bitter days built himself a little fire in the bottom of the car to keep from freezing.

The old-time engineers, by force of necessity, were compelled to be mechanics of considerable ability. They knew their engines from inside out and were usually able to bring them home at times under the serious handicaps of breakdowns and other disabilities. Their pride was centered not only on the appearance of their engines, but particularly on performance in speed and power. Many a classic of performance in these old days still survives in railroad annals and in the memories of the old-timers, to be retold and pondered over with other stirring tales of heroism, narrow escapes and many real tragedies of hazardous days in the old town.

In the old days of railroading every man started as a brakeman. His first duty usually was that of flagman, and from that position he was promoted through the various grades of brakeman to front man and assistant fireman, then to fireman, conductor and engineer. The man who arrived at the coveted position of engineer had been trained in the whole curriculum of train operation, and it was a poor engineer, indeed, who couldn't, and wouldn't, give the train dispatchers and train-masters, and, perhaps, even the superintendent himself, some valuable pointers on how trains should be run, whether these pointers were well-taken or not. But, speaking for Delano and the Mahanoy Division of the Lehigh Valley in those early days, there was a deep mutual respect between officials and men, each recognizing genuine railroading ability in the other and holding for each other an esteem that did not always show on the surface, but that was genuine nevertheless. These were days of direct personal contact instead of the present-day system of representative administration.

Among the engineers who drove the first locomotives in Delano, these names will be recalled by many Delano people: Fred Rutay, Nick and Fred Shillinger, William Luckenbill, John McCarroll, Joshua Riegel, Nick Weaver, John Kepp, Edward Kemmerer, William Stevenson, Edwin Fox, John Lyons, James and Michael Kelly, Stephen Koons, Harry Kistler, William Arner and William Opp. Many of these men came from Mauch Chunk, being experienced engineers before they came to Delano, and in the employ of the Lehigh Valley Railroad. A few continued in the service of the road at Delano for many years. John McCarroll and William Luckenbill came to Delano from the Mine Hill Railroad.

One of the writer's interesting recollections of railroading days in the 80's, which had not changed materially from the earliest days, is that of the pyrotechnic displays put on by the sturdy engines on dark nights. The use of anthracite as fuel in the days before spark arresters were known made every dark night the setting for displays that would put "The Last Days of Pompeii" to shame. What kid of those times has forgotten the sight that trailed after a doubleheader pounding along with a long string of the little six-ton hoppers—a stream of glowing sparks flowing from each stack that rivalled old Vesuvius in full eruption. The trainmen who had to ride the little hoppers did not always enjoy the display, for the hot sparks had a disconcerting way of landing on sensitive necks.

Mention has been made of the small coal cars used for many years before gondolas and present-day battleships came into existence. These cars, without automatic couplers and air-brakes with retaining valves, added greatly to the hazard of the work. A brakeman who had mastered the technic of running over a string of fifty or one hundred of the empty little hoppers when in swift motion might well have qualified for the slack-wire artist's job in a circus. When the ice and snow of severe winter days coated the naturally treacherous footing on the narrow sides and cross beams, the task was immensely more complicated and dangerous.

In bringing to mind the sight of one of those early trainmen in full flight over the funny little coal cars, it has often since occurred to the writer that the company should have maintained a training school with a competent dancing master to teach the rookies the steps before letting them risk their lives out on the road. For really, they performed very much like the dancers in a ballet. First the left foot on the end cross-piece (an up-ended plank about three inches wide), then the right foot to the right side, left foot to the sloping middle cross-piece (iron sheathed), right foot again to the side, left foot to the front cross-piece, bringing the right foot up to join the left; then start all over again on the next car, and so on from car to car as far as the journey had to go. And it had to be done swiftly, for when the engineer blew for brakes, he meant it. A Rocky Mountain sheep might well have become green with envy after watching an old-time Lehigh Valley brakeman do his stuff on a train of empties.

The hazards were not all in running over the cars. The oldfashioned three-link couplers added their terrors. The brakeman had to lift the heavy end link with one hand, or, if he had a good strong arm, with his brake-stick, while signalling the engineer with the other, see that the link properly caught the hook, and at the same time make sure that he himself was not caught between the bumpers. Accidents were numerous and tragedies in lost lives not infrequent.

Who of those former days can ever forget the clamor caused by the taking up of slack when a long train of "jimmies" got under way? It sometimes seemed to the observer that the engine had reached its destination before the last car in the train was yanked from its place. Here, too, the trainman riding the last car had to be alert to avoid being thrown from his perch. The stopping of a long coal train was no less interesting to the youngsters of that day, for, long after the front of the train had come to rest, the rest of the hoppers kept coming, each in turn giving the car ahead a resounding bump.

Plate No. VIII, among the illustrations in this volume, shows a drawing of one of these old-time coal cars, the sight of which should bring back some vivid memories to railroaders of forty years and more ago.

So much for the first few years of railroading in Delano.

CHAPTER VI

THE SHOPS

THIS chapter can begin in no better way than to quote again from material furnished by Mr. McCarroll.

"To many old Delano residents the 'shops' were Delano.

"In a large degree they meant the life of the little town and the modest comfort of the people. And yet, very few people have any conception of the importance, the value or the development which reached far into the world of industry of the locomotive that originated in the old Delano shops.

"No account of Delano can be complete without the proper emphasis on this phase of its history. The very design of the locomotive as it is today originated in the Delano shops back in the period from 1864 to 1867, under the direction of that skilled and far-seeing mind of Alexander A. Mitchell, the first Master Mechanic of the railroad. Mr. Mitchell designed and supervised the building of the shops at this early date of 1864, and when the work was started he conceived the idea of installing what is known as a "drop pit," a device for taking the wheels out from under the locomotive. At that time the locomotive was a very small thing, but when he made this innovation he had before him a vision of the great engine he wanted to build.

"When the shops were completed in 1867, they were regarded as the most modern and up-to-date of the day anywhere in the country, for Mr. Mitchell had builded well, with an eye to the future development of the locomotive.

"The first locomotive was delivered to Delano in the fall of 1863. Many locomotives were rebuilt and built new in the early days of the opening of the Delano shops of the Lehigh and Mahanoy Railroad. This first locomotive was a second-hand engine built by the Taunton Locomotive Company, with two driving-wheels on each side and a double truck in front and weighing about twenty-eight tons. Other locomotives soon arrived, all second-hand and of different makes. They began building the shops in 1864 and by the spring of 1865 they had nine locomotives. They were all in need of repairs and attention. Mr. Mitchell soon realized his locomotives were too light and not powerful enough to do the work and he at once prepared to finish up his shops to repair and rebuild locomotives for heavier service and minor work was done on some locomotives.

"The first two locomotives that were rebuilt were the No. 66 and No. 67. They had some Indian names that were not often used. The engines had been rebuilt. The 66 was named 'Delano' and the 67 'Junction.' These two locomotives received new boilers, cylinders and frames and were made considerably larger into American type passenger locomotives. The 'Centerville,' or 68, was then rebuilt in the same style and class as the 66 and 67. The engines 69 and 70 were also of the same type. No record of their names was kept.

"Engines 69 and 70, the two largest engines of all, were then to have a good repairing. These were ten-wheel engines, three driving-wheels on a side, with a single truck in front. The boiler on the No. 70 exploded in the yard in front of the shops one morning in the summer of 1868, killing Michael Clemens.

"After the 69 and 70 had been repaired, other engines were repaired and put in good condition. Mr. Mitchell then had permission to rebuild the No. 83 into a new locomotive to his own plans, making it a larger and heavier engine than any they had before. This was to be an eight-wheel engine with three driving-wheels on each side with a single truck, boiler forty-eight inches in diameter and eighteen-inch cylinders. The boiler and frame were made by the Baldwin Locomotive Works of Philadelphia, cylinders and wheels were cast at Weatherly, and the machine finished in the Delano shops.

"During the building of the 83, he was ready to try his hand at the designing and building of a new and modern locomotive that would be capable of hauling one hundred cars up the Quakake grade—a larger engine than had ever been built anywhere. While the shops were still being built, he completed his drawings and in 1865 had some correspondence with the Grant Locomotive Works in Paterson, N. J., and with Matthias W. Baldwin Locomotive Company in Philadelphia. Neither company seemed interested because of the great size of the locomotive and the equipment of shop tools necessary to handle the work.

"However, an interview to examine the drawings was finally arranged with Mr. Baldwin, of the Baldwin Locomotive Works, and Mr. Mitchell and Mr. James I. Blakslee, then superintendent of the Lehigh Valley Railroad, went to Philadelphia with the plans. After a lengthy study of the drawings and following a conference with his shop superintendent, Mr. Baldwin told the two Delano men it would be impossible for him to build this engine because of its great size and weight, adding that he felt it would not be successful if built.

"Mr. Mitchell refused to take this decision as final. He pointed out to Mr. Baldwin that he brought his plans merely to have the locomotive constructed and not for decision or judgment on them. He said he would hold himself responsible for the operation of the engine when it had been built according to his specifications.

"Still Mr. Baldwin hesitated and declared the engine would not fulfill Mr. Mitchell's expectations of it. Mr. Mitchell lost patience and told Mr. Baldwin he had had some correspondence with the Grant Locomotive Works and that they were anxious to see the drawings. This clinched the matter and Mr. Baldwin said that what the Paterson company could do, he could do.

"The question was settled and Mr. Mitchell and Mr. Blakslee remained in Philadelphia at the Baldwin plant for one week going over and deciding on the details of the design. Mr. Baldwin promised to finish the engine in seven months.

"The engine arrived in Delano on July 10th, 1866, and was immediately put into service. From the very start it was a success, operating with perfection just as Mr. Mitchell had claimed. This engine brought Delano into almost international prominence, for it attracted the attention of master mechanics all over this country as well as many engineers from foreign countries, who traveled to Delano to see it in operation.

"The engine was numbered '63' and named 'Consolidation,' taking its name from the fact that at this time the Lehigh and Mahanoy Railroad was consolidated with the Hazleton and Beaver Meadows Railroad which terminated at Black Creek Junction.

"Those who remember the Consolidation may recall that the diameter of the boiler was fifty inches, cylinders twenty by twenty-four, steam pressure one hundred thirty pounds, and it had four forty-eight inch diameter driving-wheels on each side, a single pair of front truck wheels. This type of engine proved to be the most popular style ever built in this country and was well-received in foreign countries."

This graphic description of the achievement that is undoubtedly Delano's chief claim to industrial fame was written by a man who himself grew up in Delano and went out from there to attain a prominent place in the industrial world, serving with this same great firm of locomotive builders, the Baldwin Locomotive Company, and traveling for them in almost all the countries of the civilized world. It is a privilege to include in this book a photograph of Mr. McCarroll as his many Delano friends will best remember him.

It was Mr. McCarroll's father, John McCarroll, who had the honor of piloting this new engine wonder for many years, and the son himself occasionally fed the fires that made the steam for the old-time giant of the rail. Plate X shows a photograph of the Consolidation, taken in front of the Baldwin Locomotive Works at Philadelphia on the day it was shipped to Delano, and Plate XI shows a drawing of the same engine made by Mr. McCarroll. This famous engine was years later rebuilt in the Delano shops.

It is interesting to note that this same type of engine is still in very general use on railroads all over the world, almost seventy years after it was designed. A further technical description of it is here given for the benefit of the mechanically-inclined who may peruse these pages. This account is taken from the trade journal published by the Baldwin Locomotive Company, the issue of July, 1925:

"The general construction of the Consolidation is clearly shown in the drawing shown at Plate XI. The boiler was of the wagon-top type with a long firebox, suitable for hard coal, placed above the rear driving axle. The firebox had a combustion chamber and the grate consisted of water tubes. The boiler was fed by one injector and two pumps, the latter driven by return cranks secured to the crank pins of the rear driving wheels. The cylinders were placed horizontally and the pistons were connected, through long main rods, with the third pair of driving wheels. As the eccentrics were on the main axle, and the links were forward of the second axle, it was necessary to use long bowed eccentric rods, a form of construction subsequently applied to many Consolidation type locomotives equipped with Stephenson link motion. A variable exhaust nozzle, controlled by a hand-lever in the cab, was applied. The leading truck was of the Bissel type, and it was equallized with the driving wheels in substantially the same manner as in present-day locomotives having this wheel arrangement."

One of the Consolidation type engines was exhibited at the Philadelphia Centennial in 1876. It was Engine No. 310, with the name "United States," shown in the illustration Plate No. XII, and was built by the Baldwin Locomotive Company for the Lehigh Valley Railroad after the plans of the original Consolidation, although it had a somewhat larger boiler and had been thoroughly revised in its details. A description of this engine was published, with sectional drawings, in the London magazine, "Engineering," and republished in Railroad Gazette of New York on December 1st, 1876. This indicates the world-wide interest that had been aroused over this type of locomotive.

The Consolidation type engine was capable of hauling one hundred empty four-wheel coal cars, weighing 340 tons, at a speed of about eight miles an hour on a grade of 76 feet to the mile; not, perhaps, very impressive in this day of the modern giants, but considered marvelous in that early day.

Quoting further from Mr. McCarroll's article:

"The locomotive No. 83 was finished about this time and christened with the name of 'Advance.' Mr. Mitchell was an ardent anti-slavery man and he so named the engine as a symbol of the freeing of the slaves and of the new equality of the black man. To further emphasize his idea, he had a life-size head of a negro modeled in iron. This he had placed on the front truck center-pin bolt. When the engine was moving over the tracks, it had an up and down movement in relation to the negro's head which made it appear very lifelike. This feature was always a source of attraction for those who saw it. This engine, 'Advance,' always had the reputation by all enginemen from the very start of being very speedy and powerful.

"Mr. Mitchell then had permission to rebuild or build two new locomotives. It is not on record, but nevertheless, he had plans for two engines similar to these. He bought two new boilers and two sets of frames from the Baldwin Locomotive Works, cylinders and wheels were cast at Weatherly, and the machine finished in the Delano shops. One of these engines was to have driving wheels three inches larger in diameter and cylinders one-half inch larger in diameter than the other, otherwise they were practically the same. Both proved remarkably high-class locomotives, but the one with the larger wheel and cylinders appeared to be the favorite with enginemen.

"One of these engines was named 'New York,' with the No. 1. The other was named 'L. Chamberlain,' No. 147. These locomotives had three driving wheels on a side and a single truck wheel in front.

"Then the 'Evangeline' or the famous No. 148, appeared on the list to be built about 1868. This was to be Mr. Mitchell's masterpiece of work for a high-efficiency and beautiful-looking locomotive. The mechanics took the greatest care in fitting up the working parts and bearings. Many parts were fitted up to geometrical lines. I dare say more so than any other locomotive work I ever knew of. When finished, it was really a beautiful picture with its ornamental brass, white metal trimmings and polished steel.

"This boiler was the first boiler ever built in the Delano shops. Mr. John Weiss and Albert Knecht, the two leading boiler-makers, had charge of the work. Mr. Weiss remained in the shops as foreman boiler-maker for many years.

"This engine was the regular American type with boiler forty-eight inches in diameter, 130-pound steam pressure, cylinders 18 inches in diameter, two driving wheels on a side and double truck in front. After the locomotive was in service some time and demonstrated its efficiency of speed and power, it was arranged to be tried out in service on the Pennsylvania railroad train service. It was therefore sent to the Altoona shops of the Pennsylvania railroad to have it equipped with Westinghouse air-brakes, so it could be used in their train service.

"When the engine was in service, its performance was closely recorded and admired by railroad officials. This engine was always a favorite with enginemen and it remained in service for many years.

A Drawing of the Consolidation, by William McCarroll.
Plate XI
Text Page 34

The Consolidation. Plate X
Text Page 32

No. 310. Plate XII
Text Page 35

No. 147. Plate XIII
Text Page 36

No. 148. Plate XIV
Text Page 36

"Mr. Mitchell was always an advocate of heavier power and strong engines to get traffic over the heavy grades. In the year 1867 he had one very heavy passenger engine of the American type built at the Norris Locomotive Works at Lancaster, Pa., named 'Eagle,' No. 93.

"He was disappointed in its performance and, therefore, changed the cylinders and increased the steam pressure five pounds and increased the size of the throttle-box, dry-pipe and steam pipes and made a remarkably good engine. It was found that the increase in steam pressure added to the boiler was just up to the limit, as it always gave trouble in leaking. About this time he ordered the 'Bee,' No. 81, and the 'Ant,' No. 82. These engines were the limit for size and remained the limit for many years. They gave trouble by jumping the track when run backwards. They had five driving-wheels on each side, a single truck wheel in front, a fifty-two inch boiler, with one hundred thirty pounds steam pressure, cylinders with 22 x 24 diameter. Mr. Mitchell applied what is now known as a 'trailer' truck, to overcome the trouble in jumping the track, thus making the first trailer truck ever to be used. These engines were exact duplicates of those seen today, except for their weight.

"Mr. Mitchell also built the first still fire-box used on a locomotive, and he was the first to use corrugated sheet in fire-boxes. All of the above-mentioned items are developments of Mr. Mitchell and are in general use on all railroads of the world today. These features were developed in the Delano shops from 1864 to 1867."

Plate No. XIII shows Engine No. 147, and Plate No. XIV Engine No. 148. Both of these engines have been out of service for some years, although the 148 continued giving good service until very recent years. The writer recalls here that the first ride he ever had on a passenger engine while on a regular run was on this same famous old 148, then in charge of his father on his passenger run between Shamokin and Wilkes-Barre. It was his father's first engine when he entered passenger service in 1900. More will be said about the engine in a later chapter.

Quoting Mr. McCarroll further:

"In 1871 Mr. Mitchell was transferred to the Wilkes-Barre shops of the Lehigh Valley Railroad and while there continued his work of locomotive development. He was later made superintendent of the Wyoming Division. He was an inspiration to work under, a fine gentleman and one of the best mechanics I have ever known. I consider it an honor that I knew him and had his good advice from my boyhood days to the time of his death.

"Mr. John Campbell succeeded Mr. Mitchell in 1872 and carried on the work begun by Mr. Mitchell in constructing engines which earned him the reputation of turning out locomotives that held together better than any other engines made. Mr. Campbell built many good locomotives and organized and built the passenger car shops, which constructed many of these cars. In this period Mr. David Fletcher was general foreman of the shops. Mr. Campbell also built the first 15,000-gallon tender that had two six-wheel trucks. In 1880 large additions were built to the shops and a large carpenter shop for passenger coaches was added.

"It was my good fortune to serve my apprenticeship under these two men and able mechanics, and when I left Delano and started out in the world, I soon realized that my training was extremely valuable and sound and one of which to be proud. After leaving Delano, I was fortunate enough to become connected with the Baldwin Locomotive Works and in a few years I was traveling in foreign countries all over the world and everywhere I went I could see the earmarks of the designs developed in the famous Delano shops."

This splendid and well-deserved tribute to the genius of the men who founded and developed the Delano shops supports the expressed conviction of this writer that the high place attained by the little town in the great industrial world has been too little recognized and understood even by those who have over the years claimed Delano as their home town, and that this fame deserves to be permanently recorded for the appreciation of future generations.

At the time of the organization of the Delano shops, Mr. Charles Hartshorne was President of the Lehigh and Mahanoy Railroad Company, and it was he who procured the services of Mr. Mitchell as Master Mechanic, Mr. Mitchell at that time being connected with the Camden and Amboy Railroad at its shops at White Hill, near Bordentown, New Jersey.

SHOP FOREMEN OF THE EARLY 80's
Text Page 42

Shop Group of 70's. Plate XVI
Text Page 43

Mr. Charles Collum, now head of the Allentown Boiler Works, at Allentown, Pa., and one of the early residents of Delano, gives this information as to the various shops in existence when he came to the town in 1876:

On the north side of the railroad tracks going east stood the first engine house (since razed), with which was connected the first paint shop, in which four or five painters were then employed. The first machine shop was on the south side of the railroad, with about thirty machinists employed. Connected with this shop was the blacksmith shop, with six smithy fires and twelve men employed. The boiler shop adjoined the machine shop building, with ten boiler-makers and helpers. Connected with the boiler shop was the pattern shop.

Mr. William Campbell, a son of John Campbell (for many years Master Mechanic of the Delano shops), gives some valuable information about the early and later history of the shops. According to his statements, the original shops consisted of one machine shop of stone construction with ten pits; one engine house of stone construction with twelve pits; one frame boiler shop, one frame carpenter shop and blacksmith shop, with an extension for paint shop and coppersmith shop. These buildings were all located east of the station and to the south of the railroad.

The foremen who had charge of these various departments were all men of the highest type to be found in their respective trades. To quote Mr. Campbell: "This plant was an ideal one, compact, and with a set of men and boys as mechanics to compare with any in the country for thoroughness and ability."

Among the pioneer foremen were these: Alexander A. Mitchell as Master Mechanic, to be succeeded later by John Campbell; David Fletcher as General Foreman in the shops; Charles Whitehead, Machine Shop Foreman; John Weiss, Boiler Shop Foreman; John S. Moore, Master Car Builder; John Hartley, Foreman Paint Shop; a Mr. Haldeman as Blacksmith Shop Foreman, later succeeded by John R. James; Joseph N. Becker, Foreman of Tin Shop; George Crossan, Foreman Coppersmith Shop; Frank H. Bickle, Air Brake Foreman; Dwight Ashby, Chief Clerk; Charles Schmidt, Frog Shop Foreman; and John Schaeffer, Tank and Truck Foreman. It is worth noting here that Mr. Becker and Mr.

Crossan came to Delano with the opening of the shops and remained in their respective positions until they were finally closed in 1899, a remarkable record. Mr. Crossan had a unique position in the shops, as his trade of coppersmith was a rare one in that section. The flues in those first locomotives were made of copper and much brass work was used, and Mr. Crossan was brought from Philipsburg, New Jersey, at the opening of the shops because of his expert knowledge of this trade.

Other veteran shopmen, who served in later years, included James Beels, in charge of the machines in the machine shop, to be succeeded by Josiah Swank, who had been connected with the shops almost from their beginning; R. F. Joslyn, who succeeded Mr. Hartley as Paint Shop Foreman, to be succeeded himself later by John Bannan; Henry Smink, who succeeded John Weiss as Boiler Shop Foreman; George Wynn, who succeeded John R. James as Blacksmith Shop Foreman; Joseph Bannan, who succeeded Frank H. Bickle as Air Brake Foreman; W. S. Campbell, assistant to the Chief Clerk until 1892, when he was succeeded by Llewellyn Bannan; Lewis Garner, who succeeded Charles Schmidt as Frog Shop Foreman. Track bosses in the shops were Joseph Gassner, Lafayette Boyle, Charles D. Bannan, George Symons, George Morgan, Charles G. Mohr, Gottlieb Miller, August F. Hoegg, Charles Meder and Edward Fletcher.

Other expert mechanics who served well in these famous shops in that day were George Porter, foreman in charge of fitting up rods and bearings; Harry Artz, John Selgrath, Webb Zimmerman, Thomas Donnelly, Matthew Donnelly, Samuel Depew, Jr., Jacob Engel, Sr., and Jacob Engel, Jr., Calvin Engel, Clinton Engel, Harry Whitehead, Eli Haldeman, Martin Neeb, John Herbig, J. Wesley Smith and his three sons, John, William and George; Samuel and Harry Shafer, and many others who came in later years. Of these, Samuel Shafer is the only one who is still at work as a machinist in the Delano shops.

Among other well-known men connected with the shop life in Delano were Michael Neary, in charge of the shop storeroom, who had a reputation for seeing that every cent's worth of company property was handled as faithfully as though it were his own; John Culliney, who had charge of the oil house; Thomas Curley, night car cleaner boss; and Tom Ross, general manager of the sand house. Many stories of shop life that have become almost legendary are woven about the names of these men.

Mention has been made of the fact that Michael Neary came to Delano in the very beginning of its history. By reason of the fact that he helped to assemble the stone out of which the shops were constructed, he was given the nickname of "Stonewall," which clung to him during his whole life. An amusing incident of shop history early in the 70's is associated with this nickname of Mr. Neary's. A new employee in the shops was sent to the supply house one day with an order for red oil for a red lantern, that being one of the favorite jokes uesd in initiating new men into their duties. He was cautioned to address Mr. Neary as "Stonewall" in placing his order. On the way to the supply house he became confused in his instructions and he called the custodian of the storehouse "Brimstone." This was more than the genial Irishman could stand, as he suspected that someone had told the new man to call him that. The greenhorn failed to get his red oil, and he reported to his tormentors that the old man had chased him with a pickhandle.

Ollie Mason relates a story of his early boyhood that has to do with Mr. Neary. Mr. Mason's father had taken him for a visit to the shops and called at the supply house to talk to Mr. Neary. Upon seeing little Ollie, Neary immediately pretended that he was a long-lost son who had been stolen from him and demanded that Mr. Mason, Sr., turn him over. Needless to say Mason, Jr., was very much frightened, for he was just about convinced that Mr. Neary's claim was good.

It has been noted that but a handful of men was employed in the shops at the beginning. When Mr. Campbell took charge in 1872, there were about one hundred men employed and this number had increased to almost three hundred fifty when Mr. Campbell was transferred in 1893.

The original purpose in the erection of the shops was the repairing of the railroad equipment. Up to 1871 a number of the Consolidated type engines as designed by Mr. Mitchell had been built by the Baldwin Works and delivered to Delano. Among those were Nos. 79, 80, 99, 100, 168, 169, 170 and others. All of these were later rebuilt at Delano.

Besides the repair work for the Mahanoy Division, the Delano shops took care of the repairs for the Wyoming Division up to 1875; also all the work for the Montrose Railroad, which was a narrow-gauge road operating between Tunkhannock and Montrose. The shops also did much repair work for the collieries in that district.

Just before the coming of Mr. Campbell as Master Mechanic, the Delano shops had begun the work of rebuilding engines and the building of new ones, as has already been mentioned. It is generally recognized that the first new engine to be constructed in the Delano shops was the No. 148, which was named "Evangeline" in honor of the wife of Mr. Mitchell. A full description of the building of this engine has already been given. While it was practically an entirely new engine, there had been an engine by that number before, so that actually it was not classed as a new product of these shops. Like the Irishman's knife, which had four new handles and twelve new blades, but was still the same old knife, this engine was new in every particular except the number.

The first entirely new engine to be built, including even the number, was No. 341, built by Mr. Campbell in 1877, and named "Alexander Mitchell" in honor of the first Master Mechanic.

From this time on the shops were busy rebuilding old engines and building new ones. A complete list of the rebuilt and new engines will be given in a later chapter.

Several very interesting photographs of shopmen taken during the period from 1870 to 1880 have been furnished for this history and the writer is pleased to present them for the pleasure of his readers, believing that they will stir memories in the minds of the old-time residents that the written word cannot reach.

The first picture, Plate No. XV, shows a group made up almost entirely of shop superintendents and foremen. The men appearing on this picture are, reading from left to right: Seated—Michael Carroll, Benjamin Williams, Theodore Howells, George Butler, James P. Swartz, Lafayette Boyle, Joshua Butler and Edward Evans; standing—John Campbell, John Weiss, James Connell, Charles Whitehead, Josiah Swank, George Burnett, George Crossan, Morris Cushing, "Dad" Jenkins, John Shaffer, Michael Neary, Charles Mills, Dennis Lynch and George Wynn.

Shop Group of 70's. Plate XVII
Text Page 43

No. 341. FIRST NEW ENGINE BUILT AT DELANO. PLATE XVIII
Text Page 42

No. 170. FIRST DELANO-BUILT "CAMEL-BACK." PLATE XIX
Text Page 44

The second group, Plate No. XVI, is made up of the following, reading from left to right: Front row—Jacob Billman, Unknown, Samuel Depew, David Fletcher, David Dreisbach; middle row—James Jackson, John Moore, Francis Billman, John Schaeffer, Albert Bast, Conrad (Uncle) Kocher, John Taylor and Rudolph Billman; back row—Reuben Minnich, John Campbell, John Weiss and Mr. Kershner.

The third group, Plate No. XVII, is made up of the following, reading from left to right: Front row—John Taylor, John Moore, John Schaeffer, Rudolph Billman, Conrad Kocher, Charles Runkle, Benneville Bensinger and Henry Barclay; middle row—Jacob Billman, John Weaver, Solomon Schaeffer, Peter Kimbel, Mr. Shuler, Francis Billman and Frank Wagner; back row—Gottleib Bachman, Frank Ebert, John Runkle, John Bair, Daniel Deichler, Calvin Engel, Jacob Schuck.

In addition to the series of shop pictures just shown, a number of interesting engine pictures are included in this chapter. These photographs have been selected from among many available because of some particularly pertinent connection they had with the history of Delano. Not all of these engines are products of the Delano shops, but they did belong to Delano railroad life, which entitles them, in the opinion of the writer, to a place in this volume.

Plate No. X, as has been mentioned before, shows a view of the famous No. 63, the first Consolidation type built, taken in front of the Baldwin Locomotive Works at Philadelphia on the day the engine was shipped to Delano. Plate No. XI is an illustration of a drawing of the same engine, made by Mr. William McCarroll. Plate No. XII is a picture of the No. 310, the Consolidation type engine exhibited at the Centennial at Philadelphia in 1876.

Plate No. XIV shows the famous No. 148, with a very familiar Delano background, while Plate No. XIII is of the No. 147, a twin to the 148 in matter of age.

Plate No. XVIII of the No. 341 and Plate No. XIX of the No. 170 are, respectively, the first new engine built in the Delano shops and the first "camel-back" engine built there. This "camel-back" or "dirt-burner" type, as it was more familiarly known, was a new design made by Mr. Campbell, providing much larger fire-box space and steam capacity. It proved very successful on the steep grades of the Mahanoy Division and many of the old Consolidation engines were converted into the new type at the Delano shops. Two of the men appearing on the picture of the 341 are Tim McCarthy, engineer, and Ollie Mason (at end of foot-board). The writer is not able to furnish the name of the man nearest the cab. On the picture of the 170 are shown, left to right: Ezra Bachert, Milt Moser (engineer), William Brouse, Wallace Gerhard, Charles Bishop and Robert Burdess.

Plate No. XX is a picture of the No. 617, the last engine built in the Delano shops. This engine achieved some wonderful road records, of which more will be related in a later chapter. The men on this picture are: Edward Campbell, engineer; James Blew, fireman; Ben Hendricks, conductor; and Llewellyn Bannan, passenger-extraordinary. Plate No. XXI shows a Baldwin-built engine which was one of the first modern, large-type engines used at Delano, No. 530. The particular interest in this picture for the reader is in the person appearing on it, none other than Bill Clasby, an old-time and highly-respected former resident of Delano, who was employed in the Baldwin Shops when this engine was built, and had the picture taken because the engine was being sent to his old home-town.

A contrast of the old and the new appears in Plates Nos. XXII and XXIII, showing engines Nos. 364 and 311, respectively. The 364 was built at Delano in 1882 and gave fine service to the Lehigh Valley for many years. The crew shown consists of: On ground —William Brouse, Milt Moser (engineer), and Condy Boyle; on foot-board—John Raab, Robert Burdess and Thomas Richardson. The writer recalls here that the first ride he ever had on an engine was on this same 364, the engineer being William Opp and the fireman his own dad. It was at the tender age of four years, still in dresses, that the momentous experience came. The trip was from Delano to Logan and return. The writer sat on a board which the engineer placed in front of his seat, reaching from the boiler to the cab window sill. About the only recollection of the trip is that a hot spark from the stack dropped on his tongue and blistered it. It is perhaps not necessary to say here that, so far as the writer is concerned, the 364 was the finest engine the Lehigh Valley ever produced.

No. 617. Last Engine Built at Delano. Plate XX
Text Page 44

Bill Clasby and one of the First Big Engines. Plate XXI
Text Page 44

No. 364. PLATE XXII
Text Page 44

No. 311. A MODERN ENGINE. PLATE XXIII
Text Page 44

THE DINKEY. PLATE XXIV
Text Page 45

The picture of the 311 shows one of the modern bull-moose type engines now used. It conveys an excellent idea of the powerful machines that pull the Lehigh Valley trains today. The men on the picture are George Opp, engineer, and Howard Lorah, fireman. Mr. Opp is a son of William Opp mentioned above and is a worthy successor to a famous old-time Lehigh Valley railroader.

Plate No. XXIV is a picture familiar to Delanoites of the 90's and some years later—the old dinkey. This was not a Delano-built engine, but it pursued its fussy way about the Delano yards for many years and was one of the most familiar sights in the town during that time. The only members of the crew the writer can identify are James Perry, engineer (on the foot-board), and James Cain, conductor (in the cab). The background of this picture is a very familiar one to Delano people.

Plate No. XXV pictures an engine that broke some service records, No. 407. The crew shown on the engine are: John McMullen, engineer, and Jerry Ryan, Sr., fireman. On the ground are: Charles Whitehead and David Fletcher, machine shop foreman and general foreman, respectively. More will be said later about this engine and crew.

The picture shown on Plate No. XXVI portrays a custom that was very popular in the 80's. It was taken on July 4th, 1888, at Pottsville, Pa., and the members of the crew are: Tim McCarthy, engineer; Charles F. Brill, fireman; John McAvoy, conductor; John Oswald, brakeman, and Edward Lindemuth, baggage-master. G. F. Hartley, of Delano, also appears on the picture.

There was a great rivalry among the various train crews at Delano in the decorating of their engines on Memorial Day and Independence Day. The writer can still recall his father spending hours at night in cutting out stars and other figures from gold and silver foil, to be used for pasting on stack, sand-box, and dome. Great quantities of bunting, flags and rosettes were used in giving the engine a gala appearance. The picture here shown gives a fine idea of the effect produced.

It is said that this custom was abolished by the company the day after this picture was taken, for the reason that a serious wreck almost occurred as a result of the decorations on this particular engine. Engine 34 on this day was carrying signals for a second section and met a train bound in the opposite direction at a passing siding along the way. The crew of the other train failed to notice the signals because of the decorations and came very close to a collision with the second section.

One more picture is shown here, being that of No. 66, Plate No. XXVII. This was the engine which was given the name "Delano" and was one of the very first to be rebuilt at Delano. It continued in service for a great number of years and completed its years of usefulness on the Bloomsburg and Sullivan Railroad.

This chapter on the basic industry of Delano covers a period from about 1865 to the end of the 70's. The reader's attention is now invited to a review of community life in Delano during the first two decades of its history.

THE NO. 407.   PLATE XXV
Text Page 45

ENGINE NO. 34, ON JULY 4, 1888.   PLATE XXVI
Text Page 45

NO. 66.   PLATE XXVII
Text Page 46

CHAPTER VII

Early Community Life

TO HOLD the sustained interest of the reader in this narrative, it is necessary to preserve a certain degree of chronological sequence. Having touched upon what might be termed prehistoric conditions relating to the locality and events leading up to the founding of Delano, as well as to various aspects of industrial activity in the first two decades of its history, it is proper that we give attention to community life in general in this early period.

The seventy-year span of the town's life might well be divided into epochs of almost equal duration, the development of its varied interests falling quite naturally into time divisions of approximately ten years each. The period from 1861 to 1870 marked the pioneering days; from 1870 to 1880, the firm establishment of the basic industry; with each succeeding decade showing a pronounced advance over the preceding one in every phase of community interest, and each decade having in itself elements of individuality distinct from the others.

This chapter will undertake a general survey of the people and their personal interests as distinguished from the industrial activities during the first twenty years of the town's existence.

It must be kept in mind that the first settlers of our little mountain town, while they found themselves surrounded by the most primitive conditions, were not the uncouth and ignorant type sometimes associated with those who beat new ways into the wilderness. It has already been seen that the pioneers were men with skilled hands and keen minds, whose genius wrought things to attract the attention of the world. To people of this sort the finer things of life would be essential, and we find in the early life of Delano a deep interest in things religious, educational, social and cultural.

Even in that early day, long before the famous Rule "G" had been promulgated, railroad companies insisted upon sobriety and decency in their working forces, and nothing that would militate against the strict observance of these requirements was permitted to find a foothold in the place. This made for a high grade of good citizenship, as is well expressed in the words of Mr. Collum, one of the early residents: "Young men were sent to Delano from other towns and cities to serve their apprenticeship in different trades, mostly because it was a healthful location and a temperance town, as well as because of the high reputation of the shops there. No intoxicating liquors were allowed to be sold on the property of the Delano Land Company. The nearest hotel was three miles away, which made it uncomfortable for a few men, who grumbled at the town's loneliness, but their duration of living there was short and their departure was good riddance, thus leaving a good class of respectable, honorable and intelligent people, a blessing to live with."

This describes the feeling and standing of the first comers and explains a great deal about the foundation upon which the fine little community was organized.

The first few families to locate here occupied homes set in the heart of a great forest. When the store building was built in the late 60's, trees had to be cut down to make room for its erection, and between the store building and the railroad were thick woods and great rocks. These were later removed and a storage place for timber to be loaded on cars was placed there. This later was the location of the beautiful Blakslee gardens.

One of the first concerns of the pioneers was to establish the means for the proper worship of God. The nearest place for supplying this need in the beginning was Mahanoy City, five miles distant, with very crude facilities for getting there and back. For a time a hand-truck was used to carry worshippers to and from their places of worship, the power being furnished by the passengers themselves. Mr. Robert Martin, an old-time resident and employed at Delano until very recently, relates an amusing incident connected with this primitive mode of conveyance. A group had gone to Mahanoy City by way of the hand-truck and one man, a recent addition to the town's population, reached the station for the return trip a little earlier than the others. He seated himself on a station express truck under the impression that he was on the conveyance that would take him home, and when his companions returned they failed to notice him and left him sitting there as they

DAVID FLETCHER
Text Page 49

JOSIAH SWANK
Text Page 49

THE OLD BELL OF THE FIRST
SCHOOL BUILDING
PRESENT OWNER, AL ZIMMERMAN
Text Page 51

pushed their way home. The poor chap had a five-mile walk before him.

With the building of the first school house in the village in 1865, a community center for worship was provided and the first Sunday School was started in this building by Mr. David Fletcher. Mr. Josiah Swank was another pioneer resident who was actively associated with this early religious work and he became superintendent of the Sunday School early in its history, a position which he held from time to time through all his residence in Delano. Photographs of Mr. Fletcher and Mr. Swank appear here. The first school building was a small one-room structure, which will be described in greater detail in another part of this chapter, but it served the purpose of a common meeting place and excellent use of it was made.

The devout Catholics of the community, of whom there were quite a number, in the early days worshipped at Tamaqua, Pa., and later became members of the parish of St. Canicus Roman Catholic Church at Mahanoy City, Pa., of which church the present Catholic residents of Delano are still members.

When the four-room school building was erected at Delano in 1870, just west of the first one, the Sunday School and church services were held there. This larger building was far more convenient and commodious for the purpose and was used until the erection of the first Union Hall in the early part of 1875. The building of the new hall marked a new era in the religious, literary and social life of the town, as it provided a suitable building for those activities, being constructed for that very purpose. Its size was about thirty feet by forty feet.

This building as originally constructed continued in use for about twenty-two years, when, in 1897, an addition twenty-eight feet by thirty feet, or almost as large as the original, was built; and this enlarged building served the religious and literary needs of Delano for another period of twenty-three years, when it was razed and replaced by a beautiful, modern chapel.

The first preaching services conducted in Delano were in charge of several denominations. The Lutheran Church of Mahanoy City during the period from 1867 to 1880 was served by these pastors: Rev. I. C. Burkholter, 1867-1869; Rev. Reuben Weiser,

1869-1871; Rev. D. Beckner, 1871-1875; and Rev. J. M. Steck, 1875-1880. These pastors also served the Delano charge during that time on alternate Sundays. The St. Paul's Reformed Church of Mahanoy City also sent its pastors to serve the Delano people during this period. The Rev. Mr. Wood, of the Presbyterian Church of Mahanoy City, preached in Delano for some time, but the writer has not been able to learn the dates of his service. The Rev. Mr. Fischer, of the Reformed Church of Tamaqua, Pa., also preached in Delano for many years.

The people of the little town were a God-fearing people and the high standing of the community throughout the years is directly attributable to that fact.

Military Records

Delano from its beginning has had an enviable record for patriotism. The town was born just at the opening of the Civil War and many of its early residents, with some who came to the town later, had fine records of service with the Union Army. The following is a roster of Delano residents who served in the great rebellion: George Gasser, Isaac Mason, Abraham Markle, John Schuler, Jacob Kerschner, John Richardson, Thomas Smith, John Weiss, John Runkle, Charles Derr, Washington Zimmerman, Jacob Engel, Sr., and Josiah Swank. The writer is not able to supply any information as to the service records of these men.

Educational Activities

During the period covered by this chapter, Delano was a part of Rush Township. It has been said that the sturdy people who made up the population of this important township were outstanding from the beginning in their interest in sound education, and made great sacrifices that their young people might have the benefit of the most advanced methods of educational training.

Delano very quickly became the most important part of this large township and its requirements in the matter of education were well provided for. As has been noted, the first school building was erected in 1865, which is the year in which the actual need for schools first arose. This little structure was twenty-five feet square, one-story high, and was built right in the forest about seventy-five yards southwest of the store building and on the opposite side of the street. Anyone who resided in Delano as late as 1897 will remember it, as it was used for quite some time as a club house and library by the residents of the town after it had served its time as a school house and, later, as a dwelling.

It was equipped with four rows of desks, five deep, with accommodations for twenty pupils. During the first school term the regular desks and seats had not yet been placed and the pupils were seated on ordinary chairs about a table. No provision for heating the building had been made at first and pupils were sent home on very cold days. Later a large cast-iron stove was furnished, but the only fuel available was that gathered by the pupils themselves, who were sent into the woods surrounding the building to collect firewood. Later the boys in the school were sent to the coal dump for coal, until a coal shed was built, after which coal was delivered to the school.

The historian was not able to locate any pictures of this first school building, but he was fortunate enough to find a part of the equipment that belonged to it—the old school bell which summoned the Delano youngsters to their studies back in the 60's. When the building was finally razed, the bell was purchased by the family of D. W. Zimmerman, who moved to a farm above Shickshinny, Pa., after the Delano shops were closed. The bell was hung on a locust tree on this farm and, instead of calling children to school, it now called farmhands to their meals. Early in April, 1932, the bell was brought from this farm to the home of Mrs. Zimmerman, who now resides with her son, Al, and daughter, Linda, near Berwick. The writer happened to stop at the Zimmerman home the day after the bell arrived from the farm and he promptly took a picture of it to be used in this volume. It is shown here as the only thing left of that first temple of learning in Delano. On the picture also appears Mr. Al Zimmerman, the present owner of the bell, who needs no introduction to Delano people of the 80's and 90's.

Delano's first school teacher, the first to dedicate this little building to its use as a seat of learning, was Miss Miriam E. LeVan, daughter of Henry LeVan, who was the first train dispatcher at Delano. Miss LeVan came well equipped for her work, having graduated from the High Schools of Easton, Pa., in July, 1864.

The school opened that first year with eight pupils, five boys and three girls. Included among those were William McCarroll, Jerry Ryan, Sr., James Kelly and Morris Cushing. Jerry Ryan and James Kelly made their home with their grandmother, Mrs. Cushing, who was also the mother of Morris Cushing, so that almost one-half the pupils that year came out of this one family. Mr. McCarroll, of this first school group, is still residing in Philadelphia and has contributed some invaluable material to this record. It is not known whether there are any others of those first eight pupils still living, but the teacher is still enjoying excellent health at her home in Wilkes-Barre, Pa., as these lines are being written.

The studies taught in that first year were the very elementary ones of reading, writing and arithmetic. Excellent progress was made with the school and by the second year had grown so much that the room was crowded.

In the second year Miss LeVan resigned to marry Mr. Thomas Moore, then a fireman on the railroad at Delano. This wedding was solemnized in the parlor of the LeVan home at Delano and the Baptist minister of Mahanoy City performed the marriage ceremony. This was no doubt Delano's first wedding.

Mrs. Moore, as has been said, is still living in Wilkes-Barre, where the writer had the pleasure of visiting her just recently. He is indebted to her for much valuable information furnished for these chronicles. Although she is almost eighty-four years of age, she possesses a remarkable memory and spoke most interestingly of her friendship for Delano and its people. She has kept in touch with the town throughout all these years. Two photographs of Mrs. Moore are shown here, the first one taken quite a number of years ago, and the other one taken by the writer himself when he visited her in April of this year.

Among the many interesting things spoken of by Mrs. Moore, several are of interest to readers of this history for their connection with early life in Delano. Two of the guests at Mrs. Moore's wedding were Mrs. John McCarroll, mother of William McCarroll, and Mr. Alexander A. Mitchell, famous Master Mechanic.

The first baptism performed in Delano was that of a brother of Mr. Eli Haldeman, at which Mr. Bartley Brady and Mrs. Moore (then Miss LeVan), were godfather and godmother.

Mrs. Miriam Le Van Moore
Delano's First Teacher
Text Page 51

Mrs. Moore in 1932
Text Page 52

Prof. Williams
Text Page 54

Prof. John B. Anthony
Text Page 54

Mr. and Mrs. Moore left Delano almost immediately after their marriage and went to Pittston, where Mr. Moore was an engineer for the Lehigh Valley until he was killed in the service in 1887. An account of his death will be of interest to readers of this history because of his former residence in the town and the further fact that at the time it occurred he was engaged in demonstrating a device that had been perfected by a man named James Weaver in competition with another demonstration of a similar device that had been invented by Mr. Mitchell, former Master Mechanic at Delano. This device was a spark arrester, something never before used on an engine. Two engines were equipped with the respective inventions and sent down the main line to Hokendauqua, Pa., to test them out. Because of the new attachment, it was necessary to increase the length of the smoke stack to give the necessary draft, and this long stack on Mr. Moore's engine struck a low bridge near Hokendauqua, was hurled back into the cab and caused his death.

To return to a review of school life in Delano, we find that a man by the name of Stauffer came after Miss LeVan, another teacher by the name of Swicher later on, who remained only a short time. He was succeeded by a Mr. Jones and different teachers served for the period reaching into the early 70's. It is not possible to supply the names of all those early instructors.

The school soon grew beyond the accommodations of the small building and in 1870 a large two-story structure, with four rooms, was erected. This gave ample room for the schools to expand in the years ahead. In fact, only two rooms were used when it was first occupied.

With the erection of this modern building, the residents of Delano demanded of the directors of Rush Township that a longer term be permitted. This demand was granted and an additional month added to the regular term for the town. Mr. H. H. Slayd taught this extra month for a term or two when it was first authorized.

Mr. and Mrs. Sarge were the first teachers in the new building. They used half the building for school purposes and occupied the other half as a residence. Mrs. George Folweiler assisted Mrs. Sarge with her housework during the school term, coming from her home in the valley as a girl. The use of two rooms made possible a more efficient grading of the schools, which was becoming necessary with the larger numbers attending. Mr. and Mrs. Sarge remained for several terms and were succeeded by Mr. Davis, who resided at Trenton and later taught in Mahanoy Township. Mr. Davis lost his life in 1881, being a victim of the same wreck in which Mr. Michael Reynolds was killed.

Succeeding Mr. Davis was Mr. Williams, who taught for a short time until almost the end of the 1870 decade. Mr. John Anthony succeeded Mr. Williams at about the close of the period now under discussion and, at his coming, the schools had grown into four very flourishing departments. Without doubt, the names of some of the early Delano teachers do not appear in this record, but the writer has not been able to get these. Photographs of Mr. Williams and Mr. Anthony, two of the principals of the schools, are shown here, as is also one of the two-story, frame school building that was erected in 1870.

The picture of the second Delano school building was taken long after it had ended its career as a house of learning. It furnishes a striking illustration of the fate that befalls things material in this old world. Like a battered old hulk cast upon the shores of Time, it stood starkly for years in the place where once it had reared its proud height, now left ingloriously to the ravages of time and the unthinking pranks of careless youngsters, many of whom had started upon Learning's long, difficult way within its once sacred walls. The school youngsters of the 90's spent many happy hours around this old shell, making use of it in their games of "overs," hand-ball, hide-and-seek and tag. But it served its day well, and men and women now scattered to almost every corner of this land can attribute much of their success to the first steps they took along the road of learning within that old building. This writer himself will always retain the memory of two happy years spent in the room on the first floor at the southeast end, where, under the guiding hands of Miss Wickett and Miss Houseweart, he made his first venture into the mysteries of the alphabet and the old wall chart.

The facts in this brief survey of the first fifteen years of Delano's school history have been gleaned from those whose memories go back to the pioneer days. There are no written records in existence, so far as the most careful and extended inquiry has been

THE OLD SCHOOL HOUSE
Text Page 54

DR. PHAON HERMANY
Text Page 79

DR. LEWIS A. FLEXER
Text Page 80

able to discover, but what has been recovered from the active memories of the old-timers and set down here will suffice to give historic permanence to the most important facts in the school life of that early day.

Social Life

There is no more absorbing interest in life than to turn back the pages of history and look into the intimate personal activities of the people of other days. Just how did they occupy their time? What were the amusements that interested them? What were the social relationships? What means had these pioneers to advance their intellectual and cultural desires?

In this glance at that phase of life in Delano in the first two decades, it is well to remember that science and the genius of man had not yet conspired to provide custom-made entertainment, amusement and other matters of divertisement for humankind. In a time when man still relied wholly upon his skill of hand to give material form to his ideas, it was incumbent upon him, also, to order as he could his scanty leisure for the best advancement of his mental and spiritual nature. Let no one suppose, however, that people then fell behind in the development of those essential spheres of life because they lacked the equipment of a later age. Under the necessity of providing their own means of progress along the various avenues of character building, they found in that very fact an added impulse toward the attainment of their objective.

Purblind satirists may rail at Main Street, but the fact remains that the real nation then, as now, centered in the lives of those who lived and wrought in towns like the little place of which this is written.

The first ten years following the establishment of the town found the population limited to just a few dozen families. Settled in the midst of most primitive surroundings, it is too much to suppose that leisure was plentiful. Their immediate concern, outside of working hours, would be the improvement of those surroundings and the development of more comfortable living conditions. The clearing of the wilderness, the beautifying of home surroundings, the preparing of gardens—all these were without doubt first considerations with each family, and with every member of each family.

Of course, social intercourse would not be lacking. There would be matters of great interest for fruitful discussion in a small community that was so busily engaged in making industrial history. The rapid-development of the town and its industry would engage the avid attention of everyone.

We have already seen that no time was lost by the first residents in providing for the spiritual and educational interests of their families, and it is reasonable to suppose that the social amenities occupied a rightful part of the time of the people. Neighborhood parties, social calls, small entertainments, with frequent visits to the places from which they had come, and to the surrounding countryside, with the entertaining of guests, undoubtedly kept those hardy folks fully engaged during such idle moments as they were able to snatch away from the more serious business of life. In such pursuits and homely pleasures, the pioneers dwelt in a fine spirit of neighborly co-operation, happy in the contribution their little community was making to human progress.

Shopping trips to Mahanoy City were made occasionally and it is related that the railroad company placed at the disposal of the women of the town for that purpose an engine and flat car, with railroad ties laid on the flat car for seats. This open-air conveyance in fine weather was not so bad, but hot sparks from the engine sometimes proved annoying to the passengers and destructive to holiday clothes.

During the second decade of the town's existence, a period of rapid growth and increased activity in the business of social advancement was reached. During this time the greater part of the houses in Delano were constructed. According to Mr. William Campbell, from whom much valuable material for this history has been obtained, the buildings erected in the town when his father arrived to take charge of the shops as master mechanic in 1871 consisted of the store building, four-room school building, the large three-story building used for passenger and freight station, superintendent's office, boarding house and barber shop, twenty single and fifteen double residences, including the large single home which had just been erected for the Campbell family. In 1872 the houses comprising what was then known as Spring Row, just back of the Coal Dump, were built, and these were at first occupied by the Hartung, Beels, Swank, McMullen, Welsh, Dick and Haldeman families. During 1877-1878 many new homes were constructed, including those in what was known as Toney Row (now Lakeside Avenue), twelve houses in the Patch, ten on Main Street (now Hazle Street), eight along the railroad on the street known as Swamppoodle. The Blakslee home was built some time prior to 1876, as were the houses on the opposite side of that street. The exact dates when the various homes were built cannot be determined, but it is apparent from the information secured from many sources that most of them were completed by the end of 1878. This does not include the new brick office building and several large double houses built later at the east end of old Swamppoodle, nor three or four built in recent years to replace some that were destroyed by fire.

A number of small single houses located in the Patch were removed during the 80's and larger, double houses erected to take their places. These single houses were some of the original houses built when the railroad was under construction. Old-timers will also recall a few bachelor shanties, as they were called. One of these stood at the east end of Toney Row until late in the 90's, and was ocupied by several men employed in the shops whose homes were distant from Delano. Another small building located just west of the ice house at the end of the freight building was used for bachelor quarters for a long time.

Some very interesting facts concerning the social life of the town between 1870 and 1880 have been furnished to the writer by those who were residents in Delano at that time. The growth of the town and the steady increase in the size of the shops and extension of railroad business, had brought many new residents, most of them young married people, and its growing importance as an industrial town had made Delano a center of interest for many who worked there and lived in the surrounding country.

The citizens were not long in providing ways for their own entertainment and advancement along literary and social lines, and if these things may seem somewhat crude to the present sophisticated age, they, nevertheless, served their purpose well and were the means of creating a spirit of helpfulness and good-fellowship among those early residents that had much to do with the fine type of citizenship developed in the town.

One of the first accomplishments along this line was the establishing of a library in the building used for station and office purposes. This library was provided partly by the people of the town and partly by the railroad company, and it grew to large proportions and was an important factor in furnishing profitable diversion and instruction for the people. Books on mechanics were included, with a valve motion machine, for the instruction of railroad and shop men; also various games for diversion and amusement.

With the completion of the new Union Hall early in 1875, a new impetus was given to community pride and enterprise along literary paths. The historian is indebted to Mr. Charles Collum, previously mentioned in this record, for some very interesting facts about the early efforts of the young men of Delano in the histrionic field. Mr. Collum came to Delano in 1876 and learned his trade under John Weiss, foreman of the boiler shop. He had a very active part in the entertainment furnished the little town by its own thespian stars.

Mr. Collum states that literary and debating societies were organized, encouraging music, singing, reciting, poetry, prose, etc. The leaders of the first debating teams were Mr. John R. James and Mr. John Hartley, Sr. Debates were held each week and the debaters were selected from the audience by the leaders a week in advance of the time set for their appearance on the platform. Many pleasant and instructive evenings were provided for the community in this way.

There were some, however, who had no particular talent as debaters and to give them a part as entertainers a dramatic and minstrel association was organized. This proved a great success from the beginning. By the courtesy of Mr. Collum, an original program of an entertainment given by this association on August 16, 1878, was placed in the hands of the historian and a photographic copy of it is shown here. Of the men whose names are mentioned on this program, at least five are still living, so far as the writer has been able to ascertain: Mr. Martin, Mr. McCarroll, Mr. Collum, Mr. Artz and Mr. Bickle. Without doubt the sight of this old program will bring back some long forgotten scenes in the memories of these men, as it likely will in the minds of many others.

A great amount of wholesome, homespun fun was injected into the entertainments. Home-made verse and quips and jokes with a local flavor directed at friends in the audience made up much of the programs, and were enjoyed by entertainers and entertained alike. New arrivals in the little town were usually introduced to the salient points of interest about the town by some ready-made verse composed by the actors and recited whenever a new face was to be seen in the audience. An excellent sample of this was sent to the writer by Mr. Collum, having been composed by him and Mr. John Hartley, Jr. It is a pleasure to give it here in full, for its historic value and for the benefit of those who may have heard it given originally. Some of the allusions will not be understood by some readers, since they were particularly applicable to that day and to those who had part in the entertainments, or were in the audience.

DELANO

When you arrive in Delano, if you're a total stranger,
We'll tell you what you'll find when you get off the train, sir.
This town from drinking custom quite is free,
'Twas founded on the ground of aristocracy.
You first behold a structure which will likely cause remark,
"What is this great big edifice that looks like Noah's Ark?"

You are sure to get an answer, this will be your quick reply,
"It is not Noah's Ark, though you've landed very high.
It has within it many things, as you can plainly see,
Passenger, baggage, freight depot and a wonderful libraree.
With also forty boarders of many occupations,
Including all their families, with friends and more relations.

"There are also many rooms within, some narrow, others wider,
All in charge of the manager, the genial Mr. Snyder.
From the platform you may enter the temperance saloon,
There upon a chair sits a man who tires soon.
Don't bother him or ask him to give you any tick,
If you buy a cigar he'll tell you to light it with a stick.

"In the corner across the room you will see an easy chair
Belonging to our barber friend, perhaps he isn't there.
There are many fancy portraits hanging on the wall,
If you want a nice clean shave, be sure to give him a call.
And now we're out on Main Street, well-kept, with very few holes,
Whose residents take greatest pride in lofty, straight flag poles.

"Standing on the railroad, looking westward for awhile,
You'll see the tank and sand house and the place we keep the oil.
Doc. Culliney owned two chickens, a rooster and a hen,
They fell into an oil barrel and that was the last of them.
You next behold the company store, where men do often meet
And talk on many subjects, but always most discreet.

"And right up here's the school house, Teacher Anthony in charge,
Who teaches all our children about the world at large.
The Delano Dramatic Club plays there, as you will see,
With twenty pounds of white lead upon the sceneree.
Our church folks built a hall, it's just across the way,
And here they go to services on every nice Sunday.

"The shops you'll find on the east side,
Where mechanics work with pride,
When you come in the shop door
You'll find parts all over the floor.
Also locomotives scattered here and there,
With skilled mechanics working to put them in good repair.

"If you should be smoking a good cigar and feeling very proud,
Someone will quickly tell you, 'Smoking is not allowed,'
And if you fail to take the hint, thinking it just a sell,
Your cigar goes out and with it you go out as well.
The master mechanic's office is just north of the stairs,
Where men are called quite often to settle their affairs.

"On the east side stands the blacksmith shop, with fires burning free,
With a silver-bearded gentleman the men to oversee.
'Hit-em-down'—a thousand pounds—you can bet and you may win it,
Just like there is an engine going down in but a minute.
But Soldier Tom gets very tired when coming up the hill,
As home he plods at night from the little town Barnesville.

"The boiler shop has a foreman with a mustache on his face,
Attends to all the men at work and puts them in their place.
Here are the boiler-makers, with the hammers they just got;
Also rivet-heaters to make the rivets hot.
Some men do the holding, while others knock them down,
You can hear the noise they make in every part of town.

"And so, good night, and with it, we bid you all farewell,
We hope you're not offended at what we had to tell.
We think you must be pleased, if we can judge by looks;
At any rate we're mighty glad you didn't use the hooks."

These verses, making no pretence to poetic quality, served to give the stranger in a glance a very comprehensive idea of the important things in the town, and undoubtedly caused considerable

Deland Amateur Dramatic Association

Will give one of their entertainments in the New Hall, Delano,

FRIDAY EVENING, AUGUST 16, 1878.

F. J. Bickel, President; J. T. Wyatt, Treasurer; J. Ward, Secretary;
J. Barclay, Acting Manager; Charles Collum, Stage Manager;
John Weise, Property Man.

PROGRAMME—PART I.

THE BRIGAND AND HIS SON
A MELODRAMA IN ONE ACT.
CHARACTERS:

Corporal Nicolo Gamba	Mr. Charles Collum
Mateo Felcone	Mr. J. Barclay
Gianetto Sampiero ⎫ Brigands	Mr. F. J. Bickle
Brozzo ⎭	Mr. W. McCarroll
Fortunato Falcone, son of Mateo	Mr. M. Snyder

SOLDIERS, BRIGANDS, &c.

PART II.

THE HARVEST STORM
A SERIO-COMIC DRAMA.
CHARACTERS:

John Garner	Mr. T. Wyatt
Dick Darrell	Mr. W. M. Carroll
Mr. Lynx ⎫ Detective	Mr. A. Gimbi
" Barker ⎬ and	Mr. P. Nush
" Nibler ⎭ Assistants	Mr. J. Hartley
Samuel Lexicon, writing a new Dictionary	Mr. J. Barclay
Andrew Radfor	Mr. J. Ward
Michael Radford	Mr. C. Collum
Charles Cooper ⎫ Gipsies	Mr. J. Weiss
Nat Lovely ⎭	Mr. H. Artz

Sentimental & Comic Song . . . . Our Boys

THE MISCHIEVOUS NIGGER. A N...
CHARACTERS:

	Mr. T. Wyatt
	T. J. Bickle
	Mr. R. Martin
	Chas. Collum
	M. M. A.

PROGRAM OF DELANO DRAMATIC ASSOCIATION, 1878

HISTORY OF DELANO 61

mirth at the expense of those in the audience who were the victims of the good-natured twitting.

The starting of the movement for the new town hall and carrying it through to completion, are matters of interest in this historic record. In 1875 the need for a building of this kind had become apparent and, under the direction of Mr. John Campbell, a group of men, of which H. F. Bickle, Robert Martin, Thomas Wyatt, Peter Roseberry, Henry Barclay, Josiah Swank, James Ward and others were members, began preliminary work on the project. The work of clearing the ground for the foundation was done by the men of the community after their regular working hours, this labor being given without charge. In fact, there was no labor cost whatever involved in the whole operation. The total cost of the building when completed, all for material, was $385.00, this amount being contributed chiefly by the residents of the town by direct gifts and from funds raised through entertainments, with some of it coming from the railroad company.

Mr. Campbell was the treasurer of the committee and handled all the funds for the operation. When the first Sunday School was opened in the new building, Mr. Josiah Swank was named as superintendent. This was a position that, with several interruptions, he held during a large part of his long residence in Delano, and had at the time he left the town in 1899.

Upon the completion of the hall, the question came up as to how it was to be opened. Mr. Collum relates that a difference of opinion existed between Mr. A. P. Blakslee, the superintendent, and Mr. James, head of one of the debating teams, as to who should have the honor of presenting the first program. Mr. Blakslee felt that so signal an event should be marked with an unusual program and suggested getting a high-priced choir from Shamokin, Pa., while Mr. James thought Delano should reserve that honor for itself, since the people of the town conceived the plan and carried it to completion entirely by their own efforts. His suggestion was that the local dramatic association should open the hall with a minstrel performance, and that plan was adopted. The receipts of the first entertainment were $25.00, all of which was turned over to the treasurer of the building committee toward the payment of the debt. One of the high spots in this first entertainment was the presence of Superintendent James I. Blakslee, of Mauch Chunk, who brought his own family and a large delegation of people from that town to help celebrate the great event.

This was the beginning of many more of the same kind of entertainments, and many happy hours for entertainers and entertained centered about this little building. Indeed, this was a real community center, and every generation down to the present carries memories of happy hours spent within its walls.

Mr. McCarroll tells some interesting things about social functions held during the 70's, all of which helped to make life there most pleasant. Formality never entered into these affairs, which added much to the pleasure derived from them. Picnics, dances, excursions, sleighing parties and house parties were frequent. Often an informal dance would be arranged within a few hours, when someone felt the urge for such diversion. In short order a fiddler, or, perhaps, an orchestra, would be located in Mahanoy City or Shenandoah, arrive in Delano at 8:30 p. m. on one of the many trains then operating, and, in the meanwhile, the party would be rounded up at one of the homes, carpets lifted from the floors, and the dance was on. The fun and enjoyment derived from these parties were as wholesome and spontaneous as the impulses that prompted them.

The writer recalls that his Dad was occasionally pressed into service as a fiddler for these parties during the 80's, as he had developed considerable skill in scraping out the old dance tunes on his faithful violin. In fact, he can still, at 75 years of age, put the old-time zip into "Turkey-in-the-Straw," "Pop Goes the Weasel," and other famous old dance numbers. Possibly his greatest triumph as a fiddler was when he was called on one evening to furnish the music for one of those impromptu dances at the home of A. P. Blakslee, then Division Superintendent. For a mere fireman, still in his twenties, that was something.

MISCELLANY

The boarding house at Delano was always a center of interest, for here resided many of the young men who were unmarried and whose homes were in other communities. Volumes could be written of the things that occurred through the years in this ever-changing group. The first manager of the boarding house, which was located in the large building used for station, offices, etc., was Aaron Lattig, who was also assistant train dispatcher and afterwards train dispatcher. He was succeeded later as boarding house manager by Mr. William Snyder.

An amusing account of the strict rules maintained by Mr. Snyder in operating his hotel is given by Mr. Robert Martin, now of Mahanoy City, who went to Delano to work in 1873. He states that Mr. Snyder had a system all his own, that was neither European nor American. Supper was always served at 6 p. m. The man who came ten minutes too soon had to wait for the bell, while the chap who was ten minutes late stayed hungry for the night, as only the man who was there to start at scratch was admitted to the dining room. Mr. Martin also speaks of the cold winters at Delano as he experienced them in that boarding house. There was but one stove in the place and the boarders on cold nights raised their windows to let the cold out, as it was colder inside than out.

The first barber to serve the community was Emanuel Snyder, son of Manager Snyder above-mentioned. The shop was located at the east end of the building. Mr. Snyder was succeeded as tonsorial artist by John Gicking, who was later in passenger service on the railroad. Other barbers who took over the work in the decades following were Albert Gimbi and Elmer Artz and some others of whom mention will be made later.

The first store manager at Delano was a man named Watson. The business was established in the very beginning of the town's history, as would be expected. The original building still remains at the writing of this story, with few changes, and has been used for the same purpose all through these years. Before the end of the 70's, the store had been taken over by A. P. Blakslee, who operated it until his departure from Delano in 1898. The Post Office at Delano was established in the 70's and has been located in the store building from the beginning.

The town was not without its baseball team in these early days. Probably the first team organized in the town was named the "Clippers." A junior team was given the name of "Buffalos." The big team played teams of Mauch Chunk, Mahanoy City and other surrounding towns. Mr. Charles Collum was a member of this team in the late 70's and states that the last game he played with it was with Mount Carmel, which Delano lost 24-5.

The early water supply in the town was from wells and a small reservoir erected by the railroad company at the site of the present reservoirs. A plentiful water supply is a requisite to the operation of a railroad and railroad shops and this need was provided for in the very beginning of the town's history. The four small reservoirs which supplied the town for many years, and which still remain, were completed in April, 1879. These four dams are fed by a mountain stream rising from springs of purest water. No better water is to be found anywhere than that which cares for Delano's needs. Hydrants were placed at various convenient places about the town early in the history of the place and these furnished water for the householders until modern demands brought delivery right into the houses. A large wooden pipe line was the first crude method of getting water to the shops and water tanks, later to be replaced by regulation metal piping.

The Delano plateau forms the crest of a divide, part of the waters arising there flowing eastward and southward to find their way into the Schuylkill and thence to the Atlantic Ocean, while the other part flows westward into Mahanoy Creek, thence over many twisting miles into the Susquehanna near Herndon and on to the Chesapeake Bay.

CHAPTER VIII

THE CHILD COMES OF AGE

OUR story has brought us to the end of the first twenty-year period in the life of this lusty young community. A very important turning-point in the town's development is now to be recorded.

From time immemorial, under English and American law, the age of twenty-one has been considered the time of the attainment of full manhood or womanhood, with the investment of all legal rights and powers. It marks the time when young people achieve individual independence and the right to leave parental roofs and seek far countries.

By a peculiar coincidence, Delano was declared by the Courts of Schuylkill County to be an independent political subdivision on January 20th, 1882, just as it arrived at its twenty-first birthday anniversary. The husky young industrial giant cast off its childish habiliments and stepped out into the world free of its obligations to old Rush Township, from henceforth to enjoy independence under the name of Delano Township. The northwest portion of the original township was separated by this order from the parent township. Included in it, besides the town of Delano, are the villages of Park Place and Trenton.

A careful examination of the proceedings in the erection of the new township discloses some interesting things. The petition requesting the separation from Rush Township contains a not-too-subtle bit of humor that is not often found in legal papers, and that likely was not intended as humor at all. It is in the list of signers that it crops out. Because of the fact that the writer spent about as much of his life in rural Rush Township as he did in Delano, and had a wide acquaintance among the residents of that rural section, he was quick to notice this strange twist. Of the eighty-eight signers to the petition asking for a new township, not one was a resident of Delano, so far as the writer can determine.

It was the old story of the prodigal son, turned end for end. The fond father, in a tactful, but no uncertain way, invited the big child to pack up and get out. It is apparent from the language of the petition that the relations between the rural and urban sections of Rush Township had reached the place where the tail was wagging the dog.

Because of the importance of this event in the history of Delano, the whole petition and the various orders of the court thereon are set forth here.

PETITION FOR INCOPORATION OF DELANO TOWNSHIP

To the Honorable, the Judges of the Court of Quarter Sessions of the Peace for the County of Schuylkill:

The petition of the undersigned inhabitants and taxpayers of the township of Rush in the said county respectfully represents:

That your petitioners labor under great inconvenience by reason of the present formation of the said township, a portion of said township being exclusively of an agricultural character and another portion being in the mining region, containing the large and growing town of Delano, at which are also located the shops of the Lehigh Valley Railroad Company. That owing to the different wants and characteristics of the two sections, there is a continual and growing antagonism between them, in regard to roads, schools and in all matters relating to the government of said township, and that the interests and conveniences of both sections would be promoted if the said township were divided, and a new township erected out of the western part of said township according to the following division line, to wit:

Commencing at the Kline township line on the Lehigh Valley Railroad, thence along said railroad to the curve above Heiser's Mill and East of Pine Creek Gap, thence across Pine Creek Gap to the southern part of foot of mountain west of said Pine Creek, and thence along the foot of said mountain to the Ryan Township line.

Your petitioners therefore pray the court to appoint three impartial men as commissioners to inquire into the propriety of granting the prayer of the petitioners, and after making a plot or draft of the township as proposed to be divided, shall make their report at the next Court of Quarter Sessions, together with their opinion of the same.

And they will ever pray, etc.

George Loch	William Shickram	Daniel Zigler
H. A. Weldy & Co.	W. Kaup	E. K. Faust
Nathaniel Welsh	William Bachert	George Horcht
Samuel Shaffer	H. J. Bankes	Calvin Sherer
William Welsh	John Iffert	William Billy
William Neifert	John Fegley	Adam Steward
E. F. Hamsher	Samuel Neifert	Henry Hauck
Jacob Faust	Balzer Schultz	John Wetterau

Charles Herring	Jacob Leibig	D. H. Steward
Thomas M. Reed	Moses Welsh	Jonas Markel
Henry Hardranft	Eli Tillson	Condy Murrin
Joseph Bachert	Leonard Heffner	John Brobst
Isaac Blew	Cornelius Wagner	Henry Hauck
H. H. Reedy	Jacob Long	Monroe Hauck
Moses Hein	John K. Henry	Martin Wetterau
John Keller	Jacob Heckler	Thomas Coddington
Aaron Gelb	Martin Neifert	George Welsh
Josiah Keller	Charles Blew	William Kehoe
Abraham Neifert	Frank Neifert	Edward Hauck
William Iffert	Alvin Bankes	Allen Correll
Daniel Gerhard	Reuben Fogel	Jacob Beltz
David Neifert	Isaac Betz	Edward Eveland
Bernard Frank	Levi Gerhard	Benjamin Gerber
George Bankes	Albert Lindner	Philip Guenther
John Gerlach	John Lanz	Reuben Staller
Joseph Osenbach	Hermann Keilmann	Mahlon Lutz
S. P. Kester	Ben Kramer	Moses Day
James Steward	Edward Adams	Franklin Eveland
Emanuel Steward	Charles Klingeman	George Hein

And now, to wit, November 14th, A. D., 1881, at a Court of Quarter Sessions of the Peace in and for the County of Schuylkill this day held, the within report and return having been presented to the Court by H. B. Graeff, Esq., attorney, and it appearing to the Court that the commissioners appointed to inquire into the propriety of granting the prayer of the petition of sundry inhabitants of the township of Rush, asking that said township be divided and a new township be erected out of the western part of said township, made a return favorable to the erection of such new township, and reported that in their opinion it is proper that the prayer of the petitioners should be granted and that such new township should be erected according to the division line as prayed for and as set forth in said report by courses and distances. The Court order a vote of the qualified electors of the said township of Rush on the question of the division of the said township and the erection of a new township out of the western part of aforesaid township according to the division line as prayed for by the said petitioners and reported by the said commissioners, and the Court further order that the election officers of the said township of Rush shall hold an election in said township, to be governed by the laws of this Commonwealth relating to township elections, on Saturday, the thirty-first day of December, A. D., 1881, and that the Constable of the said township give at least fifteen days' notice of the time and place of holding said election by posting not less than six written or printed hand bills in the most public places in the said township.

By the Court:

E. W. Frehafer, Clerk.

HISTORY OF DELANO

And now, January 3rd, 1882, it appearing to the court that by reason of the absence from home of the constable of Rush Township at the time of the making of the former order of the court fixing the time of the holding of the special election in said township for the purpose as set forth in the said order, and the continued absence of the said constable until the time for the posting by him of the notices of said election had passed, so that fifteen days' notice of the holding of said election, as required by law, could not be given by the said Constable, the Court therefore direct that an alias order for the said election be made, and that the said election be held in said township for the purpose of the former order, at the usual place fixed by law, by the election officers of said township on Saturday, the 28th day of January, 1882, to be governed by the several laws of this Commonwealth relating to township elections, and that the constable of the said township give at least fifteen days' notice of the time and place of the holding of the said election, by posting not less than six handbills in the most public places in the said township.

By the Court:
E. W. Frehafer, Clerk.

And now, January 30th, 1882, the return of the election officers of the township of Rush, of the election held in said township on the 28th day of January, 1882, on the question of a division of the said township of Rush, and the erection of a new township out of the western part of said township having been presented to the court by H. B. Graeff, Esq., Attorney, and it appearing to the Court that a majority of the votes cast at said election are for a division of the said township, it is thereupon ordered and decreed that the said township of Rush be divided and a new township be erected out of the western part of the said township, agreeably to the lines marked out and returned by the commissioners, and it is further ordered and decreed that the name of the said new township shall be Delano, and further that the county commissioners pay the costs of the holding of said special election out of the county funds by order on the treasurer.

By the Court:
E. W. Frehafer, Clerk.

And now, January 30th, 1882, the Court direct that the place for holding the general, special and township elections for said township of Delano shall be at the public house of William Snyder in said township, and that the officers for holding the said elections until their successors are duly chosen shall be as follows: Judge, Dwight Ashby; Inspectors, John F. Mack, Jr., and W. J. Ashby. And A. A. Read is hereby appointed as Constable to give notice of the township election to be held on the third Tuesday of February next.

By the Court:
E. W. Frehafer, Clerk.

And so it was, that on the 30th day of January, 1882, at the proud age of twenty-one years, the town of Delano, by order of Court duly made and recorded, acquired political independence and a corporate entity of its own. It is interesting to note that the first official election held in the new township fell just three weeks after this date.

The writer is indebted to Albert L. Werner, Esq., present Justice of the Peace in Delano, and a resident of the town for more than fifty years, for a list of Justices and Constables who have served Delano Township since it was erected. Justices: Conrad Kocher (known to all old-timers as "Uncle" Kocher), John James, James M. Schrope, John H. Bannan, Harry E. Shafer and Albert L. Werner, the present incumbent. Constables: A. A. Read, (named specially for the first election), D. W. Zimmerman, James Scott, J. T. Wyatt, Jerry Ryan, John B. Hall, Simon Arner, William Sprague, Oscar Reigel, Harry W. Shaup, Robert Gasser and Lewis Shaup, the present incumbent.

It was during this momentous year in Delano's history that the writer first became a resident there. Mention of this fact is not, of course, by way of intimation that two great honors came to the little town in one year. But it was a matter of real personal interest to learn so many years afterward that it was his good fortune to come into the town at such an important time in its life.

In connection with this account of municipal concerns, it is well to include extracts from the records of deeds filed in Schuylkill County which cover the site of Delano. Mention has been made earlier in this volume of land titles, but readers will no doubt be interested in more specific statements of the several conveyances affecting the town plot. Such a record is important in the history of any place.

Briefly stated, these records are as follows:

Warren Delano, Jr., William Gihon, George Peabody Wetmore, Franklin H. Delano, Asa Packer, and others,
to
Delano Land Company

Dated July 1, 1872.
Consideration, $2,000,000.00.
For 5,229¼ acres on headwaters of Schuylkill River and Mahanoy Creek, Schuylkill County, Penna.

Edward King and Augusta King, his wife,
to
Delano Land Company

Dated November 22, 1872.
Consideration, $1.00.
All their interest in the above described tract of land.

Edward King, Guardian for William Henry King, to Delano Land Company	Dated November 20, 1872. Consideration, $1.00. All his interest in above-described tract of land.
Nathaniel Thayer and Cornelia Thayer, his wife, to Delano Land Company	Dated January 27, 1873. Consideration, Legal. All their interest in the above-described tract of land.
Warren Delano, Jr., and others to Delano Land Company	Dated February 6, 1873. Consideration, Legal. Interest in the above tract.
Delano Land Company to Lehigh Valley Railroad Company	Dated November 2, 1891. Consideration, $1,000.00. For 255.5 acres in Rush Township, Schuylkill County, Penna. (Delano Town Plot).

On October 1st, 1926, the Lehigh Valley Railroad Company conveyed most of the dwellings in Delano to the employees occupying them at that time, retaining just a few for the use of such of their employees whose work is more or less transient in character. More detailed information of this will be given later in this book.

CHAPTER IX

Railroad and Shops—1880-1890

POSSIBLY Delano made its greatest advances as a railroad center during the ten-year period now under consideration. Its highest point of activity in this field was reached in this decade and was maintained until about 1892, when occurred what is always spoken of among Delano people as "The Reading Deal," from which time a diminution in the importance of the town as a railroad community began, which culminated about seven years later in the removal of the shops from the place. This was Delano's major catastrophe, from which it never did entirely recover.

At about the beginning of this period, an imperative need for more shop buildings arose, due to increased repair work and the contemplated rebuilding of many old engines and the construction of new ones, with the inauguration of car building as an additional industry. Accordingly these new buildings were erected: Machine shop, blacksmith shop, boiler shop, copper and tinsmith shop, paint shop, car shop, frog and switch shop and a new engine house. These added facilities for the extension of the construction work brought new prosperity to the little town.

Besides the repair work and rebuilding and construction of engines, the plant was now prepared for new lines of work. The building of passenger cars and baggage cars was started, under the supervision of John Moore, master car builder, and this brought many new mechanics into the town. The frog and switch shop also opened a new field of industry, all the frogs and switches for the Lehigh Valley system being manufactured at Delano for many years. In these shops also were made the hubs and springs used on the entire system. The opening of the new car shops increased the demand for master painters and this shop took on a new activity.

It was at this time that the shop forces increased rapidly, reaching a total of over three hundred fifty skilled mechanics at one time. Due to the restricted building area, as has been mentioned, the town could not provide homes for all those employed there, and surrounding towns and country derived large profit from the prosperity of Delano.

A comparison of wages paid in that day with those of today is illuminating and interesting. The highest-paid mechanics were paid at the rate of $2.40 for a ten-hour day, and not many men received that much. At this time railroad engineers, the highest paid employees in road service, received $3.00 per day for a twelve-hour day, with conductors, firemen and trainmen receiving considerably less. Work was steady and it was difficult for an employee to get a day off. However, there was not much dissatisfaction with conditions at that time. Many of the things that the American workman today lists with the absolute necessities would have been considered extravagance then, and things that are still in the luxury class today were then beyond even the wildest flights of the imagination.

The personnel of superintendents and foremen in charge of the various shop departments underwent no great change during these years. The list named earlier in this volume covers this period, as well as the years immediately preceding and following.

In the railroad department in the early part of this decade the division official list was made up of Alonzo P. Blakslee, assistant superintendent (his father, James I. Blakslee, still being superintendent); Thomas May, trainmaster; Edward Glenn, yardmaster; H. V. Perry, day train dispatcher; J. J. Neifert, night train dispatcher; Thomas Reynolds, station agent, and John B. Anthony, time-keeper. Mr. Anthony was also at that time principal of the schools, doing his railroad work after school hours and on Saturdays. A. H. Butler was time clerk.

Delano at this time, both in the shops and on the railroad, was a veritable hive of industry. On the railroad at least seventeen train crews handled passenger service alone, all of these crews running out of Delano to various points. The division headquarters formed the hub of a wheel with spokes twenty miles long. These steel radii extended in every direction, reaching Mahanoy City, Ashland and Mount Carmel to the west, Pottsville to the south, Mauch Chunk to the east and Hazleton to the north, with connections to other and more distant points on the Reading, Pennsylvania and Northern Central Railways. Passenger trains arrived and departed every hour in the day at Delano and this was the changing point for travelers moving from various places in this part of the state by way of Delano and the Lehigh Valley Railroad. Who does not remember the old-style method of changing cars, when two trains pulled alongside of each other and a brakeman placed his slatted gang-plank across the opening between the car platforms, over which bridge the passengers transferred from one train to the other? The railway station was always a scene of great activity throughout the day and night. Naturally it was a congregating place for the youngsters as well as older men after school and working hours, who found a never-waning fascination in watching the outside world flow through their little transportation gateway. But the ancient and perennial joke about the villagers hanging around the depot to see the 8:15 go through did not apply here, for watching trains come in and go out had lost its novelty to these men and boys long before they had cut all their milk teeth. But they never lost interest in the ever-changing tide of humanity that passed through the town.

What a transformation in this service the years have wrought! Today but two passenger trains a day each way pass through the town. Both of these have their terminal points elsewhere. Further, neither one is drawn by the good old iron horse of other days, but, as if to add insult to injury, the fussy, sputtering gas-electric motor car clatters contemptuously through with its lone day coach trailing behind like some noisy Seventh Avenue elevated.

The first trains to operate out of Delano were coal trains from the mines to the coal pockets at East Mauch Chunk, the eastward route being through the Quakake Valley. For the first twenty years of the town's existence freight and passenger traffic was confined to the main division line between Mount Carmel and Mauch Chunk, connections on this line being made with the Catawissa Railroad at Quakake, the Hazleton and Beaver Meadow Railroad at Black Creek Junction and the Lehigh Valley main line at Mauch Chunk.

On September 6th, 1886, the first passenger train was run from Delano to St. Clair and, upon the completion of the St. Clair tunnel, the first passenger train from Delano to Pottsville was run November, 1886. On April 24th, 1887, the first passenger service from

Delano to Hazleton was inaugurated, and passenger service was opened by the Lehigh Valley by way of Shenandoah Junction to Pottsville, over the Frackville Branch, on December 19th, 1887. The Lizard Creek Branch, between Pottsville, Orwigsburg and Lizard Creek Junction on the main line, was opened for passenger service on August 18th, 1890.

The building of these radiating lines to the important towns about Delano was done over a period of a few years and brought the department of passenger service to its operating peak, which high level was maintained for about ten years, or until division headquarters were changed to Hazleton. The building of the Hazleton branch was started in July, 1886, and the engineering work was done by a corps of engineers including Isaac Dox, Chief Engineer; Jonas F. Young, W. Osterhout, William H. Sayre, Jr., S. J. Harwi and L. J. H. Grossart. The latter three had just graduated from the engineering department of Lehigh University at Bethlehem, Pa., and this was their first assignment to duty. Mr. Grossart, in a letter to the writer, relates how much impressed these men were with the friendly spirit of the Delano people during their stay, which ended in April, 1887. Mr. Grossart is now the head of an engineering firm in Allentown, Pa., and he is the husband of Miss Carolin Moore, a long-time resident of Delano.

Coal and freight were carried in ever-increasing volume over the new lines. Delano train crews at that time performed service reaching to Wilkes-Barre, Hazleton, Lizard Creek Junction, Mauch Chunk, Pottsville, Ashland, Mount Carmel, Shamokin, Tomhicken and intermediate points.

Railroading in this period had its difficulties as well as its triumphs. The winter season was then, as now, the railroader's Nemesis. Rotary snow plows, powerful engines, with modern equipment, were still unknown, but the daring and resourcefulness of these old-time knights of the rail were able to cope with the most trying situations.

The great blizzard of 1888, still recalled as the granddaddy of all blizzards, has furnished to this day a most absorbing topic wherever railroaders foregather to discuss railroading. The "I-Remember-When" clubs have never been successfully challenged in their tall stories about this noted spring uprising of old King Winter.

The snow fell in blinding clouds for three days and nights and the wind howled with the fury of a hurricane. Malone's cut, near Delano on the Hazleton line, was filled with snow to the top from end to end. Three large consolidation engines, selected for their great tractive power, in charge of their dauntless crews from Delano, were put back of one of the old-time snow plows and, under a full head of steam and at full speed, time after time they rammed the huge drifts that lifted themselves higher than the engines, but without any noticeable effect in clearing the cut. Now, if any reader thinks he has experienced the ultimate in thrills as furnished by an age that has become rather blase in such matters, let him conjure up in his mind, if he can, the emotions aroused by riding in the cab of one of those plunging ten-wheelers, with a small snow plow in front and two other ten-wheelers behind, driving full-tilt, like some jousting knight, straight at a towering snow-drift. One hundred tons of steel traveling at thirty miles an hour, hitting a hard-packed and unyielding mass. It came very close to demonstrating what happens when the irresistible force meets the immovable body. Only men of daring and courage, inured to danger as an everyday matter, could undertake that kind of a task. With those men, it was just part of the day's work.

In some respects life in a railroad town is akin to that in a fishing port, where men go down to sea while women stay home to work and weep while the harbor bar is moaning. Each day in the life of the railroad family has its anxieties and forebodings. What person who ever lived in a railroad center can forget the chills of misgiving and the pull at heart strings that came as the wreck train pulled out of its siding and started forth on its grim errand? And what the doubts that assailed each family until exact information had been obtained as to whether tragedy was to rest upon that house? How many times were the worst of these fears realized.

These reflections take the writer back to pleasant hours spent in the company of old Dad Jenkins, in charge of the wreck car, as he sat in his domain busy at his work of splicing rope and other duties while regaling his young friends with tales of adventure at sea encountered by him in his sailor days years before. It is difficult even yet to reconcile the picture of that kindly, white-bearded old sailor, in the peaceful atmosphere of the car on its siding with the grim business upon which at ever-recurring times it was sent forth.

This seems to be a very good place to relate some of the tales of engine performance and stirring experiences of this period. These are but one or two outstanding cases taken from a multitude that might be recounted if space permitted. They are used as typical of the many, for the purpose of recording a tribute to a breed of men outstanding in any time and place.

Mention has already been made of the famous No. 148, the Evangeline. A particular aura of glory seems to hover around this famous old flyer. It was constructed at a total cost said to be $20,000.00, a large sum for that day. The flagstaffs on the pilot alone cost $300.00. It was said to be the finest engine ever built by the Lehigh Valley Railroad Company. So great was its reputation that the Pennsylvania Railroad requested permission to try it out on its main line. The engine was taken to Harrisburg and was put into service between that city and Altoona. It fulfilled every expectation and made some wonderful records in speed and power. Before using it there, it was taken into the Altoona shops and equipped with Westinghouse air-brakes, the first ever seen in Delano, to which place it was returned after the Pennsylvania try-outs.

Nick Shillinger was the engineer who first had this engine in charge and his fireman was Thomas Moore, who married Delano's first school teacher, as has been noted. Mr. Shillinger was afterwards killed in 1879, when his engine ran into a landslide on the main line of the Lehigh Valley near Sayre, Pa. He was not running the 148 at the time. Mr. Moore also lost his life on the railroad some years afterwards, as told in a previous chapter.

The 148 was put into service on the main line after a time and was in charge of James Kelly. On one trip from Wilkes-Barre to Easton, a passenger requested permission to ride in the engine cab, which was given by the engineer very reluctantly. While the train was running through the Packeton yards, the left driving rod broke, plunged through the floor of the cab, pulled the passenger through and ground him to pieces. Kelly succeeded in bringing the train to a stop safely and was horrified to learn the fate of the man to whom he had given his reluctant permission to ride on the engine.

This famous old engine later came back to the Mahanoy Division where it continued in useful service for many years. As stated

History of Delano

before, it was the first passenger engine used by the writer's father on his run between Shamokin and Wilkes-Barre. Later it was used at Hazleton on a combination freight and passenger run and was finally sent to the Bloomsburg and Sullivan Railroad, running from Bloomsburg into the Dushore and Montrose section for some years until it came to the place of all things mundane, the scrapheap. It was equipped with a deep-toned, steamboat whistle, and this writer can still hear its long, resonant call coming in at night from Pottsville as it approached Delano Junction.

A record that was a classic in its day was that made by engine 407 in charge of Engineer John McMullen and Fireman Jerry Ryan, Sr. A run was made from Pottsville to Hazleton, by way of Delano, in which this engine pulled five loaded passenger coaches up grades that are as high as 160 feet to the mile. Over one four-mile stretch on this run, on the heaviest part of the grade, eleven minutes time was consumed. The entire run was made on schedule time, an accomplishment that was declared impossible with that tonnage before it was done.

Another thrilling experience that is often recalled by Delano railroaders of the old school was that of Ollie Mason and his crew and passengers when the main driving axle on his engine, No. 147, broke just as he started to cross the high bridge near St. Clair. Fortunately the drivers held the rail and the train was safely run across the bridge and brought to a standstill. Anyone who knows that bridge can visualize the result of an engine leaving the rails while crossing it. The passengers, of course, were totally oblivious to their close call, but the cool-headed engineer certainly must have breathed a fervent prayer of thanks to the Providence that guarded him and his precious cargo that day.

Another triumph of a Campbell-built engine was the performance of the No. 617, the first and only camel-back passenger engine built at Delano, as it was also the last engine built there. This record properly belongs to a later day, but may be told here with those of the earlier time. The 617 was used on the Delano-Pottsville run, with Edward Campbell, a son of the builder, in charge. It made such a fine impression among railroad men that when the Philadelphia and Reading Railway assumed control of the Lehigh Valley in 1892, it was transferred to the North Penn Division of the Reading for service there, running in passenger service between Bethlehem and Philadelphia. The 617 soon established the reputation of being the best engine ever used in that service on the Reading, making better time, pulling at least two more coaches and using less water and fuel than the other engines used on the same run. It was kept on that division for one year and was then sent back to Delano for repairs. This engine was noted not only for stellar performance, but for appearance as well. The illustration found elsewhere in this volume shows the trim, sturdy lines that made the 617 a sensation in its day.

It would require many books to relate all the stirring tales of accomplishment and heroism that might be told about the men who have made railroad history in Delano during the 70 years of its life. Many of them died at their posts, as bravely as any soldier on any field of battle. Many more carried through life the evidence of injuries sustained in shops or on the road.

Advances in equipment on the railroad during this decade included a new coal platform and water station and a new brick office building, which was built in 1880. The first engine to be equipped with a device for heating passenger coaches by steam while on the road was the 34, this improvement being used first on April 25th, 1889.

It was early in this decade that the management of the boarding house came under the control of Edward Glenn, who was also yardmaster at Delano. Mr. and Mrs. Glenn continued in charge of this hotel until it was discontinued during the late 90's.

CHAPTER X

COMMUNITY INTERESTS IN THE 80'S

IT IS necessary at the opening of this chapter to retrace our steps for a little space, to catch up a few threads of the pattern into which this record is being woven. No mention has been made thus far of a service that is indispensable to every community and touches the most intimate family life of everyone in the community —that of the medical profession.

In many respects the town of Delano was fortunate from its very beginning in having unusually good medical service, both from the standpoint of skillful physicians and the promptness with which the service was always available. In spite of the fact that there was no resident physician in the town for many years, this was not a serious inconvenience, for the railroad company was ready at a moment's notice to provide an engine and crew to make the run to Mahanoy City when the doctor was needed in a hurry, and it was a very common thing to send a crew on such an errand at any time of the day or night.

Probably the first doctor to practice at Delano was Dr. Phaon Hermany, of Mahanoy City, who received his degree in medicine from the University of New York on March 3rd, 1863, and immediately began the practice of his profession in Mahanoy City, which practice he continued until his death on November 18th, 1916, a total of fifty-three years. It is doubtful if any name could be mentioned that would arouse greater interest among the people who lived in Delano between 1863 and 1916, than that of Dr. Hermany. His face and form were as familiar to Delano folks as they were to his friends in Mahanoy City. It is a privilege to be able to include in this volume a sketch of the life of this distinguished man, as well as a fine portrait of him.

Dr. Phaon Hermany was born in Jacksonville, Lehigh County, Pennsylvania, on September 16th, 1840. He was educated at Mount Pleasant Seminary and in the University of New York, graduating from the latter institution on March 3rd, 1863. He started practice in the same year at Mahanoy City, Pa., and continued his practice there for fifty-three years. He was successful in his profession from the start, and attained a high place not only in medical circles, but in community life generally.

He was married to Mary J. Bowman, of Mahanoy City, on December 6th, 1863. There were four children of the union: Dr. Horace, who died October 21st, 1918; Robert K., who died in 1872; Sallie, now living in Mahanoy City; and Susan, wife of William Dyatt, of Hazleton, Pa.

Dr. Hermany was active in church and school matters in his home town, serving on the school board for over seventeen years as president of that body. He was active in the St. John's Lutheran Church, and was physician for the Lehigh Valley Railroad Company for fifty-two years. At one time he operated drug stores in Mahanoy City and Delano. He was a 32nd degree Mason, a member of the Schuylkill County, Lehigh County, Pa., and the American Medical Societies. He was a charter member of Asa Packer Lodge of Odd Fellows at Delano and belonged to other fraternal organizations. He was an elder in St. John's Lutheran Church and a teacher of a Bible Class for many years.

Another physician who practiced in Delano for many years, and later was a resident there, and who was as well-known and as highly regarded as the venerable Dr. Hermany, was Dr. Lewis A. Flexer. The compiler is pleased to be able to present a sketch of the life of this eminent physician, as well as a photograph of him as he was best known to his Delano friends.

Dr. Lewis A. Flexer was born in North Penn Township, Schuylkill County, Pennsylvania, on March 4th, 1853. He received his education in the public schools, Kutztown State Normal School and Kutztown Seminary of Kutztown, Pa. He completed his medical training in the medical college of Ann Arbor, Michigan, in June, 1879, receiving his degree in medicine at that time.

In July, 1879, he began the practice of medicine in Tamanend, Pa., just east of Delano, and continued there until January 2nd, 1900, when he located in Delano, where he remained until his death on February 28th, 1910. He died a martyr to his profession, as he contracted blood-poisoning in an operation performed on one of his patients. Being very busy in his work at the time, he paid little attention to the infection, which in three days caused his death from a heart collapse.

Dr. Flexer was especially noted in the practice of surgery and attained a high degree of skill in this branch of medical science. He was particularly expert in eye surgery and removed many cataracts in his practice. His practice was so large at one time that he had Dr. Bedline as an assistant. He was called to many towns distant from his home as a consulting physician and he also served as a surgeon for the Lehigh Valley Railroad for many years.

A picture that often comes to mind with those who knew Dr. Flexer in his earlier practice is that of his distinguished-looking person in a swanky buggy or sleigh, driving through the community behind a thoroughbred, spirited, fast-stepping horse. He always drove the best of horses and occasionally, during the absence of the doctor in the home of a patient, the horse would take fright at a train or from some other cause and bolt for home over the mountain. In these headlong flights, leaving robes scattered along the way, track records were equalled, if not surpassed; and the doctor's many friends, beholding the runaway and not certain whether the doctor was in the vehicle, had many a heart spasm over the possible outcome.

These two noted physicians were closely identified with life in Delano for many years and gave to the people of the town a quality of service not surpassed in any community, large or small. They were both of the old school type of doctor, skilled in general practice, faithful to the trust imposed by their profession, and beloved by generations of grateful patients who had benefited by their healing ministry.

The Drug Store

Closely allied with the practice of the medical profession is that of the pharmacist. Delano has had the service of a drug store throughout most of its history. In the early days the store was owned by Dr. Hermany and was in charge of a qualified druggist. Various changes in ownership took place throughout the years, coming into the hands of Mr. J. A. Depew early in the 80's. For many years Mr. Reynolds, of Mahanoy City, was in charge as pharmacist, the store being then located in the small building erected for that purpose just southwest of the general store. In later years this building was removed and the business transferred to the west end of the old railway station, in what was one time the men's waiting room, where it remained for a period of about thirty-two years, or until the old building was torn down, when it was transferred to the east side of the brick office building across the railroad. It is still located in that building at this writing. Samuel Depew operated the drug store for many years, with one of his sons as the pharmacist, who was succeeded by James Kelly Shaup, son of Harry Shaup, who is the present owner and pharmacist.

The writer has pleasant memories of the delicious sodas concocted by the genial Mr. Reynolds in the days before ice cream sodas were known. Mr. Reynolds always used as a base for his drinks about an inch of rich cream, into which went an honest-to-goodness quantity of flavoring syrup before adding the carbonated water. And all this in a tall, full-sized glass for the exact sum of one nickel. Oh Time, who wouldn't turn thee back in thy flight, if for but a moment, to live again those childhood joys?

A photograph of the portion of the old station building after it came into use for drug store purposes is shown here, together with another one of the station building as it was originally.

The Delano Band

One of the outstanding organizations of Delano was the band. The historian is indebted to Mr. Henry Perry, its leader, and to Mr. Frank H. Bickle, a pioneer resident of Delano, now residing in Plainfield, N. J., for the information here given about this important institution in the life of the town. Mr. Perry and Mr. Bickle were both interested in the organization of the band and Mr. Perry was its director and cornet soloist for most of its history. Mr. Perry is now residing in Bloomfield, Conn., where he has been for the past thirty-two years. He was recently retired by the New York, New Haven and Hartford Railroad after many years' service in its operating department. The picture of him shown in this volume will be interesting to the many Delano people who were old-time friends of his in Delano. Mr. Herbert Perry, a son of Henry Perry, who was also a member of the band and who now resides in Hartford, Conn., has also furnished some valuable facts about the activities of the organization.

THE ORIGINAL STATION BUILDING
Text Page 82

DRUG STORE, PART OF OLD
STATION BUILDING
Text Page 82

HENRY V. PERRY
BANDMASTER
Text Page 82

The idea of a band for Delano first originated in the home of Mr. David Fletcher late in the 80's. The organizers were H. F. Bickle, Edward Fletcher, George Burnett, Henry V. Perry, Joseph Becker, Harry Artz, Willie Hughes and Clinton Engle. The money for the purchase of the first instruments and equipment was advanced by David Fletcher and was later repaid by funds raised on an excursion to Glen Onoko, for many years a favorite spot for picnics.

The first band was directed by Mr. George Burnett, one of Delano's pioneers. Besides directing the band at that time, Mr. Burnett also played E-flat cornet and the trombone. The other members of the band, with the instruments they played, as nearly as they can be recalled, are: Henry V. Perry, B-flat cornet soloist; a man from Park Place (name forgotten) B-flat cornet soloist; John Bannan, first B-flat cornet; John Hartung, E-flat cornet; Joseph Becker, B-flat clarinet; Clinton Engel, alto soloist; Joseph Purcell, first alto; Harry Artz, first tenor; Griff Griffiths, second tenor; Andrew Lynch, second tenor; another Park Place man (name forgotten) baritone; Frank Bickle, E-flat bass; William Mull, bass drum and cymbals; and Reuben Markel, snare drum. Edward Fletcher, Willie Hughes and some others were also members of this first band, but the writer is not able to state the instruments they played.

Band practice was held in a room in the rear of the freight house building. Band practice nights were always occasions for the congregating of the youngsters of the town outside of the band room, to enjoy the free concerts. The writer can still see his old chums, the Perry boys, who joined the band in later years, in their respective places, hard at work on the intricacies of instrument and music as their father swung the baton and made his criticisms.

Mr. Burnett did not long continue as director of the band and requested Mr. Perry, whose musical ability was a native gift, to take it over. Mr. Perry continued as director until the dissolution of the organization in the late 90's.

The work of this band was of a high quality. Delano was fortunate in having many men of genuine musical ability, in spite of its limited population. And, as is often found in small communities, the pride of accomplishment was strong in them. To reflect credit upon their town was a strong inducement to them in giving their time and their best talent toward the success of the band. They were most fortunate, too, in having a leader that knew and loved music and gave without stint of his own time to develop a worthwhile organization.

The first engagements for the band were for local dances in the Delano grove, and it was soon very much in demand. Picnics, parades, lodge functions, social affairs, all made bids for the services of the band, and these invitations came from all over that section. Many were the triumphs scored.

The band was later enlarged and, as re-organized, included these members: H. V. Perry, leader; Clinton Engle, Llewellyn Griffiths, John Hartung, John Bannan, Jacob Engle, William Smith, Joseph Purcell, Andrew Lynch, Griff Griffiths, Fred Raeder, Herbert Perry, George Perry, Charles Perry, Reuben Markle, William Mull, Robert Zimmerman, George Harris and Con Donnelly.

During the time of this second organization, some special engagements were filled, much to the credit of the band and the enhancing of the reputation it had for producing fine music. About 1897 or 1898 it played with other bands at the state convention of the P. O. S. of A. held in Tamaqua, and received high praise for its work. It was said at that time that the lack of uniforms was the only thing that kept it from getting first prize. On another occasion, in a parade at Pottsville, it was given credit for being the best band in line. Herbert Perry, who played B-flat bass in the Tamaqua parade, states that the band played there all day and halfway through the night and that the lips of the players were still in good shape at the finish.

During the period of the Spanish-American War, the band was active in furnishing music for flag-raisings and other patriotic affairs occasioned by the wave of patriotism that swept over the land.

A third re-organization was effected in the personnel before the band was finally disbanded on the removal of the shops. The members of this third organization, as nearly as can be recalled, were: H. V. Perry, leader and solo cornetist; Andrew Lynch, treasurer and first trombone; Herbert Perry, secretary and B-flat bass; John Bannan, first cornet; William Smith, second cornet;

The Store About 1884, With Some Old Timers

A Store Group in 1910
Text Page 90

William Perry, second cornet; John Hartung, E-flat cornet; George Perry, baritone; Charles Perry, solo B-flat clarinet; Simon Arner, B-flat clarinet; Griff Griffiths, second clarinet; John Becker, second clarinet; Joseph Purcell, second trombone; Frank Bitler, E-flat bass; Lewis Markle, snare drum; Robert Zimmerman, bass drum; Charles Miller, cymbals; Clinton Engel, solo alto; Leo Sparr, first alto; H. V. Clemens, piccolo; George Bannan, second alto; Fred Miller, first tenor; Robert Shafer, third clarinet.

This third organization continued the good work of providing high class music for the town and surrounding territory until it disbanded about 1899. This musical body was one of Delano's real assets. Just how much it contributed to the enjoyment of its citizens and to the reputation of the little town for producing worthwhile enterprises cannot be measured, but delightful memories will linger long in the minds of those who had the privilege of hearing and seeing the Perry Band on parade.

Fraternal Societies

It was during this time in the history of the town that the fraternal spirit manifested itself in the organization of various lodges.

The first fraternal organization was the Patriotic Order Sons of America, which was organized and chartered March 27th, 1878, with the following charter members: Robert J. Orr, David Bechtel, Joseph A. Depew, Charles Vaughn, Harry Artz, William Wildes, Eli Haldeman, H. C. Faust, D. W. Zimmerman, Robert Martin, Joseph Bannan, William Opp, John R. James, William Depew, Henry Lattig, John Wentz, J. B. Beels, George Butler, Francis Billman and James Swartz. Of these, the following are still living at this writing: Harry Artz, Altoona, Pa.; George Butler, Weatherly, Pa.; Robert Martin, Mahanoy City, Pa. D. W. Zimmerman and Francis Billman died just a few months ago.

Mr. George Butler is generally credited with being the moving spirit in the organization of this lodge and for many years he has been known as the father of Camp 72. The first meetings were held in the Union Hall, continuing there for about six months, when they were transferred to a room over the paint shop in the old round house. This was used for about a month and again the lodge transferred to the school building, where meetings were held until Delano Township was erected in the early part of 1882, when Union Hall again came into use for this purpose. Upon the completion of the large three-story freight house in 1883, a room was especially fitted for lodge purposes on the third floor of that building and Camp 72 moved into those quarters, which it has occupied ever since.

It was a fixed custom in Delano for every young man who arrived at the age of sixteen years, if otherwise qualified, to affiliate with Camp 72. The writer had that privilege when he became sixteen and still retains the most pleasant memories of his connection with the order. For some time in the middle 90's he had the honor of being assistant secretary to Llewellyn Bannan, secretary, and it was an honor that sat quite heavily upon him in that day. Among other memories of those days that cling tenaciously are those of the series of debates held in the lodge hall on the free silver question during the McKinley-Bryan campaign of 1896. Professor J. M. Schrope, although a consistent Democrat, took the gold standard side of the question, and Simon Arner, also an ardent Democrat, championed the Bryan cause.

Still fresh, too, is the memory of the twenty-fifth anniversary of the founding of Camp 72, on which occasion the writer acted as master of ceremonies. At this celebration, State Secretary William Weand made the address of the evening, with William Mull, a noted local orator of that time, representing the Camp, and Miss Ethel Butler (now Mrs. William Symons), as daughter of the father of the Camp, giving the welcome to the distinguished visitor.

On October 9th, 1883, Asa Packer Lodge No. 328 of Odd Fellows was granted a charter, with the following officers and charter members: Edwin F. Joslyn, Noble Grand; Anthony Loftus, Vice Grand; W. S. Robinson, Secretary; Andrew Klinger, Assistant Secretary; John McCarroll, Treasurer; D. B. Shaffer, Samuel Bowers, Dr. Phaon Hermany, Jacob G. Engel, James P. Swartz, John B. Anthony, Harry F. Bickle, Hiram E. Blodgett, J. A. Depew, Thomas Hughes, Theodore Howells, John Shaffer, John Taylor, John Weiss, Charles Witman and Samuel Flowers.

Of these charter members, the following are still living, so far as can be ascertained: H. F. Bickle, Plainfield, N. J.; Andrew Klinger, Allentown, Pa., and Charles Witman, New Ringgold, Pa.

The new lodge occupied quarters from the beginning in the new lodge room on the third floor of the freight station, where it continues to this day to meet. It has been throughout its history a credit to the order of which it is a part and has done much to uphold the best standards of life in Delano. It is still in a very flourishing condition and more will be said about it in a later chapter.

The Knights of the Golden Eagle maintained a lodge in Delano for many years and was very active in the fraternal life of the town during that time. It surrendered its charter, however, in 1905, due to the loss of many members through removal, and it has never been re-established. It is impossible to give a record of its membership here.

The women of Delano have also been interested in lodge activities, and two fine orders have been in existence for many years: The Patriotic Order of Americans and The Sons and Daughters of Liberty. Both of these lodges were instituted a long time ago and have continued their work to the present time.

Recreational Interests

One of the centers of great activity in the little railroad town during this decade and down to the end of the next one was the "Picnic Ground," that marvelous grove of giant pine trees which stood on the western edge of the town at the place still known as "over the hill." Here was provided a playground supreme, not only for the people of Delano, but, by the enterprise of the railroad company, for the whole surrounding countryside. It did more, probably, to make the town well known throughout the anthracite field than any other single thing.

The selection of this spot and its development were due to the pride and devotion of the small group of men who made possible the building of the town hall, baseball grounds and other things of community interest. Nature had already provided the natural setting with a heavy growth of great trees, and the untiring efforts of the pioneers in clearing the undergrowth and improving the surroundings completed the work. The railroad company later became interested in the project and furnished much equipment for the entertainment and amusement of those who visited the grove.

In the beginning, the grounds were used by the residents of Delano for their family and community picnics and dances, but the railroad company was not long in recognizing in it a source of revenue for its stockholders. With this recognition came the period of great excursions and picnics from all over the region. There were few people residing within a radius of twenty miles of Delano who did not at some time in the twenty years or more of the existence of this recreation center visit it. It was without doubt the outstanding amusement place of that day in Schuylkill and adjoining counties.

Picnic days were always gala days for the youngsters of Delano. Early in the morning of any of those big days great activity was afoot in that immediate vicinity. The work train crew was hard at work hauling sawdust to be placed under swings, drums, Flying Dutchmen, and other equipment. This writer can recall a diminutive Czech who was a member of the work train crew at that time carrying a large barrel of sawdust on his back, unassisted, at one of those picnic occasions, on a wager that he couldn't do it. He did it, too. And then, when the excursion train pulled in and the picnickers began to detrain, laden with lunch boxes, baskets, etc. The big time was on. In just a few minutes pole swings, boat swings, Flying Dutchmen, drums, seesaws, and all the other devices for creating pleasure, were going full tilt, and kept going full tilt all through the day.

Frequently the townspeople would make these excursion days the occasion for picnics of their own and would join with the visitors in the good time. Of course, all the kids of the town who were foot-loose made it their business to attend the big picnics, whether the rest of the town participated or not.

But sic transit gloria mundi. The demands of commerce and the avarice of man combined to bring the beauty of this spot to destruction. With the removal of the coal from beneath the site, came the danger of surface subsidence and the use of it for pleasure purposes was soon made impossible. The giant trees that had given majesty to the spot for so many years were cut down, others were left to die a lingering death, and now, where once the exuberant voices of happy merrymakers rang out, naught remains but desolation. Other places have since been provided for com-

FAMILY OF JOHN MACK IN 1887

The Teaching Staff in 1886-1887
Text Page 94

munity outings, but the days of great outland excursions passed into oblivion with the going of the famous old "Picnic Ground."

House parties were a popular form of entertainment in this decade. Birthday anniversaries were made the occasions for many happy social gatherings. And they were always well attended and thoroughly enjoyed. It would be a most interesting experience to visit the homes of those good housewives who lived in Delano in the 80's and examine the collections of china and glassware that were received by them as gifts at those birthday parties. Who does not remember the tall glass cake plates, made to hold the skyscraper layer-cakes so popular in that day, or the setting hens, so lifelike in clear or opaque glass, resting upon dishes used for catchalls? The gifts were always useful and, of course, a very important part of the affairs.

In such ways were the simple social and recreational desires of the good people of Delano served during this important period in its life.

Some important events in the town's main business place, the store, occurred during this decade. The store was then owned by Mr. A. P. Blakslee, assistant superintendent of the Mahanoy Division, with Mr. J. A. Depew as manager. Two men who have had a large and important part in the life of Delano became identified with the store in 1882—George W. and Charles F. Hofmann, brothers. Perhaps no two persons connected with Delano history are better known or more highly regarded than the Hofmann boys. They are still, at this writing, actively in charge of the store, operating it now for Mrs. J. A. Depew, the owner. Mr. George Hofmann has been for many years postmaster at Delano.

A rare old picture of the store, taken about 1884, is shown here. The names of the persons appearing on it will be interesting especially to residents of that period. They are as follows: Adults, left to right—David Dress (of Fish-O fame), George Geiger (Lehigh Valley Railroad Police—what kid of the 80's and 90's does not remember him?), J. A. Depew, T. Nelson, Leon Beels, George Hofmann, Charles Hofmann, Charles Blakslee, Dr. Hermany. Seated in front, left to right—James Crossan and James Irvin Blakslee. Boys in rear, left to right—Horace Hermany (son of the doctor, later a doctor himself), Seth Purcell and Mitchell

Blakslee. Children at extreme right, reading left to right—Nan Blakslee, Mary Depew, John McCarroll, Charles Meisel (a boyhood chum of the writer's, whose name was forgotten until this picture was located), girl not known. Boys standing in rear of children—George Hartung and William Opp, Jr.

A later store picture, taken about 1910, and showing the adjoining buildings, is also shown here, with the names of the adults appearing on it as follows: Seated on wagon at extreme left, Frank Bretz; standing at next wagon, Al Zimmerman, boy with bicycle not known; next, James Engel, Cyrie Hofmann, Charles Hofmann, George Hofmann, Josiah Shafer, Mrs. Pierce Schlier and J. A. Depew.

Mr. George Hofmann has furnished some interesting facts about conditions when he and his brother first came to Delano. At that time the store was like any other country store, selling everything from a needle to a haystack. Clay pipes and tobacco were usually found on the counter, inviting the male customer to buy and enjoy a smoke before leaving. The store opened for business at 6 a. m. and remained open until 9 p. m. every day except Christmas and July 4th. In the early days, it was the custom for patrons to come to the store once a month, usually on pay-day, and make purchases for the whole month, one such an order usually being large enough for a separate delivery. As time went along, changing customs elsewhere became effective in Delano. Advance purchases were made for just a day or two and, at present, only for the day's needs.

A remarkable record achieved by Mr. Hofmann, who has been bookkeeper of the business throughout all his years of service, is the making of every report for the Post Office since 1882. Besides his position as bookkeeper for the store, Mr. Hofmann has been postmaster for many years, has been township supervisor since 1896 and treasurer of the school board for many years.

An exciting event in the history of the town that will be recalled by residents of fifty years ago, was the robbery committed by a gang of men one night and the severe beating of Charles Hofmann. After beating Mr. Hofmann into unconsciousness, the men bound and gagged him and escaped into the mountains. A hastily-formed posse searched the mountains for miles around, but without locating the robbers. The outrage kept the blood of the residents at the boiling point for a long time.

A representative Delano family of the 80's is that shown in the photograph presented here of Mr. John Mack and his children, taken at the Rocks by Mr. Al Werner in the summer of 1887. This was for years one of the best-known families in Delano, and this is a particularly fine picture of it. Those shown are Angie (Mrs. Robert Moyer), of Bethlehem, Pa.; Sue (Mrs. Charles Martz), of New York City; George, of Bethlehem; Elizabeth, of Bethlehem; Mr. Mack, now deceased; Fred, of Bethlehem; and Mary (Mrs. George Rohrer), who lived in Orwigsburg, Pa., until her decease just two weeks before these lines were written. It is a pleasure to make this group a part of the record of Delano's history, for it depicts graphically the character of the residents of the town in that early day.

CHAPTER XI

Education and Religion in the 80's

THE religious life of the community was established on a more permanent basis in this period. At least three Protestant denominations served the town at some time in these ten years. The Lutheran and Reformed churches of Mahanoy City continued to supply the pulpit regularly, among the Reformed pastors being the Rev. Mr. Keiser and the Rev. Mr. Kerschner, while the Lutheran pastors were the Rev. J. W. Lake, the Rev. W. H. Lewars, the Rev. J. R. Sample and the Rev. I. P. Zimmerman.

The Episcopalian Church of Mahanoy City also maintained a ministry in Delano during this time, the Rev. Mr. Kilgore being the first rector, and later the Rev. Mr. Turner, who for a time was a resident of Delano. The St. James Protestant Episcopal Church held its services and Sunday School on the second floor of the freight station building.

A Union Sunday School service was conducted every Sunday in the Hall under the leadership of Mr. Josiah Swank. This school is still in a very flourishing condition at this writing.

The writer has delightful memories of his attendance at the Episcopalian Sunday School services in the old freight station in the 80's, and at the Union Sunday School services in the 90's. Another week-day service that was held for the particular benefit of the school children in the 80's was conducted by Mrs. A. P. Blakslee in Union Hall at 4 o'clock in the afternoon on certain days of the week. The children were taught the prayers and hymns of the Episcopalian church.

The matter of education in Delano took on a new impetus in this period. With the assumption of the duties of principalship on the part of Mr. John Anthony, a more complete grading of the school was made, as well as the adoption of a higher course of studies. No effort was made to inaugurate High School courses, the highest grade under Mr. Anthony's direction being the ninth.

Three of the school rooms available were used at the beginning of the decade, with the fourth coming into use about the middle of

The Highest Grade in 1887

The Fifth and Sixth Grades in 1887
Text Page 95

the 80's. The length of the terms was nine months, as it is today, with salaries ranging from $40.00 to $50.00 a month. These salaries in that day ranked with the highest paid in towns much larger than Delano. In fact, this little town has always had an enviable record in the standing of its school system.

The erection of the township of Delano in 1882 created at the same time a new school district and gave the people of the town a better opportunity to develop their schools according to their own ideas. This made for improvement in every way. Under Mr. Anthony's direction, great advances were made. For his day, he had an excellent reputation as an instructor, as well as for a conscientious regard for his work and a deep-seated interest in the welfare of the students under him. It is said by some of his students that he did more than teach the youngsters from the books, that he invested his own funds in equipment for their amusement and recreation out of school hours. He stressed particularly the matter of thoroughness and those who sat under him still speak highly of the splendid influence his work had upon their lives.

A number of the young people who finished the schools at Delano in this period took advanced work in other schools. Mr. Robert Swank, who has been for many years one of Schuylkill County's foremost lawyers, took his college work at State College after completing the work at Delano, having taken special instructions under Mr. Anthony in preparation for college. Several pupils, including Alvin Read, Katie Becker, Leroy Swank and Jerry McAvoy, after finishing the work at Delano, attended the Shenandoah High School and graduated from there.

Three teachers were engaged in the first year of the new school district—1882-1883. Mr. Ahthony was the principal, but the writer has not been able to get definite information about the others. It was early in this decade that Miss Mattie Whetstone and Miss Jones (later Mrs. J. P. Swartz), became members of the corps. The salaries this first year were $50.00 for the principal and $38.75 for each of the other teachers. The enrollment of the whole school for this term was 188, with 80 males and 99 female students. The term was nine months long, in contrast with six months in Rush Township, from which Delano had just been separated. The tax rate for school purposes was 8 mills.

Among the teachers who served at Delano during the early part of this period, whose exact terms the writer cannot specify, were Miss Ida Kistler and Miss Wickett. It is known that in 1885-1886, Mr. Anthony, Miss Kistler and Miss Wickett were three of the teachers, while in 1886-1887 the teachers were Mr. Anthony, Miss Kistler, Miss Jeanette Marshall and Miss Linda Houseweart. This corps of teachers is shown in the series of pictures of the schools taken in April, 1887, and included in this book.

The writer considers this series of pictures one of the prizes of this history. It includes a group picture of the four teachers, as well as group pictures of the four schools. Two of the pictures were furnished by courtesy of Mrs. Anna Swank Bailey, two by Miss Linda Houseweart and one by Mrs. Charles Struthers (formerly Miss Marshall). In getting the latter three, the writer had the very great pleasure of renewing his acquaintance with those two former teachers after a lapse of forty-five years. Miss Houseweart now resides in Lopez, Sullivan County, Pa., and Mrs. Struthers at Audenried, Pa. Of the other two teachers on this group, Mr. Anthony died several years ago in Philadelphia, and Miss Kistler (later Mrs. John Smith), died in Bethlehem, Pa., several years ago.

The writer is able to give the names of most of the children on these four groups, about half of them being identified by himself and the rest by the assistance of friends. There will probably be some differences of opinion among the readers as to the correctness of some of these identifications, but assurance is given that practically all of them are right.

The first picture shown is the group of teachers: Left to right—Miss Linda Houseweart, Miss Ida Kistler, Miss Jeanette Marshall and Mr. John Anthony.

The second is the school taught by Mr. Anthony: Front row (with feet on ground) left to right—Edna Bailey, Katie Becker, Ria Moore, Jerry McAvoy, Linda McCarroll, Mitchell Blakslee, Arthur Howell, Edward Thamarus, boy not known. Next row, left to right—Boy not known, George Bannan, Alex Artz, Wallace Wagner, Mr. Anthony, George Faust, Roy Swank, Fred Wagner, Alvin Read. Next row, left to right—Albert Symons, Elizabeth Moore, Lillian Blodgett, Emma Markel, Bertha McCarroll, Emily Butler, Lizzie Hein, Angie Mack.

The Third and Fourth Grades in 1887

The First and Second Grades in 1887
Text Page 95

The third is the school taught by Miss Kistler: Front row, left to right—Charles Price, John Becker, boy named Platzu, Leon Bailey, John Derr. Next row, left to right—Susie Wentz, Harry Shafer, Dora Allen, Miss Kistler, Emma Whitehead, George Smith, Annie Derr. Next row, left to right—Katie Houser, Annie Bretz, Lizzie Scott, John Shiley, Kate Smith, Edward Crossan, Annie Reynolds, Carrie Wanamaker, Annie Fritz, Mary Mack, Will Davenport. Back row, left to right—Nell McAvoy, Katie Bretz, boy not known, Mary Lynch, Thomas Hartung, John Butler, Katie Faust, Josiah Shafer, boy not known.

The fourth is the school taught by Miss Marshall: Front row, on lower step and ground, left to right—Sylvester Bretz, Al Zimmerman, Harry Evans, James McCarroll, Phoebe Swartz, Lizzie Butler, Robert Gasser, Charles Loftus, Martha Phillips, Edward McAvoy, Arthur Kimbel, Tom Lynch. Next row, left to right—John Clasby, Art Davenport, Edward Clay, Annie McCarroll, Miss Marshall, John Glenn, Lizzie Mack, Mary Cushing, Will Glenn. Next row, left to right—Boy not known, Walter McCarroll, Clara Shoup, Anna Swank, Lillie Bitler, Mary Martin, Hattie Shafer, Annie Zimmerman. Back row, left to right—Frank Burnett, Gus Beltz, Robert Zimmerman, Carrie Moser, Anna Faust, Dora Hoats, Margaret Cushing.

The fifth is the school taught by Miss Houseweart: Front row, left to right—Frank Bitler, Winnie Clay, Lizzie Moser, Edna Shiley, Dedie Crossan, Lillie Bretz, Katie Kimbel, Gertrude Boyle, Ada Clay, Ida Moser, boy not known, Bertha Allen, Ollie Moser (the writer), Herbert Perry, Charles Miller. Next row, left to right—William Martin, Lydia Wynn, girl not known, Harry Zimmerman, Nan Blakslee, Miss Houseweart, Clara Kimbel, Bess Wynn, George Perry, Gomer Sykes, Lewis Markel, boy not known. Next row, left to right—Edward Whitehead, Dan Payne, John McCarroll, Mary Depew, Edward Shaup, Irvin Houser, Herbert Hassler. Next row, left to right—Not known, one of McCarroll girls, Ella Sykes, Emma Artz, Zillah Fritz, Bertha Depew, Fred Miller, girl not known, John Long, Will Bretz. Next row, left to right—Art McFetridge, Annie Opp, Millie Smith, girl not known, Emily Wanamaker, Lizzie Markle, Clare Bickel, girl not known, Gussie Hein. Back row, left to right—George Price, Bob McFetridge, Mary Wagner, Alice Scheid, Howard Correll, Charles

Gasser, boy not known, girl not known, Edward Phillips, next two boys not known.

It is the sincere wish of the writer that his readers may derive the same degree of pleasure from looking into the faces of these youngsters of forty-five years ago as he did when the pictures came into his possession.

Mr. Anthony remained at the head of the schools for most of this decade, or until June, 1889. During that time he was also time-keeper for the Lehigh Valley Railroad Company, a position to which he gave all of his time for some years after resigning as principal of the schools. He was succeeded as principal by Mr. J. Harry Eisenhower, who was principal for the 1889-1890 term, which closes this ten-year period in the school life of the town. Mr. Eisenhower died several years ago.

The names of all the teachers up to 1888 cannot be stated with certainty, but from that time down to this date a complete record is given in this book. The corps for the term of 1888-1889 was made up of Mr. Anthony, Miss Minnie Pinkerton, Miss Sadie Lime and Miss Lillian Wilcox, teaching the grades in the order named. In 1889-1890, the corps was: Mr. Eisenhower, principal; Miss Anna Bomberger, Miss Sadie Lime and Miss Florence Richards, the grade teachers in the order named.

The officers of the school board at the close of this decade were as follows: A. P. Blakslee, President; J. Wesley Smith, Secretary; and A. A. Read, Treasurer.

Miss Florence Richards, a teacher for thirteen years in the Delano schools, supplies this very interesting information about the last days in the old school building. Quoting Miss Richards:

"In June or July, 1889, Professor G. W. Weiss, county superintendent of schools, conducted an examination for teachers in the high school room of the old building. That was the last examination for teachers in Delano, and, strange to say, the staff for the year was not selected from those examined that day, as then and later Delano teachers held permanent certificates or Normal diplomas.

"On that day of the teachers' examinations, the cellar of the new building was already dug; at the opening of school, September, 1889, the brickwork had advanced almost to the middle of the first story, but the building was not ready for occupancy until September, 1900. Construction forty years ago, especially on the mountain top, was slower than now.

"Eagerly in free hours, teachers and pupils watched the laying of the bricks, and anticipated the comfort of well-lighted, well-ventilated rooms, spacious halls and easy stairways; all heated by the Smead system, with its fine sanitary arrangements. In the old building each teacher swept and dusted her own room, built and cared for the fires in the old cannon stoves which heated the rooms. Nevertheless, the year in the old building was a happy one, and it was with reluctance that the doors of those old rooms were locked for the last time.

"Strange to say, not one of the old staff, after the transference to the new building, ever revisited the old one. For many years I passed it daily to and from school, yet my steps never turned toward it. Nevertheless I think that I could draw even now a very creditable plan of the old school house. As to the new building, like Mary Tudor with Calais, that is sketched on my heart."

And so came to a close a very interesting and very important ten years in the history of the Delano schools.

CHAPTER XII

Delano in the Gay 90's

IN MANY respects the ten years between 1890 and 1900 were epochal in the life of Delano. The year 1900 marked more than the turning point of a century—it brought to a completion a most disastrous turn in the fortunes of the little town.

Early in this decade there were indications of increased prosperity for the town. The Lehigh Valley shops at Weatherly were closed in 1892 and a number of the mechanics employed there were transferred to the Delano shops. The closing of the Weatherly shops naturally increased the work at Delano and required more mechanics there.

Just at this time, however, occurred the drastic change in railroad management which set in motion the forces that later wrought such havoc in the well-ordered life of Delano. The Lehigh Valley Railroad fell upon evil times for a space, the outcome of which was the leasing of this railroad and the Central Railroad of New Jersey to the Philadelphia and Reading Railway Company, a transaction that has become historic as "The Reading Deal."

To the employees of the Lehigh Valley Railroad at Delano, as elsewhere, this was a shock not only to their pride but to their material welfare. These men were Lehigh Valley men—they were born that and the idea of the superiority of their road over all others was inbred in them. To suffer the humiliation of submitting to the dictates of a foreign road was more than distasteful, it was disgraceful. To add further indignities to an already intolerable condition, the new managers transferred some of Delano's best engines to their own road, returning them for overhauling after they had been badly used up through lack of care and mishandling.

The strike of 1893 was an outgrowth of this deal, although it was of very short duration so far as Delano was concerned. In fact, it lasted there but one day. It had its inception on that part of the road known as the "lower end" and the men at Delano were called out without any opportunity to organize, and, in fact, without hav-

ALONZO P. BLAKSLEE
SUPERINTENDENT OF THE MAHANOY
AND HAZLETON DIVISION OF L. V. R. R.
Text Page 101

MRS. A. P. BLAKSLEE
Text Page 101

ing a definite idea of what the strike was all about. Word was passed around to the various homes late at night to those men who were not then on duty, and the next day the division was tied up. A conference with the superintendent during that day, however, convinced the men that their best interests lay in returning to work. Quite a bit of bitter feeling was engendered in some quarters and some of the malcontents refused to return, finding work later in other places.

In the shops the work of engine building came to a close at about this same time. The last new engine turned out there was the No. 617, the only "camel-back" passenger engine constructed in Delano. This engine was built in 1892. An account of this famous engine has been given in a previous chapter. The shops, however, continued working at capacity on repair and reconstruction work until the end of this period.

Mr. Campbell, who had held the position of master mechanic from 1871, was transferred to the same position in the Lehigh Valley shops at Buffalo in 1893. He was succeeded by John McGraw, general road foreman of engines, who was acting master mechanic for one or two years, when the shops of the coal branches were merged under the charge of David Clerk, master mechanic at Hazleton; and Mr. C. H. DeWitt, a son-in-law of Mr. Hofecker, master mechanic at the Weatherly shops for many years, was assigned to the Delano shops as general foreman. Mr. DeWitt occupied the house that had been built for Mr. Campbell and he remained in Delano until the shops were closed.

The following is a list of engines built and rebuilt in the Delano shops from 1869 to 1892, as furnished the compiler of these chronicles by several men connected with Delano shop life for many years: 63, 66, 67, 68, 100, 147, 148, 168, 169, 170. Also these: 64, 65, 69, 70, 72, 73, 74, 75, 76, 79, 80, 99, 340, 341, 342, 343, 359, 364, 365, 366, 367, 387, 388, 389, 390, 401, 402, 403, 404, 405, 406, 407, 408, 409, 410, 443, 538, 542, 575, 614, 617.

This is likely not the complete list, nor does the writer undertake to say which were entirely new engines and which rebuilt. Some of the engines were rebuilt twice, while some, like the 148, were virtually new engines except that they took a number formerly in use. Still others were new in every respect, number and all.

Whether the list as given is complete or not, enough is shown to record the fact that the Delano shops were a very important cog in the industrial machinery of a great railroad company.

The following are cars used in passenger service that were built at the Delano shops: Nos. 91, 93, 95, 97, 121, 160, being regular day coaches 50 feet long; car No. 161 being a 60-foot day coach; two combination cars, baggage and smoking, Nos. 401 and 403.

About the middle of this decade began the first migrations from Delano that were soon to assume flood proportions. Two crews operating the fast Empire freight between Mount Carmel and Packerton were moved to Mount Carmel; the family of Pierce Hoffman, engineer, being the first to leave, in October, 1896. The family of Millard Moser, the other engineer, moved in April, 1897.

On October 24th, 1898, the first step toward ending Delano's importance as a railroad center in this section was taken when division headquarters were moved to Hazleton. Sometime prior to this the Hazleton, Beaver Meadow and Mahanoy Divisions had been merged under the name of the Hazleton and Mahanoy Division. A new superintendent in the person of Mr. John T. Keith replaced Mr. Blakslee, who had been connected with the history of Delano from its beginning. Naturally Mr. Keith had no sentimental attachment for the town and business considerations made it advisable to change the division headquarters. Hazleton was more central under the merger of the divisions and, at the same time, it could provide hotel facilities for strangers coming to transact business with the superintendent. After being the center of things in a railroad way for over thirty-three years, Delano was forced to yield this advantage to the larger town.

Mr. Blakslee's resignation as superintendent took effect on April 1st, 1898, and on the evening of March 21st preceding a mass meeting of Delano people was held in Union Hall to pay tribute to him and his family. The hall could not accommodate all those who came to pay respect to the Blakslee family. Mr. Josiah Swank was chairman and Mr. John B. Anthony made the address of the evening, conveying to Mr. Blakslee and the members of his family in glowing language an expression of the feeling of esteem and regard in which they were held by those who had served the Lehigh Valley Railroad under his leadership. At the close of the address, a 250-piece set of fine chinaware was presented to Mr. and Mrs. Blakslee

HISTORY OF DELANO 101

from the people of the town, with some cut glass and a silver carving set. The Delano band provided the music for the occasion and Mr. Blakslee responded feelingly to Mr. Anthony's address.

This one quotation from Mr. Anthony's speech was prophetic of the drastic change in conditions that was shortly to take place in Delano: "It can hardly be expected that your successor will closely identify himself with this community. You have been one of us, rejoicing in the success of the prosperous and aiding the unfortunate."

Just six months after these words were spoken, Mr. Blakslee's successor removed the division offices to Hazleton, Pa.

Excellent photographs of Mr. and Mrs. A. P. Blakslee appear here.

At the time the offices were taken to Hazleton, the personnel was as follows: John T. Keith, superintendent; George W. Brill, train dispatcher; J. J. Neifert, chief dispatcher; F. A. Breisch, E. E. Smith and W. R. Perry, dispatchers; M. J. McCullough and J. H. Walsh, telegraphers; W. C. Keiber, superintendent's clerk; J. N. Haines, stenographer (Mr. Haines has since advanced to the place of general manager of the Lehigh Valley Railroad); Wallace C. Wagner, stenographer; John B. Anthony, accountant; F. W. Gilcreast, division engineer; E. C. Churchill, assistant engineer; F. W. Packer, division engineer's clerk; and Harry Hoskins, transitman.

A very interesting picture of the office personnel taken about 1890 is shown here. Those appearing on it are: Front, left to right—Edward Glenn, trainmaster; Thomas Sanger, draftsman; George Bannan, message boy; W. C. Keiber, chief clerk; John Anthony, chief accountant; Elmer Newhard, telegrapher; Henry V. Perry, yardmaster. Rear, left to right—George Haas, train runner; John J. Neifert, chief operator; William S. Campbell, shop clerk.

At about this same time many freight crews and a number of passenger crews were transferred from Delano to Mount Carmel, but the freight crews were returned to Delano after a period of about three or four years.

THE EXODUS

In October, 1899, one year after the change in division headquarters, came the great hegira. In that month the shops were removed from Delano to Weatherly. With the exception of a comparatively small group of mechanics, which was retained to take care of emergency repairs to engines and equipment, the entire personnel of the shops was taken from the town. It was as though a great cyclone had swooped down suddenly upon the place and with one monstrous twist picked up shops, equipment and men and carried them to distant places, scattering the men and their families as a giant sower might broadcast his seed over wide areas. A great many of these expert mechanics, who, with their fathers before them, had given the town a bright spot in the industrial sun, did not remain in the employ of the Lehigh Valley Railroad. They sought other fields in many places and soon fitted themselves into niches of usefulness in their new homes. Today Delano is represented by its sons and daughters of other years in more than half the states of the Union. The hands that acquired skill and cunning under the guidance of master craftsmen in Delano have stood them in good stead in these new homes, for they have reached places of leadership in every place they went.

The changing of railroad headquarters to Hazleton also resulted in transferring many of the passenger crews and the discontinuance of Delano as a center of this service. Some of the crews were sent to Hazleton and a number to Mount Carmel. The transformation in the industrial scene in the town was almost revolutionary.

But this is not a story of defeat and extinction, for Delano still lives and, in recent years, has witnessed a revival in community enterprise that shows a survival of the old pioneering spirit, with a promise of new triumphs to come.

A number of very interesting pictures of shop buildings and shop groups is shown here, giving an idea of the force employed during this period, as well as recalling to those who have not seen Delano for many years some familiar scenes. There are a few shop building scenes that will need no labelling.

Shop Plate No. XXVIII shows a group of Delano shopmen as follows: Seated, left to right—F. Wolff, Joseph Bannan, J. Herbig and Charles Whitehead, Jr. Standing, left to right—C. Becker, Daniel Mills, James Beels, R. Benson, A. Wolff, Henry Faust, Gottlieb Miller and Edward Runkle. This picture was taken in

Office Employees About 1890
Text Page 101

THE ENGINE HOUSE AND SHOPS, 1890
Text Page 102

SHOP GROUP, 1890
Text Page 102

1888 in front of the engine room of the machine shop and consists of the lathe hands.

Shop Plate No. XXIX includes these men: On ground, left to right—William Wagner, John Richardson, George Light, Curtis Kimbel, Edward Joslyn, John McHugh, Garrett Hartley, Jeff Haverstock, Frank Hassler, John Boughner, Sr. Sitting on car bumper, left to right—Jacob Engel, Jr., John Bannan. On steps and platform of car, left to right—James Jackson, Michael Carroll, Albert Bast, Thomas Reddy, Patrick Neary, man unknown, Jacob Engel, Sr., John Boughner, Jr. In rear, at car door, left to right— J. N. Swartz (now Dr. Swartz), Harry Reicheldeifer. These men were employees of the paint shop.

Shop Plate No. XXX includes these men: Bottom row, left to right —Harry Perry, John McHugh, Peter Endt, James Wynn, Thomas Marsden, Frank Murphy, John Fritz. Next row, left to right— Man unknown, August Shickram, man unknown, August Hoegg, James Warren, man unknown, Charles (Brigham) Young, Frank Schlier, Levi Heistler, William Freudenberger, Martin Neeb. Next row, left to right—John Ryan (on way to school), Willie Hughes, John Bickleman, John Carroll, James Scott, Samuel Clouser, Joseph Bachert, man unknown, man unknown, Frank Bankes, man unknown, Albert Bast, Daniel Messersmith, man unknown. Next row, left to right—Harry Opp, Joseph Arner, Thomas Stahler, Gus Beltz, George Light, man unknown, Charles Bailey, Edward Houser, James Hartung, Benneville Bensinger, man unknown, Elmer Dentzler, Harvey Bachert. Next row, left to right—Edward Thamarus, Josiah Shafer, Fred Arner, John Schmerfeldt, Zach Pugh, Ben Walters, Walter McMillan, Thomas Fleming, Robert Trickey, Joseph Purcell and Joseph Bennett. Upper row, left to right—Harry Stahler, William Houser, Edward Ellsler, Quintus Bachert, Arthur Cook, Carl Warning, Andrew Lynch, Lester Hendricks, Charles Bineman, James McCarroll, James Crossan, Charles Hendricks, William Perry, George Wynn and John Hartung. These men are nearly all machine shop employees.

Shop Plate No. XXXI is a group of machine shop men. The writer does not have the names of these, although he is able to recognize many of them. Undoubtedly the reader will be able to do the same.

CHAPTER XIII

Advances in Church and Schools

THIS particular period was marked by some noted advances in the religious and educational life of the town, from which, indeed, there has been no recession in spite of the blow that fell upon the place at the close of the decade.

The church needs of the community were still being looked after by the Lutheran and Reformed churches of Mahanoy City, their ministers preaching at Delano on alternate Sunday afternoons. The removal of practically all the members of the Episcopalian congregation caused the withdrawal of that denomination from Delano. The Lutheran ministers who preached in Delano in this decade are: The Rev. I. P. Zimmerman and the Rev. L. L. Lahr.

The coming of Professor J. M. Schrope in the summer of 1891 to take charge of the schools was the beginning of a new era not only in the school life, but in the religious activities as well. Both Mr. and Mrs. Schrope had long been interested in church work and sensed the need in this new home of a more definite religious work for the young people. A flourishing Sunday School had been maintained in the town almost from its beginning, but there was nothing to occupy the time of the young people on Sunday evenings.

In the early autumn of 1891 Mr. Schrope organized the first Senior Christian Endeavor Society in Delano and, at the same time, a Junior Society. Both were very successful from the start, and the Junior Society actually became the model for similar societies throughout Schuylkill and adjoining counties. Most of the young people of the proper age, and including many older ones, united with the Senior Society, which met each Sunday evening in the hall. These meetings proved to be both interesting and profitable spiritually and in other ways. It was the means of bringing the young people together for an hour of instruction and worship and usually, after the service, in the summer and early fall, a most pleasant close to the day was found in a long walk to the top of Quakake mountain and back, participated in by the whole group.

A Shop Group. Plate XXVIII
Text Page 102

A Shop Group of Late 80's. Plate XXIX
Text Page 103

Miss Florence Richards, who was very active in the work of the Junior Society, has furnished an interesting account of the accomplishments of this organization, which is here quoted:

"From the first, and throughout my knowledge of it—the Junior Society was quite large, numbering sixty or seventy and consisted of all ages, from the tots of five to girls and boys of fourteen and fifteen.

"I was the superintendent and Mrs. J. M. Schrope the assistant, and these officers remained in charge until June, 1902, when Mrs. L. A. Flexer succeeded me, with Mrs. Schrope as her assistant. At first the meetings were held Saturday afternoon, but later were changed to Thursday evenings.

"In 1894 the Delano Junior Society became the center of Junior Christian Endeavor work throughout the county, and became also the model for many of the societies organized later in Schuylkill County. At that time there were eight societies and on October 27, 1894, a rally of these Juniors was held in St. John's Lutheran Church in Mahanoy City. There was an almost one hundred per cent. attendance of the Delano Society, both at this rally and also at the subsequent ones held successively at Ashland in 1895, Pottsville in 1896, Pottsville in 1898, Mahanoy City in 1899, Minersville in 1900 and St. Clair in 1901.

"I have been wondering how many of the Juniors of those distant nineties recall the operetta, "Cinderella in Fairyland," which they gave in Union Hall about 1893 or 1894."

Of the work of the Sunday School and the Senior Society, Mr. Schrope has this to say: "The Sunday School work and the Christian Endeavor in the old Union Hall form an interesting chapter in the history of Delano. There never was any finer co-operation in the community work than that which emanated from Union Hall."

In 1895 a new denomination arose over the religious horizon of Delano. The Methodist Episcopal Church, with its aggressive policy of sending workers into fields where no regular ministries are maintained, felt that Delano should have a resident pastor, and at the annual conference in March, 1895, the Rev. W. W. Hartman was assigned to the new charge, to be known as the Park Place and Delano Charge. This was the beginning of a very successful work by this church and the station was maintained without interruption for a period of twenty years, when it was found necessary to discontinue it.

Mr. Hartman lived in the home of Albert Dent and was married during the year he lived in Delano. Preaching services were held in Delano on Sunday evenings and in Park Place on Sunday afternoons.

There follows a list of all the Methodist ministers who served the Delano charge, with the years of their ministry, and their present locations:

1895	Rev. W. W. Hartman, now deceased. Widow living in Delaware, O.
1896	Rev. F. C. Buyers, now deceased. Widow living at Selinsgrove, Pa.
1897	Rev. J. C. Grimes, now deceased.
1898	Rev. E. E. McKelvey, now preaching at Everett, Pa. Served to 1900.
1900	Rev. Wilson Vandermark, present location not known.
1901	Rev. Frank Brunstetter, now deceased. Widow living in Williamsport, Pa.
1902-04	Rev. Frank Curry, now deceased. Widow living at Williamsport, Pa.
1904	Rev. Otho C. Miller, now Superintendent Children's Home at Mechanicsburg, Pa.
1905	Rev. J. C. Wilhelm, present location not known.
1906	Arthur Santinier, present location not known.
1907-11	Rev. George Duvall, now pastor at Bedford, Pa.
1911	Rev. Harvey Young, present location not known.
1912	Rev. Philip Thomas, now residing in Ashland, Pa.
1913	Rev. William Shannon, present location not known.

The membership of this charge in 1896 was 31, while during the pastorate of the Rev. Mr. Duvall it reached its highest point of 119 in 1910.

With this great increase in church activities, the seating capacity of Union Hall was found inadequate to meet the needs, and several public meetings were held early in 1897 to consider the matter of increasing the size of the hall. Much discussion was had over the proposed improvement and considerable doubt was expressed as to the wisdom of taking such a step in the face of the discouraging outlook for the town. However, there were enough optimists to

A Shop Group of Late 80's. Plate XXX
Text Page 103

A Shop Group of the 80's. Plate XXXI
Text Page 103

HISTORY OF DELANO 107

carry the project through and two committees were appointed to lay plans for the work. The finance committee consisted of Martin Neeb, chairman; James I. Blakslee, secretary; H. F. Fritz, treasurer; D. W. Coder, Simon Arner, J. M. Schrope and C. E. Depew. The building committee consisted of Josiah Swank, chairman; J. M. Schrope, secretary; C. E. Depew, Llewellyn Bannan and J. C. Grimes.

The building committee proposed a 28-foot addition to the rear of the old hall of the same width as the original building, these two portions to have a rolling partition by means of which they could be used as one room, or divided into two rooms. This plan was accepted and the finance committee prepared a plan for raising the money to pay for the improvement.

Certificates calling for subscriptions of $12.00 each to the Union Hall Extension Fund were issued, payment to be made in twelve installments of one dollar each per month. Letters were sent to the people of Delano, explaining the plan and urging the purchase of the certificates. On the back of the letter was a plan of the proposed addition, so that people could visualize the improvement for which they were being asked to pay.

The committee met with gratifying results in the disposal of the certificates and the addition to the hall was completed in the summer of 1898, giving the town a community meeting place of almost twice the size of the old building. Needless to say, payments on the certificates issued were met with the same fidelity that supported all community undertakings in Delano. The confidence and leadership of a few of Delano's outstanding people, backed by the co-operation and support of the others, made the venture easily attainable.

It is timely here to tell the story of a Delano boy who has reached a place of high distinction in the noblest profession in life, that of the Christian ministry. So far as the historian knows, the Rev. Dr. Frederick Runyan Wagner is the only Delano boy to hold that honor. It is a privilege to make his life story a part of this history, as well as to present a photograph of his distinguished self. The writer holds cherished memories of having been the recipient of many kindnesses at his hands when they lived in old Swamppoodle.

Dr. Wagner was born in New Market, New Jersey, May 30, 1873, the son of George and Agnes Wagner. He came to Delano in 1880, where his father was employed for some time as a painter.

He began his school life in the two-story frame school building, with Miss Martha Whetstone as his first teacher and with Miss Jones and Mr. Anthony as later teachers. After completing his school course under Mr. Anthony, he picked slate for a time in the Park 2 breaker at Trenton, then worked as an engine wiper at Delano and later became an apprentice painter in the paint shop.

In the early 90's he united with the Lutheran church at Delano at the Easter service following special services conducted by the Rev. Isaac Zimmerman, of Mahanoy City, Pa., and felt then the call to preach the Gospel. In the autumn of 1893 he began studies in Missionary Institute at Selinsgrove, Pa., graduated from Wittenberg College, Springfield, O., in 1898, and from Gettysburg Theological Seminary in 1901. The same year he accepted a unanimous call to become pastor of St. Paul's Lutheran Church, at Frostburg, Md. He was ordained a minister of the Gospel by the Maryland Synod, at Boonsboro, Md., in October, 1901.

He was married, October 10, 1901, to Miss Sara B. Toot at her home in Gettysburg, Pa.

March 1, 1910, a call was accepted to become pastor of St. James Lutheran Church at Huntingdon, Pa., where he served for ten years, helping to build an entirely new church, Sunday School building and brownstone parsonage in that charge. During this pastorate he was elected President of the Allegheny Synod. In 1917 Susquehanna University honored him with the degree of Doctor of Divinity.

He has been a delegate to several General Conventions of his church, including the Merger Conventions in Chicago and New York. March 1, 1920, he became pastor of St. James Lutheran Church, of Martinsburg, W. Va., where he has served for the past twelve years. This congregation was organized in 1770, and has a present membership of about 800 members.

Dr. and Mrs. Wagner have four children and one grandson. A daughter, Agnes Elizabeth, now the wife of Ralph A. Beebe, Professor of Chemistry, at Amherst College; a daughter, Harriet Frances, now Mrs. W. F. Warren, of Washington, D. C.; a son, John F. Wagner, a post graduate student of the University of Michigan, and a son, Richard H. Wagner, in the Junior class of Michigan University.

Dr. Wagner has made literary contributions to various church and other periodicals, assisted with two Synod Histories, and has traveled extensively throughout the United States and in Europe.

He is at present a member of the executive committee of the Maryland Synod, of the Board of Trustees of the National Lutheran Home for the Aged in Washington, D. C., of the Free and Accepted Order of Masons, and the Rotary Club.

In a letter from Dr. Wagner to the historian, he states that he has always had high appreciation for the kindness of his Delano friends and that he regards them as "the very best."

School Activities

These were momentous days in the school history of the town. It has been noted in a previous chapter that the work of erecting a new, modern school building had been undertaken early in 1889. This building was ready for occupancy September, 1900. At that time it was a model school building in every respect. Built of brick, it was two stories in height, with two school rooms on each floor, a smaller room on the second floor for laboratory purposes, and with wide halls, staircases and cloak room. The heating system was the latest then in use, known as the Smead system. It not only furnished heat for the building, but circulated fresh air throughout the whole building. In that day no janitors were provided and the principal was charged with the care of the heating system, but even that was a vast improvement over the old stove which was used in each room of the old building, with each teacher her own janitor. The bell installed in this building was purchased from a Port Carbon church.

The teaching staff in the first year in the new building, 1890-1891, was made up of Mr. Kreider, from Hazleton, principal; Miss Anna Bomberger, from Berks County, grammar school; Miss Sadie Lime, from Port Carbon, Pa., secondary school; and Miss Florence Richards, from Minersville, Pa., primary A and B. Mr. Kreider died the following year at his home in Hazleton; Miss Bomberger some time later in the State of Washington; Miss Lime for several years after leaving Delano taught in a Presbyterian School for Colored Children in Alabama, and is now residing in Los Angeles, Cal., while Miss Richards now resides in Minersville, Pa.

In the terms of 1891-1894 the teaching corps was made up of Prof. J. M. Schrope, of Hegins, Pa., principal; Miss Ida Kistler, of Nesquehoning, Pa., grammar school; Miss Ida Hepler, of Eldred, Pa., secondary school, and Miss Richards, primary A and B. Mr. Schrope, who remained at the head of the Delano schools until 1895, later taught in Port Carbon, Pa., and for many years has been assistant county superintendent of schools of Schuylkill County, with his residence in Hegins, Pa. Miss Kistler was married in 1894 to John Smith, a well-known resident of Delano, and she died several years ago in Bethlehem, Pa., where her husband still resides. Miss Hepler was later married to Robert Swank, Esq., and resides now in Mahanoy City, Pa.

With the coming of Mr. Schrope, great changes were made in the school system. The modern school building just completed moved the school board to establish more up-to-date school courses, with an approved high school course. Except in the larger towns, high schools were unknown in that day, but the people of Delano had always been interested in keeping pace with the best to be had in the educational field. Mr. Schrope, who had organized the high school of Porter Township at Tower City, was elected supervising principal with full power to organize such a school. The purchase of new books, with necessary equipment and supplies, was authorized, and a two-year high school course decided upon.

The first class to graduate from the new high school had two members: Leon Bailey and Hattie McMullen. This class graduated in 1893. A photograph of the members of this class, with Mr. Schrope, is included in this book, together with a photograph of the graduating class of 1932. Space did not permit the using of pictures of all the graduating classes and the writer decided upon the first and latest for purposes of illustration and comparison. The class of 1932 consists of nineteen members.

The names of the 1932 graduates as they appear on this picture are: Back row, left to right—Louise Bones, Ardella Fegley, Betty Steimling, Mary Sharkey, Rita Bell, Loraine Fegley and Isabelle Long. Middle row, left to right—Evelyn Folweiler, Ruth Edinger, Clara Lindner, Myrtle Riddle, Edith Seltzer and Thelma Maurer. Front row, left to right—Clayre Matz, William Moschock, Eugene Houser, Charles Diefenderfer, Edwin Singley and Arthur Becker.

The historian is able to present here another complete series of pictures showing all the schools at Delano as they were constituted in the spring of 1895. So far as known, the names of the pupils are here given.

High school picture is made up of these students: Front row, left to right—Herbert V. Clemens, Dedie Crossan, Charles Perry, Ethel Butler, Robert Houser, Carrie Billman, Fred Mack, Maude

THE REV. DR. FREDERICK RUNYAN WAGNER
Text Page 107

FIRST GRADUATES AND PRINCIPAL, 1893
Text Page 110

LATEST GRADUATING CLASS, 1932
Text Page 110

High School, 1895
Text Page 110

Grammar School, 1895
Text Page 111

Tansey, Edward McAvoy, Mattie Sykes and Robert Shafer. Rear row, left to right—Edgar Witman, Hattie Shafer, Will Schrope, Maud Dent, Prof. J. M. Schrope, Millie Smith, Oliver Moser, Clara Kimbel, Katie Moyer and Lizzie Butler.

Grammar school as follows: Front row, left to right—Thomas Crossan, Lewis Billman, George Eisenbach, Bert McAvoy, Edward Long, Fred Perry, John Folweiler, Winfield Markle, Alonzo Glenn, Ward Packer, Eugene McAvoy and a visiting boy. Middle row, left to right—Bertha Schlier, Corrine Derr, Katherine Kimbel, Essie Billman, Lizzie Burnett, Annie Doyle, Stella Boyle, Lizzie Doyle, Katie Bowman, Mamie Hartung, Emma Dent, Maggie Lynch and Miss Hepler. Rear row, left to right—John McCarroll, Fred Phillips, Tillie Hartung, Annie Shaup, Lottie Shiley, Sallie Gasser, George Mack, Mary Connell, Lizzie Depew, Katie Allen, Carrie Gouldner and Bert Gouldner.

Secondary school as follows: Front row, left to right—unknown, Elvin Neeb, Oscar Bretz, Oliver Bitler, George Depew, unknown, unknown, Leon Long, Ambrose Grossman, George Bretz, Earl McAvoy, unknown, Cyriak Hofmann, unknown, unknown. Middle row, left to right—unknown, Oliver Fredericks, Norman Swartz, Katie Depew, unknown, unknown, Bert Sykes, Katie Hartung, Hattie Davenport, Audrey Price, Anna Veletchko, unknown, unknown, Ruth Depew, Linda Depew, Mary Hoffman, unknown, Dolly Preston. Back row, left to right—unknown, Albert Bretz, John Sharp, Dora Butler, Hannah Miller, Mida McCarroll, Tillie Hartung, unknown, unknown, Mary Hoffman, Bessie Collins, Bertha Boyle, Miss Corrine Kirke.

Primary A and B school are as follows: Front row, left to right—unknown, Lloyd Shaup, Jerry Ryan, Roy Phillips, unknown, —— Bachert, Worthington Packer, Elmer Clemens, —— Arner, Charles Hoeflich, Elmer Koch, unknown, Charles Engle, Charles Hoffman, unknown, William Gasser, George Bretz. Middle row, left to right—Katie Connell, Bessie Neifert, —— Gouldner, Florence Allen, Mary Lynch, unknown, unknown, Katherine Folweiler, Bessie Moser, unknown, May Walters, unknown, Eva Billman, Minnie Miller, Nellie Brill, Mary Strocko, Albert Depew, unknown. Back row, left to right, unknown, unknown, Elsie Faust, unknown, unknown, unknown, unknown, unknown, May Houser, Christine Depew, Bessie Perry, unknown, unknown, Miss Florence Richards.

The graduating classes during this period, following the first one in 1893, were as follows:

1894—Katie Smith, Anna Faust, Gertrude Mowery, Anna Swank, Mabel Packer, John M. Shiley, Thomas Hartung and William Glenn.

1895—No graduating class.

1896—Millie Smith, Clara Kimbel, Lizzie Butler, Dedie Crossan and Oliver Moser.

1897—Harry Zimmerman, William D. Schrope and Katie Moyer.

1898—Mary Depew, Herbert Clemens and Henry Weaver.

1899—No graduating class.

The year 1899 was the first year of the removal of the shops and the high school classes were seriously affected, resulting in a lapse of several years before graduations were again possible.

The faculty for the term of 1894-1895 was made up of Prof. J. M. Schrope, principal; Miss Ida Hepler, grammar school; Miss Corrine Kirke, secondary school, and Miss Richards, primary A and B. Miss Kirke came from Pottsville and taught in Delano just one year. She later taught in the Philadelphia schools, where she now resides. She is now Mrs. Thomas Cain.

For the term of 1895-1896, Mr. Schrope was principal, Miss Hepler in charge of grammar school, Miss Salina Beatty, of Minersville, secondary school, and Miss Richards, primary. Miss Beatty taught just this one year and later was married to William Parry, of Minersville, Pa., after several years moving to Philadelphia, where she has been a member of the public school teaching corps ever since.

The corps for the two terms, 1896-1898, was made up of Mr. Schrope, principal; Miss Hepler, grammar; Miss Margaret Dengler, of Shenandoah, Pa., secondary, and Miss Richards, primary. Miss Dengler, at the end of the 1897-1898 term at Delano, taught for a time in Newark, N. J., and later married a Mr. Hawk, of Tower City, Pa. Miss Hepler was married to Robert Swank, Esq., at the end of this term.

For the term of 1898-1899, Mr. Schrope was principal; Miss Millie Smith, assistant principal; Miss Anna Clauser, grammar; Miss Anna Faust, secondary, and Miss Richards, primary. Miss Smith and Miss Faust were the first graduates of the Delano High School to teach in the Delano schools.

The terms from 1899 to and including 1902 had for the faculty Mr. Schrope, principal; Miss Richards, assistant principal; Miss Clauser, grammar; Miss Anna Faust, secondary, and Miss Millie Smith, primary. At the close of the term in June, 1902, Miss Clauser was married to Mr. Wasley, of Shenandoah, and Miss Richards resigned to go to college. Miss Richards finished at that time a continuous service in the Delano schools of thirteen years, and she has always been regarded as one of the best teachers the schools ever had.

Many precious memories of the old school days come crowding into the mind of the writer as he reviews the history of those days. Expression to the feelings that are aroused will be given more fully later on.

CHAPTER XIV

Community Interests in the 90's

THIS period witnessed many events of general importance that properly belong to this report.

Mining operations at the Park 2 colliery, located about a mile southwest of Delano, had crept slowly up to the site of the town and serious surface disturbances became frequent. The street known as Swamppoodle was the portion of town dangerously affected. It is said that one of the housewives residing in a home on that street went into her cellar one morning and found a yawning hole where the cellar floor had caved in during the night. Just under the rear porch of the home occupied by the family of D. W. Clemens a large cave-in of great depth occurred one day. The matter of every-day living in that section became most hazardous.

The railroad company finally took cognizance of the dangerous situation and, without ordering the tenants to vacate, moved the houses to a new location, the families remaining in them during the moving process. This operation provided much diversion for the youngsters of the town, as well as for many of the older people.

The method employed was novel and very efficient. The houses were first jacked up and cribbing built under them, with well-soaped skids placed directly under the sills of the houses. Cribbing was built along the way the buildings were to travel and an old-fashioned capstan, operated by horse-power, was used to furnish the pulling force. All day long the old white horse walked about this capstan in a circle, while the house being moved inched along on its soaped skids. Excellent progress was made and very little damage done. In the meanwhile, housekeeping business kept right on in the moving houses and these families found themselves in a few days after starting living in an entirely new section of town.

About ten houses were moved in this way, two of them to Brown Row, and the rest to make a new street that was at that time euphoniously dubbed "Paradise Alley."

Secondary School, 1895
Text Page 111

Primary School, 1895
Text Page 111

Thus ended old Swamppoodle, except for several large double houses at the east end, which were out of the danger zone. Former residents who have not visited the town for twenty-five or more years would not recognize the place where the old street stood. A railroad siding has been built along what was formerly the road in front of the houses, while a tangled growth of underbrush covers the place where the houses once stood.

Another important public improvement that was started in 1895 and completed that same year was the construction of a new reservoir. For many years Delano had been furnished with the finest quality of water by means of four small reservoirs located about three hundred yards north of the town, just at the foot of the higher Mahanoy range. The supply from these little dams was not adequate for the increasing needs of the town and its industries and the new reservoir was built.

It has a capacity that is quite large for a small community and, when filled, holds a plentiful reserve. In recent years the supply from the springs which feed the dam has been augmented by piping water pumped from an artesian well located in the direction of Girard Manor.

Two very interesting pictures of the old reservoirs are shown here, taken July 17, 1887. The heavy timber background shown gives an excellent idea of the wildness of the surroundings of Delano even as late as 1887. A photograph of the new reservoir taken just recently furnishes a sharp contrast in the background as over against that of forty-five years ago. On the one picture of the old dams will be found George Hofmann, Charles Hofmann, Joseph Gassner, Seth Purcell, J. A. Depew, Will Campbell, Gat Hartley, John McHugh, Tim McCarthy, Alex Butler, John Anthony and Clinton Engle. On the other appear the Misses Carolin and Ria Moore.

The completion of the new reservoir brought a glad day for the youngsters of the town, for it brought permission to use the old dams for swimming. The old Boston swimming hole was abandoned and swimming was everyday business from April to September in the clear waters of the two lower reservoirs.

Skating took on a new meaning, also, as permission was given to use the large new reservoir for that purpose. It was ideal for the purpose, and about everyone in town who knew how could be found on winter evenings, gliding over the smooth surface of the ice in varying degrees of grace and skill. In those days Bob Shafer was the champion skater, one of his feats being to jump from the square dam to the round one over the five-foot footpath that separated them.

It was during this time that most of the families in Delano had water service installed in their homes, although the old town hydrants continued in use for quite awhile longer.

The building operations at the new reservoir furnished the boys with many interesting hours. The clearing of the site, blasting out stumps, building the forms for the breast, the gangs of Italian laborers who occupied small shanties right on location and did their own cooking and housekeeping, were all things to intrigue the interest of inquisitive boys. The blasting at the noon hour, when the charges prepared during the morning hours were set off, was always a thrilling sight. From the school rooms could be seen great stones thrown a hundred feet and more into the air as charge after charge let go.

Bicycle racing first became popular about 1894 and 1895, with the invention of the safety bicycle. The Lakeside track was the scene of many thrilling contests and Delano was usually represented in those events by its crack racer, Billy Wynn, who had a reputation that extended beyond the little town. He always had plenty of friends present at the races to cheer him on and he gave Fred Bernet, of Pottsville, then the region champion, some hard brushes.

In April, 1896, Delano had its first spectacular fire, when the long freight shed was almost totally destroyed. The fire broke out early in the evening and, lacking the services of a fire company, bucket brigades fought the blaze. Another fire that threatened serious loss to the town occurred the summer before, when a great bush fire starting near Trenton one Sunday afternoon came driving through the thick tangle of underbrush across the flats west of town, with a high wind back of it, and threatened the school house and got within reaching distance of the lumber yard and the houses in Toney Row. Most of the men and boys of the town were impressed into service that day and only the use of a locomotive, with fire hose connections, saved the town from heavy damage.

An organization that left its impress on the town and whose influence undoubtedly has not yet spent all its force, was the Sons of Temperance, established in 1895 following a temperance lecture delivered by a temperance orator of that day. It started with a very fine membership and for several years was a center of interest for the young people of the town. Mr. Schrope was the chief moving spirit in its organization and retained an active part in its activities during the time it existed. One of the outstanding events in its history was the visit of the Jeanesville lodge, when about twenty-five or more young people from that town came to spend an evening with the Delano group. The meetings were held in the lodge room in the freight house building and many delightful sessions were enjoyed there.

Election days were always exciting and interesting events in the town. In the 1896 campaign between McKinley and Bryan, great enthusiasm was manifest. Because of the free silver issue, the normally Republican majority in the town was increased, as many otherwise sound Democrats could not accept this doctrine. The election returns were received by the telegraphers in the division offices and sent to Union Hall to be announced to the voters who had congregated there. The victory of Mr. McKinley met with general approval in Delano and several nights later a torch-light parade was arranged so that the Democratic losers might be started on their trip up Salt River with ceremonies befitting the occasion. This parade was a somewhat nondescript affair, but all the thrill of victory was in it and the result was completely satisfying.

In September, 1896, occurred a record-breaking hail storm such as had never been experienced in the town before and has not been since. It began late in the afternoon as a severe thunder shower, quickly developed into a hail storm in which hail stones as large as hens' eggs fell to a depth of six or more inches. The storm came from the west and not a window glass on the west side of the buildings was left intact. Large holes were made in the roofs of some of the houses on Hazle Street, and hundreds of dead sparrows were found on the ground after the storm. Trees were stripped of their foliage and many small branches broken from them.

The teachers in the school house had a serious time averting a panic among the pupils and they crowded the children to the east end of the building. Every window glass on the west side was smashed. In the shops the crashing of these great hail stones on the sheet iron roofs caused pandemonium to reign. It was said later that men who were never known to be much concerned about religious matters were on their knees earnestly praying, thinking the end of all things was at hand. Several weeks were required to repair all the damage done by the storm, and all the glass in stock in the shops was used up. The writer's sister and mother were returning from Mahanoy City by train during the storm and the passengers were compelled to get on the seats to avoid the hail stones which broke all the car windows on the side from which the storm was coming.

The social life of the town during this period was amply cared for in varying ways. House parties continued their popular appeal, dances were frequently held in the grove or in the homes. Theater parties to Mahanoy City or Hazleton became the vogue. Sleighing parties to distant towns took up the time of the young people in the winter season. The schools put on literary programs in Union Hall during the winter and these were well-patronized by the residents.

A photographic copy of a program of an elocutionary contest that was held in the hall in 1896 is shown here. The writer had a part in this contest and he feels certain that the sight of this program will bring back some pleasant memories to other participants. He does not now recall who won the contest. He knows it was not himself. Readers will note that the patrons were not overcharged for their admission to these affairs.

Delano was always interested in baseball and developed some excellent players. Among these were Tom Fleming, Bob and Jim Applegate, Wallace Wagner, Bob Shafer and others. Games were first played on the field across from the hall, which was later used for railroad sidings, after a new field had been erected across from the school house. This latter field has been in use for the past thirty-seven years. The writer had part in clearing the ground for it. Old-timers will still remember that steel arm of Jim Applegate, when he threw the ball from center field to the home plate.

Scene at Old Reservoirs, July 17, 1887
Text Page 115

Scene at Old Reservoirs, July 17, 1887
Text Page 115

The Reservoir, 1932
Text Page 115

Another interesting event in the life of Delano was the display of fireworks that was put on on the night of July 4th each year. These fireworks were supplied by the generosity of Mr. Blakslee and Mr. Depew and the shows were staged just east of the freight house building and they were well worth watching. Everyone in town came out to witness the fireworks.

The first automobile to come to Delano made its appearance in the latter part of this decade and was the property of J. A. Depew. A photograph of it, taken near the Boston bridge, with Mr. Depew and his daughter, Mary, in it, is shown here.

An interesting picture of the Depew family, taken in front of their residence, which was formerly the Blakslee home, is included here. The persons appearing on it are: Mrs. J. A. Depew, Clara (a daughter of William Depew), Christine Depew, holding a child of her cousin, Clara, Aunt Mary Richardson and Mr. Depew.

On November 2nd, 1891, the 255-acre tract constituting the Delano town plot was sold by the Delano Land Company to the Lehigh Valley Railroad Company. This transaction gave the railroad company the ownership in fee of the town site, it having already for many years owned the unchanging loyalty of a fine lot of good people.

The Spanish-American War in the latter part of this decade found ready response in patriotism from the young men of Delano. Those who served Uncle Sam in that war include: William Wynn, William Bachert, Joseph Zimmerman, Harry E. Shafer, Robert Gasser, Claude Gouldner, George Beers, Robert Anthony, James Warntz and Edward Shaup.

The writer had the privilege of making a speech at a flag-raising held by Camp 72, P. O. S. of A., during these stirring war days. The flag was raised over the lodge hall and the exercises were held from the paltform of the freight station. The Delano band participated in the ceremonies. As the writer recalls the event, the old dinkey played the most conspicuous part in it, persisting in shunting back and forth in front of the speakers' stand all during the affair.

The writer includes at this point a series of Delano scenes, showing the town as it appeared in the 90's. These pictures need no explanation.

And so we come to the close of a very important time in Delano history. A period that was marked by some paradoxical situations. In it more than half the population was taken away and yet, so far as numbers are concerned, the population remained the same. But there was a real change. What had been a railroad and shop town was now to be strictly a railroad town. As fast as the shop families vacated their homes, railroad families came in from the surrounding country to take their places, and life in Delano went on as before, with many new faces, but with the same spirit and, indeed, with a generous bit of the old leaven still remaining.

Union Hall,
Delano, Pa., Saturday,
October 10, 1896, at 7.30 P.M.
An Elocutionary Contest
for a
Demorest Silver Medal,
by the following competitors:
Miss Lizzie F. Butler,
Miss Katie L. Moyer,
Miss Kate H. Smith,
N. A. Moser,
E. D. Whitman,
E. F. Whitman.

Good addresses, good music, and a good time are promised. Come! Tickets 10c, and 5c for children.

AN ELOCUTIONARY CONTEST
Text Page 118

DELANO'S FIRST AUTO. J. A. DEPEW AND DAUGHTER, MARY
Text Page 119

J. A. DEPEW FAMILY AND FRIENDS
Text Page 119

CHAPTER XV

Personal Recollections of the 80's

THIS chapter and the next one are written for the purpose of giving to the readers some personal recollections of happy days in Delano. There may be little of historical value to them, but they will serve to recall to old-time friends some of the things that belong to the joys of youth.

No apology is offered for this personal note, but the writer does presume here to introduce himself to his readers by means of a photograph of comparatively recent date. With necessary allowances for the kindness of the photographer, it is a fairly accurate portrait. Some of the readers never knew this historian, others have forgotten him, while those who do remember his name but have not seen him for many years may be interested in knowing what Father Time has meted out to him. Hence this manner of introduction.

Early in the year 1882 the family of Millard Moser came from Quakake to Delano, their only son then just a little past two years of age. The first home occupied by the family was the east side of a small double dwelling located near the engine house at the head of the Patch. On the other side of the dwelling lived the family of Edwin Phillips, while between the Moser home and the engine house was the little single house occupied by the family of Michael Neary. Neither of the houses is now standing.

The writer does not remember his first day in Delano, but he does have many clear recollections of things that happened during the two years spent in that home. Among the earliest memories are those of the kindly Mr. Neary and his family. Kate and Bridget (or "Bee," as she was known to her friends) Neary are names that are indelibly impressed on the mind of this writer. He remembers, too, the delicious currant pie that he used to get at times when he casually dropped into the home of that motherly Irish lady, Mrs. Michael Carroll, who lived next to his home on the east side. Needless to say, he dropped into the Carroll home quite often.

There comes to mind the little narrow-gauge engine that for a time was housed in a separate part of the engine house. It was named the Montrose and had been brought to Delano for repairs from the Montrose Railroad. There is the recollection of a little colored chap brought home one evening by his father to supper. This youngster was freighting his way through Delano at the expense of the Lehigh Valley. It was the first sight of a colored person and the children could not understand why the boy did not wash his face before sitting to the table.

The Garfield-Hancock campaign occurred during this residence and the historian was the proud possessor of one of the caps that were much worn by the youngsters of that day. This cap had Garfield's name on it. An illustration of the kind of cap meant is shown in the store group of 1884 appearing in a previous chapter, being the cap perched on the head of Irvin Blakslee.

The writer remembers a well that was being dug at the lower end of the Patch and someone swinging him out over the edge of it, much to his terror. The old well has long since been filled up. He remembers also accompanying his father one evening to the home of Mr. and Mrs. Frank Bowman, who lived farther down in the Patch, and being shown a live owl that Mr. Bowman had caught and which he kept in the cellar.

The only youngsters that can be recalled of those early days are the Phillips boys, next door neighbors, and George and Kathryn Shuler, who lived nearby.

In 1884 the family moved into a house in Swamppoodle and a year later school life began, with all the joys that go with that experience. Among the clear recollections of the residence in this new location are those of the great woods just back of the street and the circuses that were put on under the big trees. Leon Bailey, Danny Payne, George and Herbert Perry, Ed Clay and others as performers, with the smaller boys and the girls as spectators. Admission, two pins. Blissful days!

There were delightful Sunday afternoon walks up to the reservoirs, when fathers of the youngsters would delight them with chestnut whistles cut out in a few minutes. The memories of the four little dams will never fade. The narrow footway between the two lower ones, leading by a few stone steps to the third one,

STATION AND DIVISION OFFICE BUILDING

FREIGHT STATION AND LODGE HALL

Text Page 119

FORMER BLAKSLEE HOME

STREET VIEW
Text Page 119

ORIGINAL BRICK SCHOOL BUILDING
Text Page 119

WHEN DELANO HAD TWO SCHOOL BUILDINGS
Text Page 119

and still another short flight of steps to the upper one. The musical splash of the stream running into the upper dam and the falls from that one into the next and then on to the lower one and over the spillway. When was music half so sweet as that?

The first school days! No others just like them. The writer had as his first teacher a Miss Wickett. The school room was the one on the first floor of the east end of the two-story frame building, a picture of which appears earlier in this book. His seat-mate the first term was John Long, now an engineer for the Pennsylvania Railroad at Sunbury, Pa. Directly across the aisle sat Clare Bickle, now residing in Plainfield, N. J. He can still recall the wall chart that was used to teach the alphabet and the formation of words and sentences, with pictures to make it more interesting. And his first piece one Friday afternoon—Mary Had a Little Lamb. Forty-six years ago! What an enduring lamb that must be.

The second school year was under the teaching of Miss Linda Houseweart. A picture of this school is shown earlier in this history, giving a fine idea of the bright youngsters of that day. A most delightful experience enjoyed by the writer since starting the writing of this history was when he found that Miss Houseweart is still living and made it a point to visit her at her home in Lopez, Pa., the first meeting of teacher and pupil since the end of that early school term.

The writer remembers a family named Kellner who lived in the old school house located just a few yards east of the one then being used. Mr. Kellner was a butcher by trade and he was kept quite busy in the fall and winter months butchering hogs for the people of Delano, most of the families in that day raising much of their own meat supply.

Many other memories keep crowding for expression. The little prayer meeting held by Mrs. Blakslee at the close of school, in which a great many of the school children joined, were important in the lives of those children. To them Mrs. Blakslee was a saint, as indeed she was to many others.

He recalls his attendance at the Episcopal Sunday School held on Sunday afternoons on the second floor of the freight house, where he learned the catechism. It was here that he had his first taste of a candy Easter egg, given the pupils at Easter-time. There has never been another just like it.

In that day Fred Wagner, now the distinguished Dr. Wagner, was a neighbor and carried the Pennsylvania Grit each week. It was the fortune of this writer to be permitted at times to accompany him on these rounds. It is a far cry from that experience to this day, when that kid is engaged in the writing of a history of the town and the same Grit Publishing Company whose paper he helped to distribute is putting it into print for him.

Is there any boy, or girl either, who lived in Delano at any time between 1886 and 1916, that does not remember Johnny Quin? It would be difficult to calculate how many yards of delicious bologna this same Mr. Quin handed out to Delano youngsters during those thirty years. And better even than the bologna were the smiles and cheery words that always went with it. Mr. Quin is still in business in Mahanoy City with his brother, Tom, and the writer has the great pleasure of showing here a recent picture of him, as well as one of the horse and wagon that used to carry him to Delano in the old days. He may be just a bit older now, but he is the same utterly good-natured and big-hearted chap as ever. The "extras" on the picture are not Delano people and they did not know when the picture was taken that they would have a place in a history of that town.

Other regular visitors to Delano that were as well-known and as highly-esteemed as Mr. Quin were Danny Hawk, the milkman; John Brill, the butcher, and others. Both Mr. Hawk and Mr. Brill served Delano customers for forty or more years.

These recollections might be multiplied times without number, but there are others of a later day to be told in another chapter.

On April 19th, 1887, the Moser family left Delano for the farm. After an absence of six years, they returned to Delano again. During this six-year period on the farm, Mr. Moser, Sr., continued his work as an engineer at Delano and boarded at the boarding house of Mrs. Glenn, while the other members of the family were making hay in the sunshine and mastering the mysteries of the Pennsylvania Dutch dialect.

CHAPTER XVI

Personal Memories of the 90's

IN JULY, 1893, the Moser family came back to Delano, this time to a home in Toney Row, now bearing the more dignified name of Lakeside Avenue. Almost four years of a very happy existence made up this second residence.

His first recollections have to do with getting re-acquainted with his former boyhood friends and with some new ones. Probably the first to welcome the wanderer back was Leon Bailey, who lived in the adjoining house. Leon had just graduated from the high school a month before. He was a few years older than the writer, but that did not prevent the forming of a close friendship, out of which came trips into the woods on hunting expeditions and other tramps together. The kindly interest of the older boy and his good advice have never been forgotten.

Another friendship that was closely cemented in those first days was with Herbert Clemens and it has never lost its warmth, although years of maturity have brought long miles of separation. Bill Bretz was an old-time friend who early came into the picture. There is a legend still extant among those who were boys in Delano in the early 90's that Bill had established a custom of looking over the new kids that came to town and if there seemed to be anything about any of them not entirely up to his specifications, the ordeal by battle followed. There was nothing at all personal in the matter, as, regardless of the outcome, a real friendship always developed. In these combats Bill was no respector of size, except that the new chap must be at least as large as himself. The writer has always flattered himself that Bill liked his looks, for he was spared this ordeal of battle.

The opening day of school is one of the vivid memories of this time. The historian was not quite certain where his scholastic attainments should place him in the scheme of things. He had evidently heard the story of the Biblical guest at the feast who was enjoined to take the lower seat first. He felt that grammar school would be about the right grade and took his place with the other pupils in Miss Kistler's room. After submitting to some questions from Miss Kistler, the answers to which must have been satisfactory, he received the glad news that he belonged in Mr. Schrope's room. This was the quickest promotion he ever experienced.

The class with which he resumed school life in Delano had in it a number of those with whom he had started school there some years before, among them, Herbert Perry, Millie Smith, Dedie Crossan, Clara Kimbel, Nan Blakslee, while Hattie Shafer, Ted Witman, Ed Whitehead, Art Davenport, Ed Crossan, and some others made up the remainder of the class.

The writer is constrained here to pay a personal tribute to Professor Schrope, principal of the high school at this time. Mr. Schrope is noted as an educator in many ways and his influence upon his pupils was always exerted toward character-building as well as mental development. He was ever a stickler for thoroughness in all things. Under his tutelage, the student just had to get it, and once he "got" it, it "stayed got." There are many people to whom the writer is indebted for influences in right directions, but he doubts whether there is another person to whom he owes more in this way than he does to Mr. Schrope. And for this good counsel at the formative period of life, he will be forever profoundly grateful.

The august senior class was always the object of awe to the young chap who had recently come up out of the rural schools. The strange studies of Latin, geometry, algebra, etc., seemed to present unattainable heights to be scaled. So the months of this first year slipped by rapidly.

In other lines of interest there were the Sunday School which met every Sunday forenoon in Union Hall and the Christian Endeavor Society every Sunday evening, with church services by the Methodist minister who had just come to town a few months before. Mrs. George Folweiler, to whom this history has been dedicated, was the first Sunday School teacher. This saintly woman is still busy at her work in the Master's vineyard in Delano. Surely a crown with many jewels awaits her. Later, Mr. H. F. Fritz, another zealous worker for good in the community, became the historian's teacher. He will always be remembered with the

HAZLE STREET ABOUT 1900
Text Page 119

THE BOSTON BRIDGE
Text Page 119

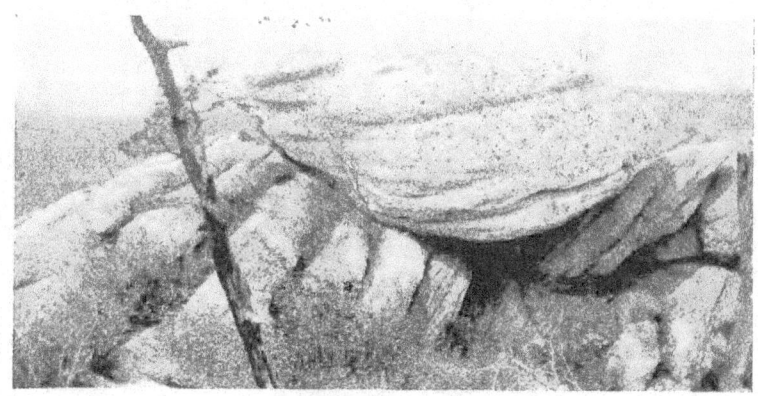

THE BOSTON ROCKS
Text Page 119

H. O. Moser, Historian
Text Page 121

deepest regard. Mr. Schrope was the superintendent of the school at the time, with D. W. Coder as his assistant. What has since become of Mr. Coder, the writer cannot say.

The Rev. Mr. Buyers, the Methodist minister who preached in Delano in 1894, was always a favorite among the boys of the community. He was a serious-minded earnest young man, tall and slim, and took an active part in the games. He was especially fond of skating and spent much of his spare time on fine winter days in company with the youngsters.

What happy days vacation times were. How many redskins bit the dust around the Boston Rocks as the fourteen-year-old scouts of Delano surrounded them there! The historian remembers well the many talks he and Charley Perry used to have about their longings to travel the great plains of the west in search of adventure. And all the while they were living the greatest adventures that can come to any life.

The old swimming hole down by the Boston switches! Just about enough depth for the kind of diving then current—in the expressive, if crude, speech of that day called "belly-floppers." The water in this hole could hardly have passed a purity test, and it had the consistency and opacity of a medium-thick soup, but that never deterred the boys from using it. One of the favorite hours for a dip there was Saturday afternoons, just after their mothers had completed superintending the week-end scrubbing process and fixed them up in nice, clean Saturday clothes. With the opening of the old reservoirs for swimming, a new day was ushered in for the boys. The battles with Indians on land were superseded by combats with pirates at sea, a big raft on the dam providing the necessary nautical equipment.

"Greenie" hunts were popular in the summer months. The stream leading into the dam and the dams themselves furnished good hunting grounds. Home cooking could never taste as good as those greenie lunches, augmented by eggs and potatoes contributed (without mother's knowledge) by the family larder. The greenie shanks might be considerably underdone on one side and badly scorched on the other, the potatoes mostly charcoal and the eggs anything from three to thirty-minute style, but no king ever feasted on viands half so rare.

Winter sports furnished their share of delight. Skating was a very popular form of pleasure and amusement and the people of Delano were fortunate in having a splendid place to enjoy it. With the completion of the larger reservoir, a new zest was given to the sport. On fine winter nights, when skating was good, a great fire built at one end of the dam illuminated it over its whole area and made a beautiful picture of the smooth body of clear ice and the swiftly moving figures gliding over it.

The hills about Delano provided fine coasting for the young and older people. Bunker Hill was the place mostly used in that day, as it made possible a fast smooth ride of about half a mile, with an easy walk back. Sometimes the Quakake side of the mountain was used. This ride had a real thrill for the coaster as he passed under the Lehigh arch some distance below the summit. Ordinarily the ground under the arch was bare and for about one hundred yards above the arch the hill is very steep. The highest speed was reached just as the sled struck the 20-foot piece of bare ground, and it took some tall holding-on to keep the coaster and his sled from parting company. Another ride taken in daylight was down the mountain leading to Grier City. This had two disadvantages—the hair-pin turn halfway down the mountain, which could be negotiated only by the use of some hard braking with the feet; and the long walk back, requiring about an hour of climbing. Two or three rides a day on that course made a pretty full schedule.

The entertainments put on by the schools in Union Hall provided diversion and entertainment for the students as well as the townspeople. The writer remembers one of those that had a few specialties that were not on the regular program. It was a rainy night, which meant a muddy night in the Delano of that day. This did not keep people from coming to the hall, however. One of the participants, whose name shall be withheld, recited very dramatically "Tam-o-Shanter's Ride," and he did it very well. On coming to the hall through the muddy streets he had rolled his trouser-legs halfway to his knees. In the excitement of the evening's program, he forgot to roll the right one back into place. In taking his place at the front of the platform when his turn came to recite, he planted this good right foot well to the fore and launched forth into the exciting story of old "Tam." The reader can imagine for himself the effect upon the boys and girls in the audience.

JOHN QUIN WITH FAMILIAR HORSE AND WAGON
Text Page 124

JOHN QUIN
Text Page 124

The first appearance in Delano of Edison's startling invention, the phonograph, was an outstanding event. It was the old-time type, wax cylinders and big horn. The audience was amazed at the marvel of it. To add to the wonder, the entertainer was prepared to make records on the spot, and Delano's premier elocutionist, Miss Kate Smith, was persuaded to recite before the big horn. In just a few minutes her recitation was repeated by the machine for the benefit of the audience. How fast the world has moved since then.

Huckleberrying and Mayflower-picking trips were often taken. Huckleberries grew thick on the flats along the Lofty road around the cross-roads and towards Trenton. Teaberry nobs were gathered on these trips, too. Blackberries were plentiful over in Nigger Hollow, but it was hard going to get there and back. In the woods back of Pine Junction the most wonderful swamp huckleberries were to be found.

The young people often had picnics up at the old picnic ground, which was then starting to lose its beauty. A new picnic ground had already been started back of Hazle Street, this being still in use. House parties played their part in providing entertainment for Delano people at this time.

The favorite promenade in Delano was the road up the Quakake mountain. On summer evenings this long straight road was filled with groups of promenaders. The writer remembers some of his chums of that day joining with him in those walks—Herb Clemens, Billy Schrope, Bill Bretz, one or two Perry boys, Ted Witman, Lew Markel and others. The urge to lift voices in song seems to develop at this age and many a popular ditty of the day was sadly mistreated by those singers, as they strolled along in the "Evening by the Moonlight."

Sometimes these good cronies would assemble on the little stoop in front of the historian's home on summer evenings. There come to him yet echoes of other voices lifted in song across the street— Katie Becker, Allie Read and their friends swinging in a hammock in the Becker yard, singing the song hit of that day, "After the Ball." Katie and Allie have long since been happily married, as they deserve to be.

Among the boyish triumphs of the time was the mastery of the curve ball. The writer's ability to put a little bend on the ball was responsible for being drafted into service one day to pitch for the Patch team of kids. The Patch team won the game, but it was due to their heavy hitting.

Coming back to school days. The second year moved quickly along. The writer's class had the distinction of being seniors for two years, as there was no graduating class in 1895. Graduation from high school is always one of the bright spots in any young person's life. There is no other graduation just like it. The historian had the honor of completing his high school course with four young ladies. Commencement Day was an event. The date was June 9th, 1896, the day was hot and the class worked hard all day getting the stage in readiness. The colors were yellow and white and the class flower the daisy, a beautiful flower in its way, but not so good when handled in bulk. No record was kept of how many thousands of daisies that class glued to the cardboard letters that spelled out the class motto and the year, but the writer, in looking back to the experience, marvels that the flower did not become extinct on June 9th, 1896.

Just before the hour fixed for beginning the program, the class assembled in the Butler home across the street, since Union Hall had no back-stage facilities by which a dignified entrance could be made. As it happened, other things intervened to mar this dignified entrance. The capacity of the hall at that time was very limited, the addition to it not yet having been built, and there were more people seeking entrance than the place could hold. In fact, the rule of capacity which says that the container must be larger than the contents, had already been badly stretched.

When the class sought entrance to the hall, the vestibule was literally packed with humanity, and it was with much difficulty that these people were persuaded that it was a custom at commencements to have the class present. The way was cleared after a bit and, once in, all was well, as a place for the class had been reserved on the platform.

Everything went off well with the program. The respective members pleased their anxious relatives in the audience, received their diplomas and the big event was over. The class motto, as the writer recalls it, was "Not Ended, but Begun," which had the merit of being good English and needing no translation for the English-speaking audience. The writer's oration that night was along the same theme, "Out of the Harbor Into the Sea." It wasn't much of an oration, as viewed from this distance, but such as it was, it was his own.

Considerable space has been devoted to a description of this particular commencement, not because it was unique in any sense, but because the writer feels that, with certain minor adjustments in names, titles and dates, the description will cover almost any similar occasion.

Many enjoyable vacation hours were spent at Laurel Junction, then in charge of Telegrapher Jerry McAvoy. Practical jokes were frequently played by and on the loafers. Mike Sullivan was a good friend of Jerry's and was often found there when the youngsters arrived. Should his eyes fall upon this paragraph, it may recall to him the day he planted his great bulk in front of the only door in the little office and poured pepper on the hot stove. The six or eight youngsters who filled the place to capacity were almost strangled before Mike relented and opened the door.

Sunday afternoon hikes were often taken by the boys of the town, sometimes to Park Place, again to Lakeside, on two occasions to the High Bridge near Hometown and at other times wherever railroad or highway might lead.

This reminds the writer of the long walks to the White Church taken in the summer of 1895 in company with Kathryn Shuler, Bob Shafer and Ted Witman. They were members of a class receiving catechetical instruction in the Lutheran Church from the Rev. Mr. Gebert, of Tamaqua, in preparation for their confirmation in the church.

On almost every one of those trips, the little group would meet on the return road with the jovial and leather-lunged Davy Dress, of Mahanoy City, in his fish wagon. Mr. Dress, as Delano people will remember, had two specialties—"FRESH FISH-O" and "DOUBLE-JOINTED, FRESH-ROASTED, CALIFORNIA PEANUTS." The capitals are used purposely, since they best express the robust manner in which Mr. Dress announced his wares to the world. The writer does not recall much about the quality of the fish, but the taste of those peanuts still lingers. They were good, no gainsaying the fact. In the store picture of 1884 shown earlier in this book is an excellent likeness of Mr. Dress.

Davy's fish and peanuts stir memories of other people well-known in Delano over a long period of time. Dieter's ice cream wagon from Mahanoy City, which usually drove into town early in the evening, when the youngsters were all home from school. Happy moment when mother sent one of the kids out to the wagon with the big pitcher. Somehow, there was a flavor and bouquet to the ice cream of those days that is no longer to be found in that dainty. What wonderful days are the days of childhood!

Mrs. Driscoll's store in the Patch was another haunt of the young people of the town. Spare change rapidly found its way into the money drawer there in exchange for candy and other things dear to the heart of childhood.

The spring hair-cut was always an important rite in the lives of the younger boys in this period. About the beginning of June most boys of a certain age visited Al Billman's barber shop in the freight house and had the closest hair-cut clippers could give, just one degree above a clean shave. With good growing weather throughout the summer, it was possible for those chaps to achieve a visible part in their hair by Christmas. That was keeping the barber upkeep down with a vengeance.

The pranks of the wiper boys kept things interesting about the engine houses. The writer missed the experience of engine wiping, but he has some good friends who did not. Many a tale was told of the knights of the road who sought shelter on cold winter nights in the warm interior of the engine houses. These unsuspecting unfortunates were always received graciously by the boys and provided with comfortable places to rest. But this rest was short-lived after the wipers got properly set. Air hose, dirty waste, coal—anything that made a handy missile—were showered upon the poor hoboes as they fled from the place. One experience was usually enough to keep them far from the place afterward. There was a haven, however, where they were able to find sanctuary. The sand house, in charge of Manager Tom Ross, was a sort of Wayfarer's Inn, and this made an ideal shelter on stormy nights, with the soft dry sand and the warm air always maintained in it. Tom was a friend to the unfortunates and permitted no foolishness by the wiper boys in his domain.

The initiation into the wiper's fraternity was rather a strenuous and exciting affair, as all those who experienced it can testify. The young fellow who survived the first night had something to remember it by. One of the milder methods used, reserved for those of more tender years, was to remove all the clothing of the noviatiate and treat him to a generous coating of engine oil and lampblack, from head to foot. This was not painful, but it surely did detract from his beauty for a few weeks.

Another tale of the mischievous bent of these young fellows is that a call boy whose duty it was to call the men for work. John Culliney, who had charge of the oil house and boarded at the Glenn boarding house, was the target for much of the mischief of the boys, and he was always watchful when they were around. On this night, the call boy had gone upstairs in the boarding house to call one of the railroad men staying there and he had with him a large bottle, to the neck of which he had tied securely a piece of heavy twine, with dark designs upon Mr. Culliney. He tiptoed into Culliney's room and found the old gentleman sound asleep. He carefully tied the loose end of the twine to one of Culliney's big toes, laid the bottle on his chest and bolted for the door with a loud yell. The old chap awoke, felt the bottle lying on him, saw his tormentor at the door and grabbed and threw the bottle at the boy with all his might. The result can be imagined. The boarders said that the old man awakened the whole house with his cries.

Who will ever forget Bausman, the crossing watchman in the 90's? He was "Bausy" to everybody. He was a good bit of a philosopher in his way and was always interesting to the boys. He had a certain pride about the way things were run about the station and the crossing that was his particular charge. Sometime about 1893 one of Glenn's boarders was lucky enough to win a cow at a raffle-match. The cow was a good cow from a utilitarian standpoint, but not strong on looks. She was large and gaunt, with plenty of angles and the head-gear of a Texas longhorn. The boarder kept the cow in a stable in the rear of the boarding house and she helped supply the boarding house table with cream. Johnny Glenn used to say that his mother used the cow for a clothes-rack for the boarders. One of Mr. Bausman's most grievous complaints on his job as crossing watchman was that this big red cow always made it a point to wander over to the railroad station just as the passenger trains came in. It was his duty to chase her from the station and to do this in sight of all the passengers was humiliating to a man of his standing, as he expressed it.

But there must come an end to reminiscing, however delightful it may be. There came a day early in 1897 when orders were given to the writer's father to locate in Mount Carmel. Shortly thereafter a house was found, furniture packed and preparations made to leave the dear old place. Good friends gave an elaborate farewell party to the family, when a few days later it was learned that the house which had been rented in Mount Carmel was not available, and the family remained in Delano for about two months longer. These same good friends were about to arrange a welcome-back party, when the flight took place.

And so came to an end the writer's residence in Delano, but not his abiding regard for the town and its people.

CHAPTER XVII

A New Century and New Conditions

THE year 1900 found Delano, now forty years old, ready to move forward, under vastly changed conditions, with the same resolute spirit that had brought it thus far along the highway of achievement. Its shops were gone and with them the sturdy craftsmen who had made them famous. Many of the people who had come in the very beginning of things had to take up the ways of life in other places. New families came to town and took up their part in community activities. These were not wholly strangers to Delano, for they were the families of the railroad men who had worked there for years. They were possessed of the same qualities of aggressiveness and community pride that characterized the pioneers. Delano in some phases of its life may have died in 1899, but—"Long live Delano!"

Almost at the beginning of this new decade the town suffered its most disastrous fire, when two double houses in Brown Row, (now Maple Street), were totally destroyed, making homeless four families. The fire occurred on the night of January 9th, 1900, and created great excitement for a town that had heretofore been singularly free of misfortune of this kind.

A direct outcome of the fire was the organization of a fire company. During the years of its existence it had its headquarters on the second floor of the freight station, with the fire-fighting equipment housed in the old band hall on the first floor of the same building. Several years passed without any call for the services of the company and it gradually fell into a state of inocuous desuetude, from which it never recovered. The old hose cart still stands forlornly in the band room, but the company itself is out of existence.

After disbanding the fire company some time between 1900 and 1910, a railroad Y. M. C. A. was organized and maintained in the same quarters. This organization held the interest of the men in the town for a number of years and then gradually disintegrated. Following this came the Railroaders' Club, which is still active.

This club serves a doubly useful purpose, in that it enables the call boys to locate the men promptly when they are needed for duty and also provides a comfortable place for the men to find diversion in idle moments.

There was no let-down in the activity of the railroad business in Delano following the removal of the shops. Many railroad men were now located conveniently near their work who before this were compelled to walk or drive from the surrounding country districts when called for duty. The full complement of railroad forces was maintained and most of the crews which had been moved to Mount Carmel in the latter part of the previous decade had now been returned to Delano. It was during this time that new engine types appeared.

The day of the consolidation engine, as originally constructed, was passing, as was also that of the rebuilt "camel-back" type. Increased tonnage in shipments required more road power. The need was met by more powerful locomotives. The same company whose founder feared to build the first consolidation engine because of its great size and weight was now designing and turning out engines that dwarfed the once powerful consolidations. Engine construction had ceased at Delano with the coming of these new giants and customs in the conduct of railroad business were changing as in every other branch of industry. Companies no longer took care of their own needs in the construction of rolling stock. The great independent locomotive and car shops supplied these needs.

With the increase in engine power came a similar change in car construction. The little six-ton hoppers passed into the discard and were followed by flat-bottomed gondolas, with 30, 40 and 50-ton capacities, and some time later by the big steel battleships, with capacities of 100 to 130 tons. Freight cars changed in size and design and the all-steel passenger coaches came into the picture. All this increase in weight necessitated the laying of heavier rails and more substantial road ballast.

Improvements in air brakes, with the adoption of the retaining valve and automatic couplers, had long ago made train operation an entirely new thing. The day of the circus stunts on the little cars was gone and safety heretofore undreamed of attended the work of the trainmen. The engineer handled trains of one hundred big cars by means of a little brass valve lever, and the brakemen needed only to watch the retaining valves on the heavy grades. Altogether a new day had been ushered in in the railroad world.

In this period stricter rules were being adopted by the companies in regard to the training and physical equipment of the employees. Train operation was becoming more mechanical, with electric block signals and the many refinements in mechanical equipment of engines and cars. The matter of hearing, eyesight, physical condition, with a proper understanding of rules, machinery, etc., assumed an important place in the railroader's life. Periodic examinations were held to test the employees—color tests, vision tests, hearing tests, and physical tests generally. An air car, fitted out with a complete air brake system, was put into use, where trainmen received careful instruction in the mechanism and operation of the system, after which they had to pass successful examinations in what they had been taught.

The book of rules became important. Examinations on rules were held and they were rigid. No guesswork was permitted in reading and interpreting train orders, signals and timetables.

It was in this decade that many of these things were first put into practice and the writer can still remember hours spent with his father in getting the book of rules down pat. In fact, he could have passed the examination on the rules with the best of them in that day. To men who had been accustomed to railroading with no more stringent rules than the use of ordinary common sense and prudence and the ability to read a passing or meet order and to know when the board was in their favor, these new requirements seemed irksome and unnecessary; but they soon came to realize that their own welfare was as much at stake as was that of the company and its patrons, and the many examinations and tests lost their terror and were accepted as a matter of fact.

The pooling of train crews became a practice about this time in the history of Delano. The old days when each crew had its own engine were gone. Crews were sent out in a rotating system, which meant that engines were in almost constant service, with a different engineer and fireman on each succeeding time out. This resulted in a number of things. Railroaders no longer had regular hours. Long use of the system, with a keen knowledge of immediate working conditions, enables them to tell with reasonable accuracy just when they are likely to be called for duty, but there is no real certainty about it, since one or more of the men marked up ahead of them may for one reason or another not be available when their time arrives, thus moving the whole board up.

Another result was the abolishing of engine wiping. The engines were never in the house long enough to enable the wipers to give them the cleaning demanded in former days. Again, the type of engines now coming into use would have required two or three boys for every one needed before, because of their greatly-increased size. A secondary result of this lack of attention to cleanliness was to create more or less indifference to appearance in the minds of the men. No more did the company take pride in turning out the fine-lined, trim-looking locomotives, with brass and copper embellishments. Utility was now the word. Great, squat, ugly monsters, with power written all over them, supplanted the lithe greyhounds of the past.

The use of soft coal also had its effect in the loss of this old-time pride. Hard coal, with its lack of soot and smoke, made for natural cleanliness, and it was comparatively easy for the crew to keep its engine spick and span under all conditions. The grime of the bituminous changed all that.

About 1903 the eastern half of the old frame station was razed. This made quite a change in the appearance of things in that vicinity, but it was only a forerunner of the razing that was to take place later among many of the buildings in Delano. Illustrations shown elsewhere in this book take note of the many changes made in this way.

The prosperity of the little town went on as in other days, with its busy railroad as hard at work as ever. Greater freight traffic than ever flowed through the yards, although passenger service was greatly reduced. The chief losses entailed through the removal of the shops were in the departure of the fine people who had so long been a part of the town's life and in the passing of the prestige that went with its position as the center of division authority.

A number of shopmen had been retained to do the needed repair work on the engines and equipment, a picture of one of these small gangs being shown. This picture was taken about 1906 between the old machine shop and the frog shop and the men appearing on it are, left to right—Lewis Markel, Harry Shafer, George Symons, Lafayette Boyle and Clinton Engel.

Life generally in the community went along in the old ways. The coming of new residents created new friendships. Without doubt there was gain to the town in the new viewpoints and ideas brought by these people from other communities. The social life of the town underwent some changes in this period, partly due to the coming of the automobile, which made access to distant places easy.

Mr. J. A. Depew brought the first car to Delano and this was followed later by others. The matter of traveling was never much of a problem to people in a railroad town, especially to people in Delano prior to this period. Everyone traveled on a pass or shop ticket and trains came and went at all hours of the day and night. But the motor car made accessible many places not heretofore to be reached and the mode of travel was much more pleasant and pleasureable.

The activity in the church life of the town continued as ever. The same denominations continued their ministries through this decade. The Lutheran ministers of Mahanoy City who served Delano through the decade were the Rev. J. F. Seebach, 1900-1907, and the Rev. Charles W. Diehl, 1908-1916. The Reformed ministers of Mahanoy City alternated with the Lutheran in the services, while the Methodist Church continued its pastorates in Delano. Many of the leading spirits in church life had left Delano in the exodus, but the newcomers brought many zealous workers in that field. The Sunday School and Christian Endeavor Societies had some of their best years in this period.

Steady progress in the schools of the town was made, with some important changes in the teaching staffs. The increased number of pupils required more room and near the end of this decade, a one-story frame building was erected to the northeast of the large building. This building contained two rooms and was used by the primary grades.

The faculties during this ten-year period were as follows: High school, 1900-1906, principal, J. M. Schrope; 1906-1910, G. W.

Hemminger. High school, assistant principal, 1900-1902, Miss Richards; 1903-1904, Miss Elizabeth Reber; 1904-1905, Howard W. Leinbach and B. Franklin Jones; 1905-1910, Maurice Singley. Grammar school, 1900-1902, Miss Anna Clauser; 1902-1904, Miss Jeanette Hornsby; 1904-1906, Miss Elizabeth Reber; 1906-1907, Miss Elizabeth Reber and Miss Gladys McMichael; 1907-1910, Miss Dedie Crossan. Miss Crossan was a graduate of the Delano schools. Secondary school, 1900-1907, Miss Dedie Crossan; 1907-1908, Miss Emma Kline; 1908-1910, Miss Laura M. Saul. Primary, 1900-1904, Miss Millie Smith; 1905-1907, Miss Emma Kline; 1907-1908, Miss Jeanette Hornsby and Miss Laura Saul; 1908-1910, Miss Sarah Prim. New building, 1908-1909, Miss Emma Kline; 1909-1910, Miss Catherine Folweiler.

The graduates for this decade are as follows:

1900—No graduates.

1901—No graduates.

1902—Thomas Crossan.

1903—Mary R. Hofmann, Elizabeth R. Doyle, James W. Engel and James W. Cauley.

1904—Blanche L. Yohe, Ruth Depew, Cyrie Hofmann and George F. Mack.

1905—Christine Depew, George Bretz, Elmer Clemens, Sarah Prim and Walter Eisenbach.

1906—Catherine L. Folweiler, John H. Cauley and Charles F. Hofmann.

1907—George Hofmann and John Hoeflich.

1908—Rosena Evans, Ethel Griffith, Margaret Driscoll, Florence E. Kline, Harold Fritz and Adam Restenberger.

1909—Benjamin Sturtevant.

1910—Irene Folweiler, Pearl Walbert, Margaret Hoeflich, Christine Hofmann, Ellen Cauley, Marie Driscoll, Fannie Doyle, Anna Arner, Albert Kleckner, John Clemens, Clarence Beltz, Harold Stewart and Graham Hemminger.

This class of 1910 was the largest yet to graduate from the Delano schools.

The greatest change in the school life of Delano in this period was the resignation of Mr. Schrope as principal, after a splendid service of fifteen years, during which the high school was organized and the general standing of the schools brought to a high level. Mr. Singley, who assumed the principalship at the end of this decade, is still in charge as supervising principal and has maintained the enviable reputation of Delano for high standards in education and has steadily advanced the interests of the schools until today they rank in the very forefront of Pennsylvania high schools. Mr. Schrope, in his position as assistant county superintendent of schools, has never lost touch with these schools.

The removal of the shops just before the beginning of this period caused a three-year lapse in graduations, but the schools recovered from that blow very quickly and have gone on from triumph to triumph through the years since.

It was the writer's privilege to make an address at the commencement in 1902 and, again, about 1905, he represented the alumni of the schools in an affair held at Delano. A banquet was held by the alumni at that time, the only meeting ever held by former graduates of Delano high school, so far as he knows.

It was during this decade that Dr. Flexer became a resident of the town, coming there January 2nd, 1900, and remaining until his death in February, 1910. Dr. Flexer was the first, and one of the very few, resident physicians Delano has had. Upon his death, his practice was taken over by Dr. J. M. Kuhns, who resided in Delano for several years and has since moved to some place in the South. Dr. Hermany continued to practice at Delano all through this period.

The barbers who served Delano through this period were A. E. Billman and Harry Evans, both known to everyone in Delano over a long period of time. Mr. Billman has been for a long time a realtor in the city of Allentown, Pa., and Mr. Evans is still following his old trade in the city of Newark, N. J.

The town throughout its whole history always had an enviable record in the matter of law observance. The only major crime to mar this record occurred on November 21st, 1909, when an Italian named Tony Fagain was shot to death in a fight among a group of Italian laborers which occupied temporary quarters in freight cars between Pine and Laurel Junctions, in what was known as Camp Gibbon. These men were not residents of Delano, but had been brought there by the railroad company for a short time to do some special work for the company.

Harry Shafer was justice of the peace in Delano at the time and, upon information made before him, he issued a warrant for the arrest of Patsy Atlas, accused of the murder. The warrant was placed in the hands of Oscar Riegel, who was constable for Delano Township, and in a very short time Mr. Riegel located his man between Delano and Lofty, placed him under arrest and brought him before the justice, who remanded him to prison at Pottsville to await trial. Three witnesses, Charles Fawyo, Tony Capiano and Tony Francis, were also held for the trial.

Both the justice and the constable displayed commendable zeal and courage in handling the case in such an efficient and speedy manner. It was quite in the Delano manner of doing things, short shrift being made of any who had the temerity to defy the rules by which the tranquil order of the town was preserved.

So life moved forward in Delano, its people always alert to the things that made for progress. Social life kept pace with the march of the rest of the world, the spiritual interests of the people were ministered to most effectively, in the educational field nothing was overlooked that might in any way promote the highest welfare of the young people. Industrially, the town had safely ridden out the severe tempest that had threatened to engulf it, and in every way the best traditions of the founders were being maintained.

CHAPTER XVIII

THE DELANO OF TODAY

NO revolutionary changes have taken place in the life of Delano within the past twenty years. The people who make up the population today are pretty much the same people who were living in the town in 1910, except for the normal changes that take place in any community. Some new families have come in during that period, a few have left the town, while some of the young folks have sought larger fields of endeavor in other places and other young men and women have united their fortunes and established homes of their own in the place of their fathers.

The final chapters of this story shall treat this twenty-one year period as the modern era of Delano's history.

During the first ten-year portion of this time occurred the great World War. In keeping with its patriotic record, Delano sent a large group of its boys into the service of their country, of which group a complete record is given here, including the units with which the boys served, so far as the information has been available:

Robert Applegate, 2nd Lieut. U. of V. Va., Co. N, Plattsburg, N. Y.; Monroe Adams, Base Hospital Corps, No. 71, A. E. F.; Edward Breitmeyer, Co. E, 112th U. S. Inf., A. E. F.; Harry Brill, Co. B, 5th Prov. Batt., E. M. P., Ft. Benj. Harrison, Ind.; Corp. Edward Cowley, Co. H, 5th Div., 11th Inf., A. E. F.; Harry Depew, 28th Balloon Co., A. E. F.; Edward Doyle, Corp. 135th Co. Transportation Corps, A. E. F.; Charles Donat, S. A. T. C., Co. E, Carnegie Tech. Institute, Pittsburgh; John Degris, 5th Park Co., 279th Aero Squadron, A. E. F.; Charles C. Engle, Sgt. Hdq. Co., 344th Batt. Tank Corps, A. E. F. (Mr. Engle was wounded in action in the St. Mihiel Sector in France); Harold Folweiler, Co. C, 103rd Regt. Engineers, 28th Div.; Guy Fegley, Cont. Officers Training School, Co. A; Albert Folweiler, Co. D, Ord. Dept., Camp Aberdeen; James Folweiler, 14th Grand Div., 22nd Co., A. E. F.; John Frey, Batt. D, 311th Field Art., 79th Div.; Frank Faust, Co. B, 81st Regt. of Engineers; Thomas Gothie, 325th Aero Squadron, A. E. F.; Charles Hofmann, 1st Lieut., Co. 3, M. T. R., Unit 306,

Camp Holabab, Baltimore, Md.; Leo Hofmann, Chief Yeoman, U. S. N. Naval Reserves, 4th Dist., League Island, Pa.; William Kemery, Co. F, 118th Engrs., Camp Upton, Benj. Harrison, Ind.; George Lazurick, 314th Field Art., A. E. F., 80th Div.; John McAndrew, Pvt. Co. M, 18th Replacement Training Center, Camp Lee, Va.; Warren Patterson, 18th Co., 154th Depot Brig., Camp Meade; Ronald Perry, Corp. Btn. C, 6th Regt., F. A. R. D., Camp Zachary Taylor, Ky.; Walter Strack, Co. L, 63rd Inf., 11th Div., Astoria, L. I.; William Straub, Co. G, S. A. T. C., Carnegie Inst., Pittsburgh; Frank Stahl, Co. L, 5th Pioneer Inf., Camp Wadsworth, S. C.; John Sharkey, M. T. C., Richmond College, Va., Med. Dept., Gen. Hospital 41, Staten Island, N. Y.; Elmer Sharkey, Med. Dept., U. S. A., Gen. Hospital 41, Staten Island, N. Y.; Guy Smith, Co. F, 304th Div. Supply Train, 79th Div., A. E. F.; Calvin Williams, 41st Div., 4th Batt., A. E. F.; Harry Cauley, Martin Cauley, Edward Brown, Thomas Farr, Philip Jacobs, Joseph Jacobs and August Edinger.

The first Delano soldier to give his life in the service of his country in this war was Harry Brill, son of Mr. and Mrs. Lewis Brill, who died October 12th, 1918, at Fort Benj. Harrison, Ind., and the second was Fred Kemery, who died October 14th, 1918.

A radical change in property ownership took place in October and November, 1926, when the Lehigh Valley Railroad Company sold to its employees in Delano the homes then occupied by them, with the exception of a few that were retained for the use of such employees as were subject to frequent transfers.

The total number of buildings in the town at this time, exclusive of railroad and shop buildings, was ninety-one. Seven of these were single residences, eighty-one double residences, one a fourdoor residence, one general store and one drug store. There were also, of course, the church and school buildings. The houses sold were four single residences, sixty-nine double residences and the four-door residence.

One of the first results of these sales was the great improvement of the homes. Most of the new owners lost no time in effecting improvements both in the convenience and appearance of their homes, and the enhancement in the appearance of the whole town was very noticeable, especially to former residents who have since visited the town after absences of many years. Thousands of dollars were spent by some owners in making their homes modern in every respect.

Another outcome of the beautifying of the homes was the improvement of the streets two years ago. Hazle Street, Lakeside Avenue and Maple Street were given a hard, smooth surfacing, greatly increasing the attractiveness of the town.

With the replotting of the town for the purpose of selling the homes, new names were given to the streets. For the information of the readers, the changes in names are given here: Swamppoodle to Birch Street; Paradise Alley to Willow Street; Main Street to Hazle Street; Toney Row to Lakeside Avenue; Brown Row to Maple Street; Railroad Street to Locust Street; Coal Dump Row to Cedar Street, and the street running from the rear of the brick station to Lakeside Avenue being now named Chestnut Street.

A number of fires occurred during this period. On May 23rd, 1924, the single house occupied by Lewis Shaup and family was almost totally destroyed. The fire started at 6:30 a. m. and the Shaup family lost about half of its furniture. The house was not rebuilt, but later was sold by the company to Melvin Straub, who erected a bungalow, which is now occupied by him and his family. The building destroyed was located east of the old frame station.

Sometime later the double house occupied by John Hentosh and John Korinchalk, located at the extreme lower end of the Patch, was totally destroyed, both building and furniture being a total loss. This building was never rebuilt.

In 1929 the remaining portion of the old passenger station was razed. This had been occupied by the town drug store for about thirty-five years. It was one of Delano's landmarks, having been erected almost at the beginning of the town's history.

On November 24th, 1926, the double house occupied by William Rhoads and Raymond Lindemuth, located at the upper end of Hazle Street, was badly damaged by fire. The Lindemuth side was a total loss. This home was later rebuilt.

Doctors

After Dr. J. M. Kuhns left Delano some time after 1910, he was succeeded by Dr. R. A. Dengler, who came from Gilberton, Pa. Dr. Dengler practiced in Delano for quite a number of years, also residing there. He left the town for a larger field in Allentown, Pa., where he still resides. He was succeeded by Dr. Dever, of McAdoo, who is Delano's physician at this writing. Dr. Dever never moved to the town, but maintains an office in the railroad station building. Thus Delano in the matter of medical service has reverted to its original status, without a resident physician.

Fraternal Organizations

Camp 72, P. O. S. of A., is still in a very flourishing condition. It has occupied its present quarters since 1883, and is the town's pioneer fraternal body. Its present roster of officers is as follows: President, James Lindner; Vice President, David Edinger; Master of Forms, Raymond Hartzel; Recording Secretary, Philip Edinger; Financial Secretary, John E. Houser, and Treasurer, Harry E. Shafer. The membership of the lodge is one hundred thirty-five.

Asa Packer Lodge, I. O. O. F., No. 328, has never lost its strength since organized in 1883. The present officers are: Noble Grand, Raymond Hartzel; Vice Grand, Melvin Straub; Secretary, John E. Houser; Treasurer, Warren Patterson. The membership is one hundred sixty-four.

Two women's lodges are still very active in the life of Delano.

In addition to these organizations, Delano has two railroad brotherhoods: the Brotherhood of Railroad Trainmen and the Brotherhood of Locomotive Firemen and Enginemen.

Social Life

Social life in Delano has kept pace with the times. Various organizations of the town still provide entertainment of different kinds and, of course, the residents are in close contact with the outside world and seek much of their diversion and pleasure in other places. The automobile has become well-nigh universal and the people of Delano are well provided with this means of travel. Lakewood and Lakeside Parks, located within a five-minute ride of the town, have their attractions for all ages, and the moving picture theaters in nearby cities are as conveniently located to the town as though within it.

Delano has not lost its standing as a clean little community of high moral standards and it is still at work in the business of developing fine character and upstanding citizenship. In its physical aspects, it is vastly improved over former years, with modern homes, well-paved streets and the conveniences that belong to any progressive community. Its citizens are intelligent and thoroughly alive to everything that is modern and worth striving for.

Several photographs of the town taken very recently are shown here. One of Hazle Street shows the improvement in homes and streets. The woman standing on the porch of the first house on the picture is Mrs. Harry Shaup, formerly Miss Bertha Depew, a lifetime resident of Delano.

Another modern photograph which it is a pleasure to include in this history is one of Mr. and Mrs. Jonathan Bretz, taken several years ago on their golden wedding anniversary, the picture being taken on the porch of their home in Delano. Mr. Bretz has since left this vale of tears, but Mrs. Bretz still resides in the homestead and is enjoying excellent health.

The writer feels that there should be a place in this history for another former Delano couple whose connection with the town extended over a period of many years—his own father and mother. A photograph of them as they appear today is presented. They are both enjoying excellent health at their home in Mount Carmel, to which place they came from Delano thirty-five years ago.

CHAPTER XIX

Present Day Railroading

PROBABLY at no time in Delano's history did its sole industry reach the present low level of operation. This is due to several things. As all the world knows, the railroad business is undergoing its most trying times in these days. With this, every business has suffered during the past few years. In spite of these discouraging circumstances, Delano is not in despair. It believes that there is a better day coming and that the coming of that day will have its effect on the prosperity of the town as well as elsewhere.

In 1922 occurred quite a serious shop strike, in line with a general strike over the Lehigh Valley system. While the forces at the Delano shops had been very greatly reduced through the changes of 1899, the strike resulted directly in additional reductions in the forces. With the exception of a handful of mechanics left to take care of the emergency repair work, a strong retrenchment was put into effect at Delano and most of the work that had been cared for there was from this time forward handled at Ashmore.

The writer is indebted to Mr. U. G. Fetterman, at present Assistant Trainmaster in charge of railroad operation at Delano, for detailed information about railroad business there at this time.

The shop forces employed there at this time are as follows: Round house foreman, Michael Sullivan; gang leaders, Clarence Steiner and Joseph Cauley; crew dispatchers, C. R. Engle and Ferdinand Wehy; machinists, Samuel Shafer, J. A. Shafer, Robert Gasser, Charles Engle, William Thamarus and E. L. Stickler; machinist helpers, Metro Muelka, Clinton Gouldner and Harry Perry; boiler makers, Lee Watkins and Milton Matz; engine hostlers, John Houser, Bernard Herman and A. J. Long; fire cleaners, Joseph Lestoskey and Thomas Folweiler; sand house man, Harry Dudra; outside laborer, Paul Okal; locomotive crane operators, Harry Wiley and William Dennis.

The first engine house built at Delano has long since been torn down, as have almost all of the shop buildings. The engine house

SHOP GROUP, 1906
Text Page 139

HAZLE STREET, 1932
Text Page 147

SITE OF SHOPS, 1932
Text Page 149

MR. AND MRS. JONATHAN BRETZ
ON THEIR GOLDEN WEDDING DAY, APRIL 9, 1920
Text Page 147

at the south end of town still remains and the machine shop is located at the west end of that building. The old carpenter shop is still standing, but not used. The new carpenter shop located across the railroad from old Swamppoodle is still standing and is now used as a basketball hall by the schools, an ideal building for the purpose. The oil house still remains and is still used for that purpose. The old coal dump has been abandoned and a small dock built near the present engine house. A photograph taken by the writer very recently and shown in this volume gives an excellent idea of the great vacant space existing where once the busy shops of Delano were humming with life.

In the railroad service, the personnel is made up as follows:

Yard office force: U. G. Fetterman, assistant trainmaster; H. M. Michael, H. W. Vogelson and G. P. Schwartz, yardmasters.

Car inspector forces: H. L. Reinmiller, foreman; inspectors, Elmer Matz, Walter Faust, Walter Herb, Calvin Evans, Frederick Bertens, Harold Bawn, Harold Folweiler, Albert Levy and John Sheeler.

Station force: Charles North, agent; Mrs. Annie Beltz, janitress.

Pine Junction force: A. L. Werner, Martin Downey and J. H. Blakslee, towermen.

Laurel Junction: Oliver Riegel, towerman.

Delano Junction has been abandoned for a number of years.

Maintenance of way forces: A. B. Shimer, assistant supervisor; A. L. Hartung, Mike Hentosh and Wasil Raddick, section foremen; Wasil Mostick, extra gang foreman.

There are three yard crews on the railroad; two local freight crews operating from Delano; two through freights between Mount Carmel and Coxton; and five mine crews. No passenger crews operate out of Delano, excepting a church train on Sunday. The only passenger service now enjoyed by Delano is made up of two electric-gas motor trains running between Mauch Chunk and Mount Carmel and Easton and Mount Carmel—two trains each way a day.

Some idea of the change in railroading conditions at Delano may be gathered from the fact that there are many men who have been qualified engineers for fifteen years or more, some of them in regular service as engineers for many years, who are now firing and others who are out of work entirely. One of the reasons for this unfortunate condition is found in the fact that one train crew today handles a train of one hundred thirty-nine loaded cars from Delano to Packerton, these cars being the great battleship type as compared with the little six-ton cars of years ago. Forty years ago twelve crews would have been required to handle what one crew now handles.

Many of the old-time family names are still to be found in the lists of Delano employees, the second and third generations now carrying on the work of the fathers. These bits of leaven from the original lump retain for visiting old-timers the home-like atmosphere so much coveted.

This account of present conditions furnishes a clear picture of railroading in Delano as set over against the days of fifty years ago. The conviction grows in the mind of the outside observer that the good people of the old town should organize themselves into a corporate community, with the view of using the many natural advantages of the town to attract other industries. With cheap fuel, fine transportation facilities, ample space and other advantageous elements, there should be a splendid opportunity to give Delano a bright new spot in the industrial sun. May its present residents, having now a real, personal stake in the welfare of the town, envision this opportunity and bring the happy day of returning prosperity close to hand.

CHAPTER XX

Twenty-one Years of School Life

WHATEVER may have been the effect of the various retrenchments of the Lehigh Valley Railroad Company as concerning the town of Delano, the schools have gone forward in a steady progression toward the highest levels attainable. The attention of the reader is called to the fact that the Delano High School is classed as a first class school under the requirements of the Pennsylvania State Department of Public Instruction, an eminence that is not reached by schools located in many towns much larger than Delano.

About 1926 or 1927 it became evident to the school board of Delano that the town had outgrown its present school facilities and that it was very necessary to provide additional rooms and more modern equipment in order to maintain the policy that had always been a cardinal principle with Delano people, to give its young people the benefit of the most advanced courses in education. A vote on the proposal to put a large addition to the school building and to float a bond issue of $40,000.00 to cover the cost was taken and was carried with only three dissenting votes.

No time was lost in getting the construction of the addition to the building under way. The contract was given to the Tamaqua Construction Company and on Friday evening, February 17th, 1928, the formal dedication exercises were held in the spacious auditorium of the new portion. This was an outstanding evening in Delano history and some noted speakers were present for the occasion. They included Professor Maurice Singley, supervising principal of the schools; Professor J. M. Schrope, assistant county superintendent of schools and a former principal of the Delano schools; R. P. Swank, Esq., of Mahanoy City; Dr. Joseph F. Noonan, of Mahanoy City, a noted educator and at that time president of the Pennsylvania State Educational Association; Mr. Walter Patterson, of Delano, then president of the school board; and Dr. William Bristow, assistant director of secondary education in the State Department of Education. The Delano school orchestra participated in the program, as did the Rev. J. A. Aman, pastor at that time of St. John's Lutheran Church of Mahanoy City.

Addresses were made by the men named, the principal address being given by Dr. Bristow. A number of guests were introduced by Professor Singley, among them principals of several schools of towns in that section, and Mr. James Sullivan, a representative of the Record-American of Mahanoy City.

An inspection of the new building followed the exercises and a social hour closed the evening, the girls of the domestic science department serving ice cream, cake and coffee.

The school board at this time was composed of Walter Patterson, president; Griffith Lindner, vice president; Matthew Riddle, secretary; George Beers, treasurer, and William Long, with R. P. Swank, Esq., solicitor.

Splendid tributes were paid to the people of Delano, the school board, to Mr. Singley and his corps of teachers, for placing the school affairs of the little town on this high plane. In a separate chapter to follow this is a detailed account of the schools of Delano, with courses, grades, equipment and work done, prepared by Mr. Singley at the request of the writer. The whole matter of the modern school system now in effect in Delano is so well covered in that article that no more will be said of it here.

The faculties of the schools from 1910 down to the date of this history, which includes the term of 1931-1932, were constituted as follows:

High School: Supervising principal, 1910 to this date, Maurice Singley; assistant principal, 1910-1914, Christine Depew; 1914-1916, Quincy Rohrbach; 1916-1917, Christine Depew; 1917-1918, Harold Dietrich; 1918-1919, Ellen Cauley; 1919-1921, Ellen Cauley and Thorne Harris.

In the fall of 1921 the high school and grammar school were reorganized, combining grades 7 and 8 with the high school, making a Junior-Senior High School of grades 7 to 11, until 1927, when grade 12 was added, at which time the addition to the high school was erected. High school instructors from 1921 to date have been as follows:

Mr. and Mrs. M. F. Moser
Mother and Father of Historian
Text Page 147

School Building in 1932
Text Page 155

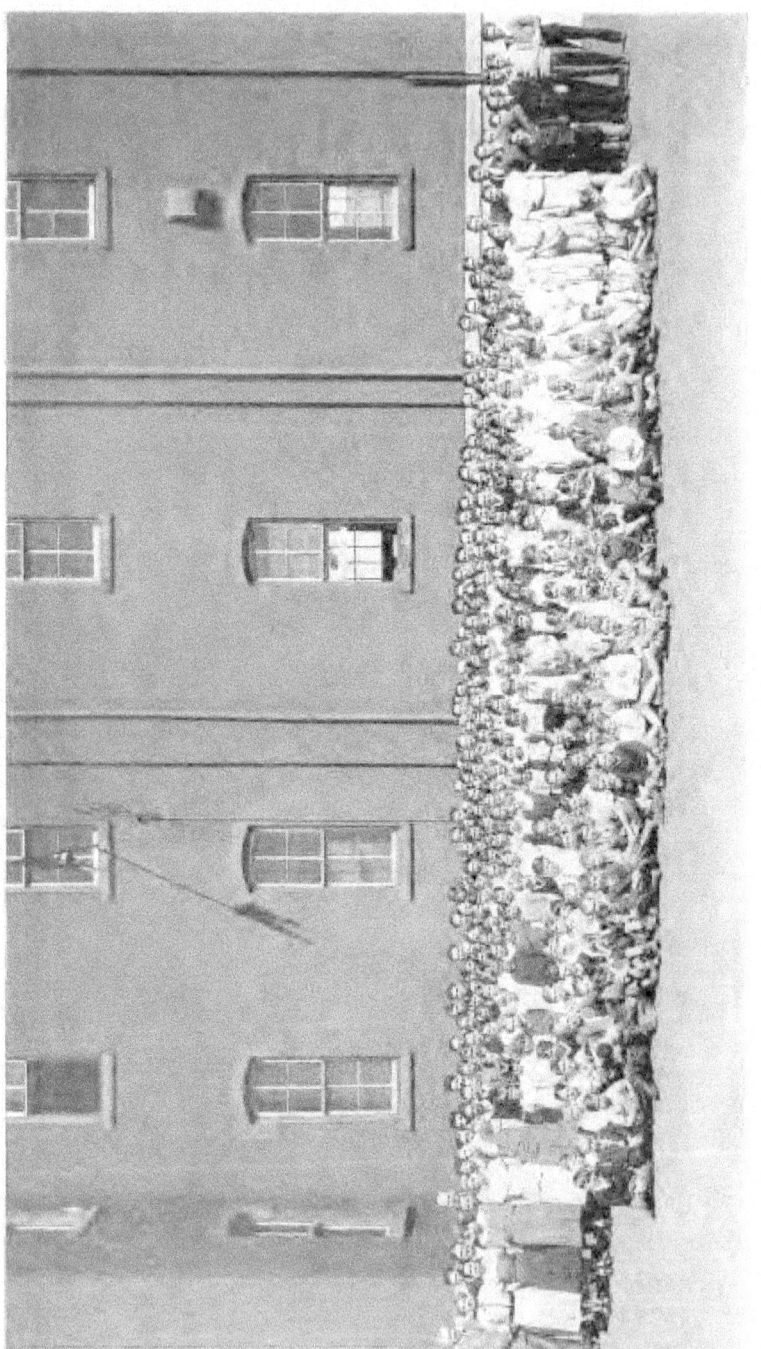

Delano Schools, 1932—Twelve Grades
Text Page 155

History of Delano 153

Supervising principal and science and manual training, 1921-1927, Maurice Singley; manual training and science, 1927-1932, Maurice Singley; mathematics and domestic science, 1921-1922, Jennie Applegate; 1922-1925, Julia Purcell; 1925-1926, Ruth Gaines; 1926-1927, Isabel Roberts. Mathematics and science, 1927-1928, John Holland; 1928-1929, James Abbott; 1929-1930, James Abbott and James Nash; 1930-1932, Stanley Mihalick. English and Latin, 1921-1923, Ellen Cauley; 1923-1925, Ruth Gaines; 1925-1926, Luther Lengel; 1926-1927, Eleanor Trinkle; 1927-1928, Eleanor Trinkle and Mary Gallagher; 1928-1932, Mary Gallagher. English and domestic science, 1927-1929, Isabel Roberts; 1929-1930, Virginia Marshall; 1930-1932, Anna Ryan. History and Geography, 1921-1929, Harris Wertman; 1929-1930, Marshall Wertman; 1930-1932, Harris Wertman. Music, 1921-1928, Guy Dower; 1928-1932, Helen Gregas. Art, 1927-1931, Mrs. James Kilroy; 1931-1932, Henry Klock.

Grammar School: 1910-1912, Dedie Crossan; 1912-1916, Sarah Prim; 1916-1918, Margaret Driscoll; 1918-1921, Jennie Applegate.

From 1921 to this date, the 7th and 8th grades comprising the grammar school have been a part of the high school, which is now a Senior-Junior High School. The teachers since 1921 are listed under the high school above.

Fifth and Sixth Grades: 1910-1912, Sarah Prim; 1912-1916, Margaret Driscoll; 1916-1918, Florence Kline; 1918-1919, Wilma Kistler and Lulu Laudenslager; 1919-1922, Julia Purcell; 1922-1923, Laura Kistler; 1923-1925, Margaret Purcell; 1925-1926, Mae Brennan; 1926-1927, Rhea Newton; 1927-1932, Theresa McAndrew.

Third and Fourth Grades: 1910-1912, Margaret Driscoll; 1912-1916, Florence Kline; 1916-1918, Ellen Cauley; 1918-1921, Julia Purcell; 1921-1922, Laura Kistler; 1922-1929, Joanna Patterson; 1929-1932, Jane Zimmerman.

First and Second Grades: 1910-1912, Florence Kline; 1912-1916, Ellen Cauley; 1916-1918, Jennie Applegate; 1918-1919, Kathryn Cauley and Ruth Edwards; 1919-1920, Ruth Edwards; 1920-1921, Laura Kistler; 1921-1922, Joanna Patterson; 1922-1932, Mildred Anthony.

The graduates for the period from 1911 to and including 1932 are as follows:

1911: Fred Faust, Vera Faust, Jennie Applegate, Augusta Depew, Ruth Patterson and Theresa Cauley.

1912: First class in three-year course—Harris Wertman, Howard Wilson, Harry Depew, Emily Klinger, Olive Griffiths and Emily Reinhart.

1913: John Sharkey, Harry Brill, Leo Faust, Wilma Kistler, Helen Walbert, Mary Purcell and Freida Sharkey.

1914: Robert Applegate, Dorothy Taylor, Caroline Kline, Violet Ecker and Edna Jenkins.

1915: William Gouldner, William Straub, William Cavage, Julia Purcell and Kathryn Cauley.

1916: Elmer Sharkey, Arner Prim, Guernald Taylor, Harry Moses, Melvin Straub, Philip Kline, Anna Fleming, Ruth Edwards, Kathryn Lawler, Laura Kistler, Minnie Faust and Walter Shafer.

1917: Joseph Cavage, Leonard Applegate, Charles Depew, Ivy Ecker, Joanna Patterson, Anna Benson and Agatha Hofmann.

1918: Hubert Hofmann, Carrie Anthony, Pauline Kistler, Mary Wichalonis and Mabel Gerber.

1919: Gertrude Guldner, Mildred Anthony, Mary McAndrew, Arva Derr and Margaret Purcell.

1920: Charles Sharkey, Donald Faust, Lester Neifert and Jane Depew.

1921: Thomas Edwards, Ellsworth Opp, Ralph Applegate, Charles Faust, Ella Wichalonis, Jessie Patterson and Eleanor Opp.

1922: George Guldner, Ellsworth Lindner, Maurice Shafer, Paul Hofmann, Leroy Gerber, Herbert Neifert, Alfred Faust and Josephine Gothie.

1923: Eugene Singley, Samuel Blew, David Purcell, John Lisowsky, James Gouldner, Wilbur Krause, Joseph Gothie and Charles Bair.

1924: Dale Anthony, Walter Patterson, Edward Shafer, Burton Zimmerman, John Daugherty, Albert Long, Edward Purcell, Marl Faust, Isabel Derr, Mary Guldner, Kathryn Lindner, Theresa McAndrew and Margaret Sharkey.

1925: Alfred Trout, Jane Zimmerman, Christine Warntz, Thelma Krause, Marion Flexer, Elwood Faust and Herbert Purnell.

1926: Edward Derr, Harry Engle, Edward Gaval, Hollis Neifert, Agnes McCarron, Ellen Polinkis, Anna Chescattie, Dorothy Brill, Earl Beltz, Noble Clemens, John Bonavich and Valleda Neifert.

1927: No graduation class because of change to four-year course.

1928: Elbur Bair, Ralph Deeble, David Patterson, Edna Anthony, Ruth Blew, Dorothy Edwards, Viola Heckman, Madeline McAndrew, Marion Trout, Lois Flexer and Robert Shafer.

1929: Glenn Singley, Alwin Lutz, Melvin Lindner, John Faust, Charles Michael, John Okal, Edmund James, Charles Wentz, Helen Carl, Anna McCarron, Anna Opp and Naomi Blew.

1930: Lowell Bankes, Clayton England, Alvin Jones, Charles Shafer, Garfield Stauffer, Thelma Bankes, Katherine Becker, Cathrine Bell, Emma Clemens, Ruth Eisenbach, Evelyn Lindner, Eleanor Ryan and Emma Tarn.

1931: Joseph Becker, Clarence Diefenderfer, Harry Gasser, Clarence Jones, James Patterson, Alfonso Bonavich, Iva Davis, Elizabeth Engle, Alyse Houser, Anna Levertavich, Ella Levertavich, Margaret McCarron, Anna Polit, Mary Reese, Claire Shea, Sara Seltzer, Laura Haldeman, Rebecca Powell and Olive Powell.

1932: Edwin Singley, Arthur Becker, Charles Diefenderfer, William Moschock, Clayre Matz, Eugene Houser, Louise Bones, Ruth Edinger, Clara Lindner, Isabelle Long, Myrtle Riddle, Mary Sharkey, Reta Bell, Ardella Fegley, Loraine Fegley, Evelyn Folweiler, Thelma Maurer, Edith Seltzer and Betty Steimling.

The classes of 1931 and 1932 each contained nineteen members, these being the largest classes graduated by the Delano High School.

Several pictures of the schools as they are constituted today are shown here, including the school building as enlarged, a group of all the students of the schools, the high school orchestra taken in the auditorium, the manual training rooms showing some of the handiwork of the students of that department, and the faculty of 1931-1932.

156   HISTORY OF DELANO

A second picture of the 1932 graduating class is shown here on which two members of the class, Clara Lindner and Ardella Fegley, are missing, having been absent when the picture was taken.

The names of the 1932 graduates as they appear on this picture are: Girls, left to right—Edith Seltzer, Mary Sharkey, Myrtle Riddle, Evelyn Folweiler, Louise Bones, Betty Steimling, Isabelle Long, Ruth Edinger, Rita Bell, Thelma Maurer and Loraine Fegley. Boys, left to right—William Moschock, Arthur Becker, Eugene Houser, Clayre Matz, Edwin Singley and Charles Diefenderfer.

The faculty is constituted as follows, as appearing on the photograph: Men, left to right—Mr. Singley, Mr. Mihalik, Mr. Wertman and Mr. Klock. Ladies, left to right—Miss Ryan, Miss Zimmerman, Miss Gregas, Miss McAndrew, Miss Gallagher and Miss Anthony.

Photographs of Professor Singley and Professor J. M. Schrope, former principal, are included here.

Teaching Staff, 1931-1932
Text Page 156

High School Orchestra—Interior Auditorium
Text Page 155

CHAPTER XXI

Delano School System

THIS chapter is a contribution from Professor Maurice Singley, who has been supervising principal of the Delano schools for the past twenty-two years, and under whose efficient and far-sighted management the town can boast of a school system that measures up to the highest standards set by the State of Pennsylvania for secondary schools. The writer acknowledges his debt to Mr. Singley for much of the information contained in this volume touching on the school subject, as well as for help in other ways.

By Mr. Singley

The present brick school house was erected in 1889, when Mr. J. Harry Eisenhouer was supervising principal. In 1891 Mr. J. M. Schrope was elected as supervising principal with the understanding that he organize a high school in Delano. Mr. Schrope put the Delano High School into operation and had his first graduating class in 1893, which consisted of two graduates: Hattie McMullen and Leon Bailey. Classes have been graduating from the Delano High School ever since 1893, with the exception of a few years, when there didn't happen to be a class ready. The total number of graduates, including the class of 1932, now numbers 248.

When I came to Delano in 1905 as assistant principal to supervising principal J. M. Schrope I found here a school system consisting of the elementary grades and a high school. There were five teachers, three teachers teaching the elementary grades, including the work of about the first seven grades. The A Grammar grade, or what now corresponds to our eighth grade, was the first grade of high school. The teachers in the high school completed the work of the elementary grades and in addition to that did what would now amount to at least two years of high school work. The high school grades were taught by the supervising principal, who was a full-time teacher, and by the assistant principal.

The schools became over-crowded, and in order to do better work it became necessary to erect another building. A two-room frame building was erected and was put into use in 1908, when another teacher was added. The schools were now graded so as to give each of the four teachers two grades, thus making eight grades below the high school. The grades were not changed in the high school until the term of 1910-1911, when it was decided to do no more grammar school work in the high school. There were from now on three grades in the high school doing strictly high school work.

When the State Department of Public Instruction began to classify the high schools in the state the Delano High School was classified as a third grade high school. This, of course, was true of many of the high schools in the state. In some much larger districts than Delano the high schools were at first classified as only third grade. This was because the courses of study at the time did not comply with the courses outlined by the state. With the three grades doing strictly high school work, we were now in a position to comply with the state's requirements and in 1911-1912 Delano High School was recognized as a second-grade high school.

The course of study offered in the Delano High School in 1905 was about on a par with the course given in the Normal schools prior to 1903, with the exception that there were no courses given in education—such subjects as psychology, school management and methods of teaching. In book-keeping, Delano offered a course in double-entry, while the Normal Schools in their regular course gave only a short course in single entry. More Latin was taught than in the Normal Schools, German was also taught. Other subjects offered were elementary and advanced algebra, plane geometry, general history, physics, English, botany and public speaking. Delano was one of the first schools in the county to introduce supervised vocal music and art. In later years it was also one of the first to introduce instrumental music, domestic science and manual training. A library containing several hundred books was also in operation.

The teachers of the entire township were Normal School graduates. I am told by Mr. Schrope that this standard of teacher qualification was maintained since 1895 and, from some time prior to that time, permanent certificates were required. This standard of teacher qualification has not been deviated from since that time. Today all the teachers from grades one to six are Normal School graduates and from grades seven to twelve are college graduates. When the salaries of the teachers of the state were fixed by law at $35.00 per month, Delano was paying $45.00 per month.

In the spring of 1906, Mr. Schrope resigned and went to Pottsville and took charge of one of the grammar schools there. During the next four years Mr. George Hemminger was supervising principal. In 1910 I was elected supervising principal. In 1911 the standard of the high school was raised from a third grade high school to a second grade. This was the rating of the Delano High School until 1921, when it was recognized, by permission of the State Department of Education, as a junior-senior high school on the six-five plan. This plan was not satisfactory to the district, nor to the department, as it did not give the pupils a complete four-year high school course, so the district was advised to furnish transportation to the Mahanoy Township High School for grades eleven and twelve, or else provide more room and add an additional teacher and make the high school a six-six system. That is, the high school including grades seven and eight.

When the school was reorganized in 1921, manual training, domestic science and instrumental music were introduced. Manual training was taught in the coal bin of the old heating system, the old heating system having been changed and the coal bin being no longer used. Domestic science was taught in one of the rooms of the two-room building that had been erected in 1908. Instrumental music was taught in the old Union Hall, which was also used as a church.

These conditions were very unsatisfactory, so the community voted on a $40,000.00 loan for the erection of an addition to the old brick building, which had been erected in 1889. The loan went through with only three votes against it. The school board at this time consisted of the following directors: Walter Patterson, President; Matthew Riddle, Secretary; George Beers, Treasurer, and Directors Griffith Lindner and William Long. These directors deserve a great deal of credit for their interest and foresightedness in the education of the children of the district.

The brick addition, a structure 40 x 80 feet, was erected in 1927. This addition gave us an auditorium, three class rooms, an office, a domestic science room, a laboratory, and a manual training room. Delano was very much in need of a building such as this, not only for school purposes, but also as a community center. It was also felt that Delano would be able to maintain a better school spirit if all of the activities of a high school were carried on in the district.

One disappointing feature about the new addition was that it did not provide a gymnasium to give physical training and for basketball playing. This has been partly overcome by renting from the Lehigh Valley Railroad Company during the term 1931-1932 the abandoned carpenter shop, a structure 40 x 80 feet, and now the Delano High School has a suitable place to play basketball and other indoor games. A great deal of credit is due to Mr. U. G. Fetterman, assistant trainmaster for the Lehigh Valley, for securing the old carpenter shop for this purpose. The school board put in a new floor and the expense of installing the lighting system was undertaken by the high school.

As a result of the reorganization of the schools in 1927, another full-time teacher was added and an art teacher who taught art one day a week to grades seven to twelve, giving each class one hour of art per week. The old library which had gone into disuse has also been reorganized with about one thousand volumes and twenty different magazines. The art teacher and the music teacher having at first been only part time are now full time teachers, making the number of full time high school teachers for the term of 1931-1932 seven.

Since the establishing of the complete high school course, there have been coming to the Delano High School a number of pupils from Rush, Ryan and Kline Townships. The number of pupils from these townships for the term of 1931-1932 is thirty-nine, and we have been advised by the State Department to add another full time teacher. In order to put on another full time teacher more room will have to be provided. This can be done by putting the two-room building into operation again. This building was moved back in order to make room for the new addition to the high school.

In the first year of high school work the Delano High School course offers mathematics, English, Latin, civics and general science. The second year offers mathematics, English, Latin, European history and biology. The third year offers mathematics, English, Latin, American history and chemistry. The fourth year offers mathematics, English, Latin, problems of democracy and physics. In addition to these courses, instruction is given in health, guidance, and physical education. Provision is also made for public speaking and dramatics. Art instruction is given one period a week and any pupil desiring to take instrumental music may do so. Both a band and orchestra are maintained by the high school. One period per week in vocal music is also provided for.

From now on we expect to have a full line of sports, since we have a place to play basketball. Delano has a splendid baseball field and has been noted for its baseball team for a number of years. Delano has one of the best water supplies in the state and some distance below the main reservoir is a swimming pool which provides sport and training in swimming for the boys and girls of town during the summer and excellent skating in the winter.

When the Lehigh Valley Railroad Company sold their houses in Delano to the people, they also donated a piece of land to the Delano School District for the use of the schools. The land upon which the school house stands was not definitely determined heretofore. This piece of land gives ample room for future expansion of the school system if necessary.

In its ten-year plan the State Department of Education is planning to make larger high school centers and it is hoped that in this plan Delano may be retained for one of these centers.

CHAPTER XXII

Late Church History

THE forces of righteousness in Delano have never retreated throughout the years and, indeed, have never been more aggressive and forward-looking than they are today. It is a significant thing for the future of the town that the two greatest factors in its highest development, education and religion, have never been permitted to fall back, but that the faith and courage of the residents have kept them always far to the front.

Some great changes in the religious field took place during the past twenty years and, at the writing of this record, the town has one of the most attractive and modern houses of worship to be found anywhere—all made possible by the spirit of devotion and faith that has been characteristic of the people of Delano in all the years of its existence.

Early in this twenty-one year period the Methodist Church found it necessary to relinquish its work in Delano, after a very active ministry of twenty years. The Lutheran and Reformed Churches of Mahanoy City remained in the field and are still in charge of the religious life of Delano, together with the Evangelical Church of Quakake, which began its service there some years ago. These denominations alternate in the conducting of services in the new chapel.

The ministers of the Reformed Church who served Delano during this time include the Rev. G. W. Smith, the Rev. R. G. Hartman and the present pastor, the Rev. C. M. Baver, all of these being of the Grace Reformed Church of Mahanoy City, which succeeded the St. Paul's Reformed Church in its work at Delano about seven years ago.

The Lutheran ministers have been the Rev. C. W. Diehl, 1908-1916; the Rev. Charles Ritter, 1916-1924; the Rev. John Amam, 1924-1928; with the present pastor, the Rev. Lester B. Lutz, since 1929.

The Evangelical Church is at present served by the Rev. William Friday, residing at Quakake.

The Sunday School and Christian Endeavor Societies are as active today as they have ever been. The superintendent of the Sunday School at present is Mr. Walter Patterson, Sr., a Delano veteran; assistant superintendent, Mr. Garfield James, who for the past fifteen years has been a leader in civic and religious life in Delano, having come to the town from Hazleton at that time. The Sunday School sessions are held at 10 o'clock a. m. and the enrollment at this time is one hundred seventy-six. The Senior Christian Endeavor meets at 6:30 p. m. each Sunday and the Junior Society at 1 p. m. each Sunday.

The Reformed and Lutheran Churches hold their services at Delano at 2 p. m. on alternate Sundays, while the Evangelical Church conducts a service every other Sunday at 9 a. m.

The decision of the people of Delano to construct a new house of worship was made early in 1924. It set into motion a train of circumstances out of which came a number of things that were not in the original plans, or even in the thought of the sponsors of the movement. Besides the central purpose to erect a new church home, which was carried to a most successful conclusion, there developed incidentally the first Delano Old Home Day, followed a year later by the second of those delightful occasions and the formation of a permanent organization to make the reunions annual affairs. And, as a further incident of this movement, there came the writing of this history, not such an important incident, perhaps, but one that the writer hopes shall be the means of reviving many blessed recollections of other days and more firmly cementing the old-time friendships and the making of many new ones.

A building committee consisting of Walter Patterson, Sr., president; William J. Sharkey, secretary; Garfield James, treasurer; Professor Maurice Singley and George Opp was appointed on March 15th, 1924.

Title to the church site was secured from the Lehigh Valley Railroad Company in October, 1926.

A church corporation was erected under the name of the Delano Union Church, the charter being granted on November 17th, 1926.

The plans of the Park Crest Building and Supply Company were accepted August 9th, 1929, and on the 20th of the same month the work of razing old Union Hall commenced.

Ground-breaking services were held August 22nd, 1929, these services being in charge of the Rev. Bruce Lehman, the Evangelical pastor; William Sharkey and Maurice Singley. These men removed the first ground for the excavation for the foundations. The actual building of the new church was begun on August 23rd, 1929.

The laying of the corner stone was held on September 29th, 1929, at which the Rev. W. H. Egge, of Trinity Evangelical Church of Frackville, Pa., was the speaker. The pastors of the church at Delano assisted in the services.

The dedication of the church was held on Sunday, December 28th, 1929, the first service being held at 2 o'clock in the afternoon and the other at 7:30 o'clock in the evening. The afternoon service was in charge of the pastors: the Rev. C. M. Baver, the Rev. L. B. Lutz and the Rev. Bruce Lehman, with the dedicatory sermon preached by the Rev. Dr. George W. Richards. The choir of the church had charge of the music for the occasion. The evening services were under the direction of the pastors of the church, with an address by each pastor. Two anthems by the church choir and solos by Miss Elizabeth Engle and Miss Margaret Sharkey were features of the evening service.

Dedicatory services were continued throughout the week, with the speakers for each service as follows: Monday, the Rev. George Duvall, a former Methodist pastor at Delano; Tuesday, Watch Night Service, in charge of the Rev. Bruce Lehman; Wednesday, the Rev. E. P. Wadsworth; Thursday, the Rev. Charles W. Diehl, a former Lutheran pastor at Delano; Friday, the Rev. G. W. Hartman, a former Reformed pastor at Delano.

The committees in charge of these services were:

Program—The Rev. L. B. Lutz, the Rev. C. M. Baver and Professor Maurice Singley.

Music—Misses Bretz, Faust and Sharkey, Mrs. Singley and Mrs. Donat.

Publicity—Mr. Garfield James and Miss Margaret Sharkey.

With the completion and occupation of this new church home, Delano began a new era in its religious life. Old Union Hall, that had served the community so well for fifty-five years, was gone, and in its place and on the same location, stood now a modern,

MANUAL TRAINING DEPARTMENT
Text Page 155

1932 GRADUATES
Text Page 156

PROF. J. M. SCHROPE
Text Page 156

PROF. MAURICE SINGLEY
SUPERVISING PRINCIPAL
Text Page 156

beautiful chapel, splendidly equipped for service in life's highest realm. It was the consummation of a dream long held by the Christian people of Delano. The seating capacity of the chapel is two hundred fifty, which is ample for every ordinary requirement in Delano.

Pictures of the exterior and interior of the new church are shown here and furnish an excellent idea of its fine appearance. A picture of Union Hall appears here also, as it was when torn down to make way for the new building.

The building of the large addition to the school building, with a fine auditorium with about four hundred seating capacity, removed the need for a public hall for general use, and opened the way for a building definitely dedicated to the worship of God. For the needs of these two important spheres of life, Delano is today equipped in a manner equal to the best to be found anywhere.

The story of the faith needed to make this venture and the remarkable way in which the faith was justified by the loyal support of the Delano people, is an absorbing tale. The total cost of the building and equipment was well over $22,000.00, the greater part of which has been liquidated. Surely such faith and such accomplishment are evidence conclusive that the spirit of the old pioneers goes marching on in Delano, and that greater things are still ahead for the town and its people.

CHAPTER XXIII

Homecoming Days

DIRECTLY out of the dedication of the new church came the idea for the reunions held in Delano in 1930 and 1931. The writer cannot refrain from mentioning here the little part he had in those two outstanding events in the town's history.

A letter was received from his former Sunday School teacher, Mrs. Angie Folweiler, advising him of the completion of the new church and the date of the dedication services. In his reply to this letter, he suggested that these services might be made the occasion for a special day of homecoming of former Delano residents, believing that such an arrangement would be profitable to the church organization and hailed with delight by the people who had lived there through the years and had long been separated from each other.

The suggestion was received with favor by the church people and it was decided to set aside a particular day the following summer for that purpose. A committee was appointed to make the necessary arrangements and on Sunday, August 31st, 1930, Delano's first Homecoming Day was held.

It was one of the most enjoyable days in the experience of this writer and he believes that this feeling was shared by hundreds of others who took advantage of the opportunity to meet with former friends. Most of these old-time residents had not seen each other for thirty years or more and to meet again in the old familiar surroundings was joy beyond measure.

Services were held in the new chapel in the forenoon and afternoon, the honor guest at the morning service being the Rev. Dr. Frederick Wagner, a former Delano boy. In the afternoon, the Rev. Dr. Noll, of the Reformed Church of Schuylkill Haven, Pa., made an eloquent address. The Delano choir provided fine music, with some special musical numbers by singers from other towns. Lunch was served in the basement of the church by the ladies of the church.

The day was filled with happy reunions and greetings and was all too short. Farewells were said late in the evening with great reluctance. It was the much-expressed opinion of those present that this should mark but the beginning of other happy events in future years, and the people of Delano made their decision to do their part in meeting the earnest desires of the old-time former residents.

THE SECOND REUNION

Early in 1931 a meeting of the reunion committee was called and the writer and his wife were invited to become members of it, an invitation that was promptly accepted. A number of meetings were held through the spring and summer and tentative plans made for the second reunion.

Because of the limited time available at the first reunion for the greeting of old friends, it was suggested that two days be used for the reunion of 1931, and this plan was adopted. September 5th and 6th were the days selected and a program for the two days worked out.

Saturday, September 5th, was the occasion for a big outdoor picnic held in the grove in the center of the town, with a parade by the schools and other organizations of town, led by the high school band. A speakers' platform was provided, with seats for those attending, and a program of speaking and music was arranged for early in the afternoon. The speakers were R. P. Swank, Esq., Walter Patterson, Sr., Llewellyn Bannan, Ollie Mason, L. O. Bair and H. O. Moser, Esq. Mr. Garfield James, chairman of the reunion committee, presided. The whole assembly took part in the singing of old songs and the Delano High School Band entertained with some fine music.

A series of games for the young people followed the program, while the people visited with each other and renewed the acquaintances of many years ago. There were many more present at this second reunion than had been at the first and the day was delightful in every respect.

Meals were served in the basement of the church by the refreshment committee and refreshments were also on sale in the grove. These wants were splendidly cared for by the church women of the town.

In the evening the Delano High School Orchestra, under the

direction of its instructor, Miss Helen Gregas, gave a fine concert, which was a revelation to those who heard it. The orchestra has about forty members and it played with the precision and feeling of veteran musicians. The old graduates present were proud to know that their alma mater could do such wonderful things.

Sunday was a repetition of the spirit of good-fellowship and happiness prevalent the day before. The Rev. Dr. G. W. Smith, of Akron, O., a former Reformed pastor of Mahanoy City, preached two eloquent sermons, one at the forenoon service and the other in the afternoon. The church was crowded at both services and several hundreds who could not be admitted congregated about the outside and spent the time in visiting with each other.

The parting at the close of this second reunion was as difficult as before, but this time there was the assurance that another year would bring the opportunity for meeting again in the old town.

The members of the committee which made the arrangements for these reunions and directed them to such successful conclusions are shown on the photograph included in this record, and they are as follows: On steps, left to right—Mrs. Maurice Singley, Mrs. U. G. Fetterman, Miss Annie Bretz, Mrs. George Folweiler. On ground, left to right—H. O. Moser, Mrs. John Houser, Mrs. Lewis Gouldner, Mrs. Clarence Bachert, Mrs. Sarah Hartzel, Mrs. Charles Collings, Mrs. Garfield James and Mr. Garfield James, committee chairman. Mrs. Moser, also a member of the committee, was not present when this picture was taken.

Besides the reunion committee, other committees of Delano people assisted in making the reunions a success. Refreshment, music, parade, program, meals, lodging and other committees had a large part in the happy outcome of these two big affairs.

Another photograph shown here is that of the building committee which directed the work of erecting the new Delano Union Church building. The members of the committee as they appear here are, reading left to right: Garfield James, William Sharkey, George Opp, Walter Patterson, Sr., and Professor Maurice Singley.

One other picture of general interest appears here: that of the members of the Park Crest Construction Company, which built the new chapel. The men shown are, left to right—Lewis A. Smith, Howard Shaffer, John Rang and Irwin Shaffer. It is especially interesting to note that John W. Shaffer, father of two members of this company, built the addition to Union Hall in 1897.

UNION HALL AFTER ENLARGED
Text Page 165

DELANO UNION CHURCH, BUILT 1929
Text Page 165

INTERIOR NEW CHAPEL, 1932
Text Page 165

CHAPTER XXIV

A Closing Word

AND so the story is told. Haltingly, perhaps—certainly not with the fluent speech of a seasoned teller of tales—but, nevertheless, out of a full heart, and with a feeling of deepest affection for those friends of bygone years and the little town where so many happy moments were spent.

The little journey along the paths that reach back into childhood has been a delightful one. The writer has walked with old comrades, heard their voices and looked into their faces, his heart deeply stirred at recollections of old joys and sorrows. Altogether, the task essayed by him has been a good one, worth the effort and hours of toil, and it is his hope that those who follow him through these pages will find in them some moments of happy retrospection, the awakening of memories of long-forgotten pleasures and the strengthening of the ties that bind together the old friendships.

Many kindnesses have been shown him by many friends in the preparation of this volume. More material was offered the writer than he was able to use, but he has tried to select that which would be of the most general interest and to do nothing that would cause the least bit of hurt to any of the old friends. Many books would need to be written to include the numberless incidents and happenings of life in the smallest of towns.

Without doubt, there will be some differences of opinion as to some of the statements set out in this work. Many of the earliest happenings in the life of Delano have been recorded here as they came from the lively memories of the few who still recall them. Exactitude in all details is not to be expected. There may be an occasional discrepancy in dates, or the order in which some events took place, but, in the main, the writer is certain that the story is true to facts; and, as stated in the beginning, the purpose is not so much to present a sharply-outlined etching of every detail in the seventy-year history of the town as it is to bring before the eyes of the reader a warm, soft-toned view of the life that was Delano in the old days and as it still goes on in the dear old town.

Some future historian may take up the story where this writer lays it down. Should that be so, this tale will serve the purpose, at least, of having preserved many important facts that in a few more years would have been irretrievably lost, for there is no written record before this of the things of the beginning.

In bringing this record to a close here, the writer covets for his readers the same measure of reminiscent delight that was his in the making of it.

BOOK TWO

HOMECOMING COMMITTEE, REUNION, 1931
Text Page 168

BUILDING COMMITTEE FOR NEW CHAPEL
Text Page 166

PARK CREST CONSTRUCTION COMPANY
LEWIS A. SMITH, HOWARD SHAFFER, JOHN RANG, IRWIN SHAFFER
Text Page 168

Biographical Sketches

THIS second part of the History of Delano the compiler believes will prove even more interesting to his readers than the strictly historical part. The thought of undertaking the writing of a history of the town really was first suggested to him by the many happy contacts he made with former residents at the reunions of 1930 and 1931. His own pleasure at locating these old friends led him to think that all former Delano people would be delighted to know what has become of the friends of years ago.

This portion of the record, therefore, is made up entirely of family sketches, giving as complete information about former and present Delano people as it has been possible to get in the time available. It tells where the folks came from, where they went to, where they are now living and what they are doing, with as many other pertinent facts as it has been possible to crowd into the small compass made necessary by the limits of this volume.

The writer regrets that he is not able to give a more complete record of those who one time called Delano home, but it is not because of any lack of diligence on his part. Over 700 letters were mailed, with return postage, seeking the information desired, and only about 200 replies were received. In many of the sketches given here, the writer depended upon his own knowledge and that supplied by kind friends. Wherever direct information was received from those appealed to, the record is full and complete. All of the facts herein given, however, are substantially correct.

In making up the sketches, an alphabetical arrangement has been used, which will make it an easy matter to refer to the names of families in which the reader may be particularly interested. Cross references are also made in cases where members of original families have established families of their own. The old-time family names are used largely, for the benefit of those people who have been out of touch with Delano for many years.

A separate list of the families now residing in Delano is appended to this family group, both for its historical value and that the reader may have the information in convenient form. Many of those named there are, of course, also referred to in the biographical records.

ALLEN, David—came to Delano in the early 80's from a town called Brittain Ferry. He was employed as a blacksmith in the shops until his removal to Weatherly, Pa., November 2, 1900. He resided in Weatherly until his death on May 10, 1915. Mrs. Allen died in Weatherly on February 7, 1931. Other members of the family deceased are Mary, Lottie and Robert, all of whom died in Delano. The other members of the family are Dora, (Mrs. Peter Endt), Camden, N. J.; Bertha, (Mrs. Robert Tweedle), Katie, (Mrs. George Shafer), Irma, (Mrs. John Rhode), and John Fremont, all residing in Weatherly; Florence, (Mrs. Stanley Wear), Beaver Meadows, Pa. The only son of the family, Fremont, is a patrolman on the Weatherly police force.

ARTZ, Levi—came to Delano in March, 1871, from Sugar Notch, Pa. He was an engineer for the Lehigh Valley Railroad for many years and upon his retirement from railroad service conducted the old Pefferwasser Shop for some time. Mrs. Artz died in Delano in 1882 and Mr. Artz in Delano in 1908. All of the children of this pioneer couple are still living: Elizabeth, (Mrs. J. A. Depew), Delano; Sarah, (Mrs. Porter), Mauch Chunk, Pa.; Ella, (Mrs. Jackson), Jersey City, N. J.; Alice, (Mrs. William Smith), Altoona, Pa.; Harry Artz, Altoona, Pa.; Elmer Artz, a barber, Clifton Forge, Va.; Joseph Artz, a barber, Richmond, Va. Mrs. J. A. Depew, one of the daughters, has spent most of her life in Delano.

ACKERMAN, Eli—resided in Delano with his family for many years, coming there late in the 80's and moving to Weatherly, Pa., when the shops were moved there in 1899. So far as the writer has been able to learn, some members of the family are still living in Weatherly.

ARNER, John—came to Delano early in the 80's and, with his family, had a prominent place in the life of the town for many years. Mr. and Mrs. Arner are both deceased, but the writer has not been able to learn when and where they died. Members of the family deceased are Simon, Henry, Joseph and Fred. A daughter, Mrs. Thomas Prim, of Hazleton, Pa., a daughter, Mrs. Fred Denison, of Freeland, Pa., and Francis, a son, of New Haven, Conn., are the living members of the family, so far as ascertainable. The widow of Simon Arner lives in Milton, Pa., and most of the children of his family reside in that vicinity. John and Edward live at Milton; Harry at New Columbia, Pa.; William at Mountain Top, Pa.; Joseph at Lewisburg, Pa., and Walter in Washington, D. C. There are several daughters of whom the writer has no information.

APPLEGATE, Robert—came to Delano some time during the 90's and still resides there with his family. He has been an engineer for many years. He was a noted ball player in his youth and helped the Delano club win many games. A daughter, Jennie, was one time on the teaching staff of the Delano schools.

ANTHONY, Robert—came to Delano from Hazleton, Pa., many years ago. He has been an engineer for a long time. His family has always been active in the life of Delano and one daughter, Mildred, has been a member of the teaching staff of the Delano schools for the past ten years. Two daughters are trained nurses and a son is in business in Harrisburg, Pa.

BANNAN, Joseph—came from Tamaqua, Pa., to Delano in 1871, belonging to the pioneer group. He was employed by the railroad company for many years, holding the position of Chief Car Inspector at the time of his death on March 8, 1901. Mrs. Bannan died in Delano on February 20, 1904. A daughter Mary, (Mrs. Hughes), died in Tamaqua, Pa., on May 19, 1923. The children living are as follows: Charles D., a foreman in the Pennsylvania Railroad shops at Altoona, Pa., John H., painter, Elizabeth, N. J.; Joseph V., air brake foreman for the C. R. R. of N. J. Railroad, East Roselle, N. J.; Llewellyn, an accountant for the Pennsylvania Power and Light Company at Allentown, Pa; George F., baker at Tamaqua, R. D., Pa. The Bannan family was one of the most prominent in the history of the town. Because of the important places occupied by several of the sons, separate sketches of their families are given here.

BANNAN, Charles D.—came to Delano with his parents from Tamaqua, Pa., and later worked in the shops there as a machinist until July 16, 1892, when he moved to Altoona, Pa., where he has since been employed in the shops of the Pennsylvania Railroad. His wife is the former Emma Depew, daughter of Samuel Depew, one of Delano's most prominent families. The children of the family and their residences are: Samuel Bannan, Shickshinny, Pa.; Mary Lackro, Philadelphia, Pa.; Elsie Crumbaker, Altoona, Pa., and Clara B. Rothrock, Altoona, Pa.

BANNAN, Joseph V.—came to Delano from Tamaqua, Pa., with his parents and worked in the shops until November, 1899, when he moved to Elizabeth, N. J. Mr. Bannan was foreman of the airbrake department when he left Delano and he has held a similar position under the Central Railroad of New Jersey at Elizabeth since he left the town. His present resident in East Roselle, N. J., a suburb of Elizabeth. Mrs. Bannan is the former Bessie Evans, of a long-time prominent Delano family. The deceased members of the family are: Mrs. Mary Powers, at Roselle, N. J., in 1925, and William J. Bannan, who died at the same place in 1931. Those living are: John L. Bannan, electrical contractor, Roselle Park, N. J.; Mrs. Emma Turner, Roselle Park, N. J.; Mrs. Mildred Copeland, Kenilworth, N. J.; Mrs. Grace Savidge, Kenilworth, N. J.; Leslie Bannan, coal business, Roselle Park, N. J., and Mrs. Alice Wenk Bannan, Kenilworth, N. J.

BANNAN, Llewellyn—came with his parents to Delano from Tamaqua, Pa., and resided there until October, 1900, when he moved to Elizabeth, N. J. During his residence in Delano he was employed in the shops, being chief clerk at the time he left the town. Mrs. Bannan is the former Katie Thamarus, daughter of Philip Thamarus, one of Delano's prominent residents for many years. The Bannan family at present resides in Allentown, Pa., where Mr. Bannan holds a responsible position in the accounting department of the Pennsylvania Power and Light Company. He was one of the speakers at the reunion in Delano in 1931. Both children of Mr. and Mrs. Bannan are deceased, Oliver J. dying in 1906 at Catasauqua, Pa., and Myrtle A., at Allentown just a few months ago. The daughter was present at the 1931 reunion in Delano.

BANKES, Peter—came to Delano from Quakake, Pa., in 1883, and resided there with his family until 1895, when he moved to Philadelphia, Pa., where they now reside. He was employed as a railroad fireman while living in Delano. He is employed at this time as sexton for the Calvary Reformed Church of Philadelphia. Mrs. Bankes, who was present at the reunion in Delano in 1931, died a short time afterward. Children of the family that are deceased are: Stanley and Clara, both of whom died in Quakake in 1887 and 1888 respectively. Those living are: Edward Bankes, machinist, Philadelphia, and Mrs. Ruth Smull, Oak Lane, Pa.

BACHERT, David—became a resident of Delano in 1893, coming from Grier City, Pa. He worked in the shops as a machinist. He left Delano about 1899, going to Tamaqua, Pa., where he resided until his death in 1916. A daughter, Eva Bachert, died in Tamaqua in 1904. Mrs. Elizabeth Bachert resides in Tamaqua, as do these children: Ida, William, Oscar, Charles, and Mrs. William Bryant, while another daughter, Mrs. Lamont Krause, resides in Reading, Pa.

BICKLE, Henry Franklin—first made Delano his home in 1872, coming from Barnesville, Pa. He had a very important part in the pioneering work of the town, as is noted elsewhere in this history. He remained a resident of the town until 1892, when he moved with his family to Wilmington, Del. He was floor foreman and air brake foreman in the shops at Delano and has been living retired for a number of years, now residing at Plainfield, N. J. Mrs. Bickle is the former Emma Fletcher, daughter of David Fletcher, another of the outstanding Delano families. Mrs. Fletcher came to Delano with her parents in 1862 from Port Carbon, Pa. There are two children, both living: F. Clare Bickle, who was an old schoolmate of the writer, and who now resides in Plainfield, N. J., where he is in the automobile business, and Mrs. Olive Van Zandt, also residing in Plainfield. The son was born in Mahanoy City, Pa., and the daughter in Delano.

BILLMAN, Jacob—was a resident of Delano for many years, coming there early in the 70's. The date and place of his death the writer has not been able to learn. He was employed in the shops. There were two sons known to the writer. Albert Billman, for a long time a Lehigh Valley engineer at Delano, who later moved to Lehighton, Pa., died there some years ago, and Amandus E. Billman, who was Delano's barber for quite a number of years, is now a realtor in Allentown, Pa., where he has resided for many years.

BILLMAN, Rudolph—came to Delano some time early in the 70's and was employed for many years in the shops. The date and place of his death the writer cannot state. Three of his sons, William, Francis, and Milton, were prominent residents for many years and are listed separately in this record.

BILLMAN, William—a son of Rudolph Billman, came from Trenton, Pa., to Delano in 1885, and worked there in the carpenter shop until his death in 1889. The deceased members of his family are William, Jr., who died in Delano in 1890, and Emma, (Mrs. William Hanly), who died in Weatherly, Pa., in 1925. Those living are: Lizzie Billman, residing in Catasauqua, Pa.; Mary, (Mrs. Frank Heilman), on a farm near Lehighton, Pa.; John A. Billman, fireman for Lehigh Valley Railroad at Weatherly, Pa. Mr. William Billman's widow later married Henry Friedenbach, who came from Quakake, Pa., to Delano in 1881, and moved to Lehighton in 1894, and has since died in Weatherly, Pa. He was an engineer. There is one daughter of this union, Mrs. Loretta Henry, Weatherly, Pa.

BILLMAN, Francis—another son of Rudolph Billman, came to Delano from Trenton in 1884 and resided there until about 1899, when he moved to Weatherly, Pa. He was employed in the shops while a resident of Delano. He died in January, 1932, in Bloomsburg, Pa., where he had been living for some years. Mrs. Billman died in Bloomsburg in March, 1931. All of the children of this family are still living: Lewis Billman, moulder, Weatherly, Pa.; Carrie, (Mrs. Lester), Allentown, Pa.; Esther, (Mrs. Young), Port Washington, L. I.; Ella, (Mrs. Stiles), Bloomville, O.; Eva, (Mrs. Unangst), Allentown, Pa., and Frank, who works and resides in Bloomsburg, Pa.

BILLMAN, Milton—also a son of Rudolph Billman, born in Delano, left there quite a number of years ago and now resides in Shenandoah, Pa. Mr. Billman is still in close touch with the old town.

BAILEY, G. Taylor—came to Delano about 1885, and resided there with this family until the middle 90's, when he left for the West. He was one of the prominent engineers of the town during his residence. There are no members of the Bailey family living. Edna, the daughter, died in

Denver, Colo., on November 19, 1893, while the family still resided in Delano; Leon, who was married to Anna Swank, died in Milwaukee, Wis., on April 14, 1908. Mrs. Bailey died in Denver, Colo., February 3, 1909, and Mr. Bailey in Escondido, Cal., on December 10, 1911. Leon, the son, was in the first graduating class of the Delano High School and was one of the most promising young men who ever came out of Delano. His death in his young manhood was a tragic thing in the minds of his many friends. His widow, Mrs. Anna Swank Bailey, and a daughter, Margaret Lee Bailey, who is in the employ of the Curtis Publishing Company, now reside in Downingtown, Pa.

BAIR, Levi O.—resided in Delano from 1916 to 1926, having come there from Lehighton, Pa., and moving to Park Crest, (Lakeside), Pa. He was an engineer in the employ of the Lehigh Valley Railroad and now operates a dairy. He is a son of John Bair, known to Delano people of other years. He has one son, Elbur, who resides with the parents at Park Crest.

BOYLE, Lafayette—was one of the old-time residents of Delano, coming from Mauch Chunk, Pa., in 1881, and residing in Delano until 1920, when he moved with his family to Hazleton, Pa. Mr. Boyle was one of the few shopmen left in Delano when the shops were removed. He held a position as machinist foreman during his residence in the town. He died in Hazleton in 1928, Mrs. Boyle having preceded him in death in 1921, also at Hazleton. All of the children of the family are living: Gertrude, (Mrs. Bloom), in Newark, N. J.; Stella, (Mrs. George Lukens), Wilkes-Barre, Pa.; Bertha, (Mrs. Griffiths), Hazleton, Pa., and Leroy Boyle, in Tamaqua, Pa. Mr. George Lukens, husband of Stella Boyle, was for quite a number of years a resident of Delano, having been employed there as a telegrapher until his removal to Mount Carmel, Pa.

BLODGETT, Hiram—one of the best-known engineers of the Lehigh Valley Railroad at Delano, came to the town in 1877 from Mauch Chunk, Pa. He remained there until his death in 1890. Mrs. Blodgett, who was Jennie Bowman before her marriage, now resides in Berwick, Pa., with her daughter, Mrs. Lillian Bowman. Mrs. Bowman is librarian of the Berwick Public Library.

BRETZ, Charles—was one of the pioneer residents of the town. He came to Delano about 1868 and was in the employ of the Lehigh Valley Railroad as brakeman, fireman and engineer, until his death in Delano in 1919. He had been retired for several years before his death, being at the time of his retirement the senior engineer of the division. Mrs. Bretz died in Morton, Pa., in January, 1920. A number of the children of the family died in Delano—Charles, Katie, and Sylvester, so far as the writer can recall. Albert, a son, was fatally injured at Shenandoah, Pa., in August, 1917, while residing in Mount Carmel, Pa., and died in the

History of Delano

Ashland State Hospital a week later. He was a conductor on the Lehigh Valley Railroad at the time. The children living are: Lillian, (Mrs. Claude Gouldner), Lebanon, Pa.; William, employed by the Gulf Refining Company, at Philadelphia, Pa.; Edward, in business at Swarthmore, Pa., and George Arthur, a merchant in Swarthmore, Pa. William, (Bill to his many friends), helped to build the Panama Canal, having been a machinist in the employ of the government during the construction of the great ditch. He spent quite a number of years there.

BRETZ, Jonathan—belonged to the valiant pioneers of Delano. He came there from Barnesville, Pa., in 1868, having previously worked as a wiper boy, started braking on the road that year and remained a prominent citizen of the town until his death on July 6, 1927. He was successively brakeman, fireman and engineer, and for seven years before his retirement was in charge of the air compressor at Delano, a total service for the Lehigh Valley Railroad of sixty years. His widow, Mrs. Lucetta Bankes Bretz, (of whom mention has been made elsewhere in this history), still resides in Delano with her daughter, Annie Bretz. The home now occupied by Mrs. Bretz and her daughter is the one formerly occupied by the family of John McCarroll, and is the one in which Mr. and Mrs. Bretz were married on April 9, 1870, at which time Mr. Bretz boarded with the McCarroll family. Mr. and Mrs. Bretz celebrated their golden wedding anniversary in this same home on April 9, 1920. Miss Annie Bretz is very active in the religious and civic life of the community, being also a member of the reunion committee. The other children of the family are: Frank, a car inspector at Delano, Pa., married to Annie McCarroll; Oscar, in the employ of the Lehigh Valley Railroad at Delano, and George, of Bethlehem, Pa.

BRETZ, Albert—a son of Charles Bretz, was born in Delano and moved to Mount Carmel, Pa., in 1916. He died as a result of a railroad accident in 1917. His widow, Mrs. Bella Bretz, now resides in Philadelhia, with her children: Mary, a stenographer for the Lehigh Valley Railroad, Ernest, employed by the Gulf Refining Company, and Lloyd, a secretary for the Stanley-Warner Theaters of Philadelphia. One daughter, Ruth, died in infancy in Mahanoy City, Pa., in 1919. Mr. Bretz was a near neighbor of the writer at the time of his unfortunate death. He was a devout Christian and a friend much beloved.

BURNETT, George—first made his home in Delano in 1871, coming to the town direct from Wales. He was one of the pioneers. With his family he resided there until 1899, when he left for Kansas City, Mo. He was a tool maker in Delano and followed this trade in his new home. He died in Denver, Colo., in 1931. His wife, Phillippine Burnett, died in Denver, in 1922. The two children of the family: Lizzie, (now Mrs. Anderson), and Frank, now reside in Denver. Frank is employed as chief engineer in the Children's Hospital at Denver, and Lizzie, besides her household duties, also works as a bookkeeper. Mr. Burnett was prominent as one of the organizers and for a time the leader of the Delano band, as well as in civic affairs generally. His daughter will be recalled as a very talented violinist.

BRILL, John—first made his home in Delano in 1880, coming from Barnesville, Pa. He was for many years an engineer of the Lehigh Valley Railroad and later returned to his home near Barnesville, where he conducted a meat market. He did quite a large business with his former friends in Delano, his delivery wagon being an institution in the town for many years. He died in Barnesville in 1909, and his wife died in Delano in 1912. Other members of the family deceased are: Emma Brill in 1919 at Delano; Mrs. Stanley Porter in 1925, at Trenton, N. J.; Mrs. John Marshall in 1900, at Leesport, Pa., and Maggie Brill in 1882, at Barnesville. The living members of the family are: Charles Brill, a dispatcher at Pittsburgh, Pa.; Edward, an engineer at Somerset, Pa, and Lewis, a conductor at Delano.

BRILL, George—was for many years associated with the Lehigh Valley Railroad at Delano as dispatcher and trainmaster. He left the town about 1898, when division headquarters were moved to Hazleton, Pa. Mr. Brill is now residing in Philadelphia, where he has an executive position with the Philadelphia and Reading Railway. The writer is not able to give the present locations of the children of the family.

BRILL, Lewis—mentioned before as a son of John Brill, has resided in Delano since late in the 90's. He married Clara Shoup, who has spent all of her life in the old town, in the same home which was formerly that of her parents. Mr. Brill is a conductor for the railroad. There were four sons of the family: Harry, Russell, Robert, and Wilbur, three of whom are still living, all in Delano. Harry, the eldest, died in the service of his country during the World War, being the first Delano boy to pay the supreme sacrifice. He died October 12, 1918, at Fort Benjamin Harrison, Indiana.

BECHTEL, David—was for many years an engineer at Delano, having come there in the 80's. He later worked for the company on the Lizard Creek Branch and moved to Orwigsburg, Pa. The only member of the family still living, so far as the writer can learn, is the daughter, Margie, now Mrs. Moyer, who lives in Cleveland, O.

BUTLER, Joshua—and his family have always ranked as one of the "First Families." Mr. Butler came to Delano from Mauch Chunk, Pa., in 1867, and was identified with the shops there in various prominent positions until he left the town in 1899, at which time he went to Weatherly, Pa. He died in Philadelphia in 1908, and Mrs. Butler at Weatherly in 1901. Other deceased members of the family are: Samuel, at Mauch

History of Delano   181

Chunk, Pa., in 1862; Elmer, at Mauch Chunk, in 1862; Kate, in Elizabeth, N. J., in 1898; Hattie, in Philadelphia, in 1913; Alex, in Philadelphia, in 1920; Fanny, in Philadelphia, in 1927, and John, in East Orange, N. J., in 1929. The living members of the family are: William, address not known; George W., retired, Weatherly, Pa.; Jennie E., Glenside, Pa.; Walter, trainmaster for the Wilkes-Barre and Hazleton Railway, Hazleton, Pa.; Emily, (Mrs. William Keiber), Easton, Pa.; Elizabeth, (Mrs. Dr. Charles Price), Philadelphia. Probably no family that ever lived in Delano took a more active part in the life of the town than that of Mr. and Mrs. Butler.

BUTLER, George—son of Joshua Butler, above-mentioned, came to Delano as a child, and resided there until the shops were removed to Weatherly, Pa., in 1899, when he became a resident of that town with his family, and has since resided there. Mrs. Butler was a daughter of William Jeffries, one of Delano's prominent residents for many years. The daughters of Mr. and Mrs. Butler are: Ethel, (Mrs. William Symons), Hazleton, Pa., and Dora, (Mrs. Seth Dodson), Weatherly, Pa. Mrs. Symons has a son, Harvey, who is a minister of the Methodist Episcopal Church.

BUTLER, John—another son of Joshua Butler, was born in Delano in 1876, married Sarah Merrick in 1896, and resided in Delano until 1899, when he moved with his family to Bethlehem, Pa. He was employed as ticket agent at Delano and continued in the employ of the Lehigh Valley Railroad at Bethlehem. Later he moved to Allentown, Pa., then to East Orange, N. J., where he was employed by the Edison Storage Battery Company. He died in that place in 1929. Mrs. Butler still resides in East Orange. She has two children: Kathryn, (Mrs. Daniel Tuthill), and Julian M. Butler.

BUTLER, Walter—also a son of Joshua Butler, was born in Delano and resided there until about 1899, when he moved to Hazleton, Pa., where he has resided since then. He has a responsible position with the Wilkes-Barre and Hazleton Railway. Mrs. Butler is the former Hattie Blakslee.

BURKHARDT, Edward—made his home in Delano in 1888, coming from Mauch Chunk, Pa., and lived in Delano until 1908, when he moved to Quakake, Pa. He was employed as a lineman for the Lehigh Valley Railroad. He died in Mauch Chunk in 1914. Other deceased members of the family are: Mrs. Mame Hoben, at Coaldale, Pa., in 1930, and Mrs. Theresa Julian, at Philadelphia, in 1932. Those living are: Carrie, (Mrs. George Opp), Delano; Mrs. Lillie Young, Auburn, N. Y.; August, fireman at Mauch Chunk, Pa.; Roland, brakeman at Mauch Chunk, Pa.; Lena, (Mrs. Reichert), Norristown, Pa., and Mrs. Jessie Schaub, (widow of Mr. Burkhardt), now residing in Mauch Chunk, Pa.

BLAKSLEE, Alonzo P.—made Delano his permanent residence about 1871, having worked on the construction of the Mahanoy Division in the 60's. He occupied the highest position in railroad circles in Delano, having been assistant superintendent for many years and later superintendent of the Mahanoy Division until his resignation in 1898. Upon his resignation, he left Delano for his native town, Mauch Chunk, Pa., where he resided until his death on September 27, 1911. By virtue of his position, his family always had a commanding place in the life of the town. They lived in the large home built for them in 1878, and the beautiful gardens surrounding the home were known throughout the whole region. Under the expert care of gardener Nels Nelson, and later Nels Hansen, these gardens were marvels of beauty. James I. Blakslee, the eldest son of the family, attained a prominent place in business life and the political world. He was the owner of the electric light company at Lehighton, Pa., for many years, and for several terms was a member of the Pennsylvania State Legislature, where he made a reputation for himself as an alert and progressive legislator. He was very active in the councils of the Democratic Party and was rewarded for his outstanding work for the party by being appointed Third Assistant Postmaster General in the Wilson Administration. This was undoubtedly the highest political position ever attained by anyone who came out of Delano. There are no members of this prominent family still living. Besides Mr. Blakslee, Alexander Mitchell, the younger son, died in Mauch Chunk, Pa., on August 12, 1908; James Irvin died in Philadelphia on November 29, 1926; Mrs. Blakslee died in Philadelphia several years ago, and Mrs. Annie Blakslee Tanner died in Oak Lane Manor, Pa., in November, 1931. The writer received a letter from Mrs. Tanner just two weeks before her death promising information about her family, but she died before it could be prepared and sent. The Blakslee family was closely identified with the affairs of the Lehigh Valley Railroad from its early history, James I. Blakslee, father of Alonzo P. Blakslee, having been associated with Judge Asa Packer and other promoters of the railroad business throughout that section.

BELTZ, Jacob—was for many years employed in the Delano shops and his family was prominent in affairs at Delano. He had the unusual distinction of working twenty-six years for the company with the loss of but eleven working days in that time. He moved into his home at Delano upon the completion of the house and the same home is still occupied by a member of the family, the daughter, Ida, now Mrs. William Trout. Both Mr. and Mrs. Beltz have been dead for many years. Mrs. Trout is the only member of the family still living at Delano. Deceased children are: Mrs. Rufe, Mrs. Frederick, Charles, who died in 1930, and Milton, who was killed in a railroad wreck at Mount Carmel several years ago. The living members are: Henry, a passenger conductor for the Lehigh Valley Railroad, residing at Mount Carmel, Pa.; Pierce and

William, at Hazleton, Pa.; Ida, at Delano, and Augustus at Quakake, Pa. The widow of Milton, who was Miss Annie Trout, still resides at Delano.

BOWMAN, Frank—became a resident of Delano in 1880. Mrs. Bowman is the former Sarah Mack. Mr. and Mrs. Bowman were married while Mr. Bowman boarded at the home of the writer's parents in Delano. Mr. Bowman was for many years an engineer for the Lehigh Valley Railroad and moved to Mount Carmel, Pa., in 1899. Later he went to Philadelphia, where he has resided for many years. The only daughter of the family, Kathryn, is now the wife of John H. Stevens, a business man of Philadelphia.

BITLER, Nelson—was employed as a railroader by the Lehigh Valley Railroad early in the 80's, and resided in Delano for many years. The writer has not been able to get a history of the family and does not know whether Mr. and Mrs. Bitler are still living. No member of the family resides in Delano at this time. Two sons, Oliver and Roy, are living in Mauch Chunk, Pa.; Matthias lives at Ashley, Pa., and Lillie, (now Mrs. Steiner), lives in Shamokin, Pa. Of the other members of the family no information is available.

BECKER, Joseph—located in Delano in 1875. He was employed as a tinsmith in the shops during his residence there, or until the shops were closed in 1899. Both Mr. and Mrs. Becker died years ago. Two children, Annie and Nellie, died in Delano many years ago. John, the only son, still resides in Delano, employed by the Lehigh Valley Railroad as a towerman, and Katy, (Mrs. Alvin Read), has been a resident of Pittsburgh, Pa., for a long time. The Becker family was prominent in the social and other activities of Delano during a long period of residence there.

BETZ, Jefferson—resided in Delano in the 80's and left Delano about the end of that decade. He was a railroad man during his residence. He moved to Tamaqua, Pa., where one son, Freeman, has been an engineer for the Philadelphia and Reading Railway for many years. A daughter, Mrs. Frank Koch, died in Mount Carmel several years ago. No information is available as to the other members of the family.

BOWMAN, Joseph—and family have been residents of Delano for a number of years. Mr. Bowman is in the train service of the Lehigh Valley Railroad.

BRETZ, Oscar—has lived in Delano all his life. He is a son of Mrs. Jonathan Bretz, one of Delano's pioneer residents. Mr. Bretz is employed by the Lehigh Valley Railroad.

BRETZ, Frank—is a lifelong resident of Delano, as is his wife, the former Annie McCarroll. Mr. Bretz is employed as a car inspector for the railroad for many years. Both he and Mrs. Bretz have been active in Delano affairs during the years of their residence there.

BACHERT, Clarence—came to Delano from Quakake quite a number of years ago. His wife was a resident of Delano from her girlhood, being the former Miss Reinmiller. Mr. Bachert is employed as a trainman. Mrs. Bachert is a very active member of the reunion committee at Delano.

BECKER, John—is a lifelong resident of Delano, being a son of the late Mr. and Mrs. Joseph Becker. Mr. Becker is employed as a towerman for the Lehigh Valley Railroad.

BOUGHNER, Harry—has been for many years an engineer for the Lehigh Valley. He came from Quakake a long time ago and still resides in Delano with his family.

CARMODY, John A.—came to Delano from Manchester, N. Y., in 1912, being employed as a foreman by the Lehigh Valley Railroad. He lived in Delano until 1918, when he was transferred to Jersey City, N. J., where he still resides with his family. Mrs. Carmody is the former Dedie Crossan, daughter of one of Delano's pioneer families, and is also a former classmate of the writer. Two children of this family are deceased: George C., who died in Jersey City in 1924, and Margaret, who died in Delano in 1915. Three children are living: John A., James M., and Mary M., all of whom are in school and reside with their parents in Jersey City.

CARROLL, Michael—moved to Delano with his family almost in the beginning of its history, some time early in the 70's. He was employed in the shops during his long residence there. Both Mr. and Mrs. Carroll have long since died, as has the only son, John, who died in New York City about ten years ago. Mary, who was the wife of John Flanagan, has been dead for many years and the present residence of the other daughter, Ella, who was the wife of Thomas Gloven, the writer has not been able to learn. An adopted daughter, Mamie Dodds, is married and has lived in Chicago for many years.

CLASBY, William—belonged to the list of Delano's first families, having come to the town on April 4, 1871. He started life there as a railroad man and continued at that work until he was severely injured in the explosion of a locomotive steam chest, which rendered him incapable of doing further work of this kind. He was made hostler in the new engine house and retained that position until he left Delano in 1903 for Philadelphia. In Philadelphia he was employed in the Baldwin Locomotive Works until his death in 1918. Mrs. Clasby died in Philadelphia in 1914, and one son, John, died there in 1915. The daughters, Mary (Mrs.

James Perry) and Cecelia (Mrs. Theodore Elm), both reside in Philadelphia, as does also the only remaining son, Martin, who is a city guard in Fairmount Park.

CLEMENS, D. Webster—came to Delano in 1889 from Mount Carmel, Pa. He was a yardmaster for the railroad company during his whole residence in Delano, and left the town to return to Mount Carmel in 1916. He died in Mount Carmel in 1927, having been in the employ of the Lehigh Valley Railroad Company at Mount Carmel until two years before his death. Mrs. Clemens still retains her home in Mount Carmel. One son of the family, Leon M., died in Quakake, Pa., in 1926. The living members of the family are: Olive (widow of Thomas Edwards, who died in 1932), still residing in Delano; Herbert V., now a resident of Milford, Conn., holding a very responsible position as general accountant for the New York, New Haven and Hartford Railroad; Elmer, residing in Greenwich, Conn., also employed by the N. Y. N. H. and H. Railroad as a clerk; John, a salesman, residing in Williamsport, Pa., and Mary, (Mrs. Gus Makaris), residing in Williamsport, Pa. All of the children are married and have families of their own.

COLLINS, John H.—took up his residence in Delano in 1886, coming from Jackson's, near Mahanoy City, Pa. He was an engineer for many years, until his death in Delano in 1919. Mrs. Collins, the widow, still resides in Delano, as does also a son, John A. Collins, Jr., who is a fireman for the Lehigh Valley Railroad. A daughter, Elizabeth C., is a registered nurse located at the Essex Mountain Sanitorium at Verona, N. J. One son, James, died in Delano in 1921.

CORRELL, Rolandus—was the head of one of the pioneer Delano families. He came there late in the 60's from Barnesville, Pa. He began work there as a teamster, but soon took up railroading and was an engineer until he left Delano for Mahanoy City, Pa., in 1895. He died in Mahanoy City in 1897. Mrs. Correll died in Tamaqua, Pa., in 1925. Children of the family who are deceased are: Selandus, at Delano, in 1880; Mary, at Delano, in 1880; Jacob, at Easton, in 1925. Jacob Correll was for a long time an engineer for the Lehigh Valley Railroad, both at Delano and at Easton. The members of the family living are: Katharine (Mrs. George Steinert), Tamaqua Pa.; Laura, (Mrs. Willoughby Frey), Tamaqua, Pa.; Howard, a Lehigh Valley engineer, Weatherly, Pa.; Estelle, (now Mrs. T. F. Luckey), White Plains, N. Y.; Roy, a foreman, Tamaqua, and R. H. Correll, an electrician, Tamaqua.

CROSSAN, George—and family constituted another of the First Family group. Mr. Crossan came to Delano in 1870 from Philipsburg, N. J., where he was employed in the locomotive works of Morris and Essex. He was an expert copper and brass worker, a trade that was not overcrowded even in that day. He learned of a demand for skilled workers in his line at the new shops at Delano and with several other men went there and was engaged at once. He remained in Delano, as foreman in that department, until his death in 1916. Mrs. Crossan died in Delano quite a number of years ago. Other members of the family who are deceased are: George, Jr., at Delano, in 1884; Julia, at Delano, in 1888; Margaret, in Delano, in 1892, and James, in Delano, in 1903. The living members of the family are: Mrs. W. J. Ryan, Mahanoy City, Pa.; Catharine, Sue and Dedie, (Mrs. John A. Carmody), all of Jersey City, N. J.; Edward, air inspector, Jersey City, and Thomas, chief clerk to the yardmaster of the L. V. R. R. at Jersey City.

CLAY, Edward—took up his residence in Delano some time early in the 80's. He was employed in the shops there for many years. Mrs. Clay died while living in Delano. Mr. Clay left the town some time early in the 90's, moving with his family to New York City, where he died many years ago, as did three other members of the family: Ada, Louisa, and Thomas. The members of the family living are: John, a machinist, residing in Hornell, N. Y.; Edward, a machinist, at Newark, N. J.; Mary, (Mrs. Harry Bickleman), Shenandoah, Pa.; Fannie, (Mrs. Morgan Williams), Brooklyn, N. Y., and Winnie, (Mrs. Walter Kedenberg), Great Neck, L. I.

CAMPBELL, John—was one of Delano's most prominent residents. He came to the town in 1871 to take up his duties as master mechanic in the shops. This history has already told much of the story of his fame in that position. He formerly resided in Ashley, Pa. He was transferred from Delano about 1893, going to Buffalo, N. Y., where he held a similar position with the same company. Mrs. Campbell died many years ago, as did Mr. Campbell. One son, Edward, who was for a long time an engineer for the Lehigh Valley Railroad, has been dead for some years. William, a son, at one time chief clerk in the Lehigh Valley shops at Delano, resides now with his sister, Elizabeth, in Allentown, Pa. To Mr. William Campbell the writer is indebted for some very valuable data for this book.

CUSHING, Morris—grew up in Delano from boyhood, being one of the eight pupils who attended the first school opened in the town in 1865. He came there with his mother and resided in Delano for many years, having a prominent place in the shops during that time. The writer does not know just when the family left the town, but it was some time late in the 80's or early in the 90's. They located in Waterbury, Conn., where one of the daughters,, Mary, (widow of T. F. Dodds), still resides. Another daughter, Margaret, resides in Ohio. Both Mr. and Mrs. Cushing are deceased.

CONNELL, James—came to Delano very early in the 70's and was employed for many years there in the shops. Mrs. Connell was a daughter of Michael Neary, one of the First Families. The family had a very prominent part in the life of Delano over a long period of time, moving to Weatherly when the shops were closed in 1899. Mr. Connell died there in 1914, and Mrs. Connell died in Hazleton, Pa., on May 10, 1923. Two daughters of the family are: Kathryn (Mrs. William Gillespie), Hazleton, Pa., and Anna, (Mrs. Henry W. Schliske), New York City. A daughter Mary died in Weatherly in 1913.

COLLUM, Charles—came to Delano about 1876 and was employed in the boiler shop for several years. He later returned to Allentown, Pa., where he founded a boiler manufacturing business under the name of the Allentown Boiler Works, which is still doing business. Mr. Collum still resides in Allentown and the writer is under great obligation to him for much valuable material about early Delano history. He has never lost his interest in the town and came there last year to attend the reunion.

CAMP, Roland—and family lived in Delano several years during the 90's, moving to Mount Carmel, Pa., the latter part of that decade, where they still reside. Mr. Camp was a freight conductor in the service of the Lehigh Valley Railroad, but since his return to Mount Carmel has been engaged in the carpenter trade and other classes of work.

CAULEY, William—came to Delano in 1883 and started work as a brakeman. He became an engineer in 1898 and worked until two weeks before his death on August 9, 1920. His widow still resides in Delano, as do these children: Joseph, a foreman for the Lehigh Valley; Ellen, a school teacher; Thomas, baggage clerk for the Lehigh Valley; Edward, a machinist; Vincent, supply clerk in the shops, and Julia, at home. James, a son, is employed as a special representative for the American Railway Express Company at Mount Vernon, N. Y. John is a teacher in McCann's Business College at Reading, Pa., and one daughter, a former teacher in the Delano schools, died in 1918. Joseph is married and has three children living at home. One daughter, Dolly, died in 1921.

CARL, Frank—came to Delano from Gordon, Pa., in 1914, and still resides there with his family. He is employed in the train service on the railroad.

COWLEY, Mrs.—has resided in Delano for many years. The writer has not been able to get any information about her family.

DENT, Albert—located in Delano about 1899, coming from Lofty, Pa. He was employed as an engineer on the road and continued in that employment until 1897, when he was sent to Orwigsburg, Pa., where he operated a passenger train on the Lizard Creek Branch. Later he was made road foreman of engines on the Auburn Division and moved to

Auburn, N. Y., where he remained until his death in 1925. A daughter, Mildred, died in Catawissa, Pa., before the family located in Delano. The members of the family living are: Mrs. Ella Dent, Emma R., and Alberta, all living in New Brunswick, N. J., and Maud A., (Mrs. Elwood Meitzler), of Washington, D. C.

DEPEW, Samuel—held a very prominent place in the history of Delano, which was maintained by his children in later years. He came to Delano in 1867 and built the first homes erected there before coming to make it his own home. He constructed almost all of the buildings in Delano. He was in the employ of the Lehigh Valley Railroad Company as foreman in the carpenter shop up to the time of his death. Joseph Albert, William, Edward, Samuel, Mary, Emma, and Clara are the children of the family, so far as the writer has a record of them.

DEPEW, Joseph A.—came to Delano with his parents from Tamaqua, Pa., in 1867. He resided there until his death in 1925. Mr. Depew was one of the town's most prominent citizens. He started work as a young man in the store then owned by A. P. Blakeslee, later managed the store, and finally, upon Mr. Blakeslee's departure from the town, became the owner. His family occupied the former Blakeslee home after the Blakeslee family moved from town. He was also postmaster for many years, up to the time of his death. Mr. Depew was prominent in Schuylkill County politics and in banking circles. His widow, Mrs. Elizabeth Depew, still owns the store, which is now managed by Charles and George Hofmann. She was a daughter of Levi Artz, another pioneer Delano resident. The children are: Mary, (Mrs. Thorpe), Detroit, Mich.; Ruth, (Mrs. James Engle), Delano; Christine, (Mrs. Patterson), Easton, Pa., and Linda, (Mrs. Clarence Correll), Bethlehem, Pa.

DEPEW, William—a son of Samuel Depew, lived in Delano for many years. He was an engineer on the Lehigh Valley and later moved to Philadelphia, where he died just a year ago. A daughter, Bertha, (Mrs. Harry Shaup), still resides in Delano. No information is available as to the other members of the family.

DEPEW, Samuel—for many years worked in the Delano store and also operated the drug store for a long time. He was also at one time an employee in the shops. He left Delano a number of years ago and is now residing in the West.

DEPEW, Edward—was for many years a resident of Delano and employed as telegrapher and carpenter foreman. He was appointed steward of the Schuylkill County Home at Schuylkill Haven, Pa., and took up his residence in Pottsville, Pa. He died in Schuylkill Haven in 1916. His widow, who was Hattie Shafer, a Delano girl, still resides in Schuylkill Haven with a daughter, Mary.

DERR, Sylvester Carl—came to Delano from Mahanoy City, Pa., in 1883. He was employed as a car inspector for the railroad during his residence there and moved to Weatherly, Pa., with his family in 1899, when the shops were closed at Delano. Mr. Derr died in Weatherly, January 6, 1906. Mrs. Derr is at present residing with her daughter, Vera, (Mrs. Clouse), at Bethlehem, Pa. Other members of the family are: John, a railroad conductor at Delano; Lillie, (Mrs. Edward Fletcher), Cleveland, O.; Annie, (Mrs. M. I. Price), Tamaqua, Pa., and Corrine, (Mrs. William Maury), Delano.

DOYLE, James—came direct to Delano from Ireland in 1874, placing him and his family in the pioneer class. Mr. Doyle was for many years a road foreman for the Lehigh Valley Railroad and remained in Delano until his death in 1922. His widow died in Delano, January 15, 1931. The children of this family are all living, as follows: Anna, a clerk in Hazleton, Pa.; Mrs. Lawrence Burns, Mahanoy City, Pa.; Florence, Delano; Frances, a clerk at Hazleton, Pa.; Edward, Mahanoy City, Pa., and James, Jr., a locomotive fireman at Delano.

DAVENPORT, Frank—came to Delano early in the 80's and was for many years a passenger engineer. He died many years ago and his widow and daughter, Hattie, have resided in St. Clair, Pa., since then. Will, a son, resides in Brooklyn, N. Y., and Arthur, the other son, in Owosso, Mich.

DONOVAN, Jerry—was for many years a passenger conductor at Delano. He moved from there to Hazleton, Pa., where he now resides, still employed in the passenger service of the Lehigh Valley Railroad. A son, James Donovan, is a division engineer for the Lehigh Valley at Jersey City, N. J. Information as to other members of the family was not made available to the writer. Mrs. Donovan died quite a number of years ago.

DYMAN, John—and family resided in Delano in the 80's. The writer is not certain just when they left Delano, but it was sometime late in the 80's. Two daughters are still living: Mary, (Mrs. Harrison), of Chester, Pa., and Lena, (Mrs. Heinze), of Germantown, Pa.

DIETRICH, Elmer—became a resident of Delano in 1910, coming from Grier City, Pa., and is still residing there. He is a fireman on the road. The children are: Calvin and Raymond, both of Delano, and Bertha, (Mrs. Schollas), Hazleton, Pa.

DEFREHN, Thomas—is a present resident of Delano, coming there with his family from Quakake, Pa., in 1911. He is in the train service of the railroad.

DIEFENDERFER, Fred—resides in Delano at this time, coming there in 1911 from Park Place, Pa. He is employed on the railroad. Mrs. Diefenderfer is the former Edna Hartzel, a Delano girl, and the children are: Clarence and Charles, both of Delano.

DERR, John—was born in Delano, the son of Carl Derr. He has been a conductor on the railroad for many years. Mrs. Derr is the former Bertha Neifert. There are a number of children in the family, two of whom are trained nurses.

DEEBLE, Samuel—has been a resident of Delano for quite a number of years. He is a trainman in the service of the Lehigh Valley Railroad.

DONAT, Charles—came to Delano from Quakake, Pa., many years ago. Mrs. Donat is the former Charlotte Clemens, also of Quakake. Mr. Donat has been in the employ of the Lehigh Valley Railroad since he was a youth. They are both active in the affairs of the community.

ENGLE, Jacob, Sr.—came from Mahanoy City, Pa., to Delano in 1884 and resided there until 1900, when he moved to Philadelphia. He later moved to Boyertown, Pa., where he died in 1911. Mrs. Engle died in Mahanoy City in 1906. Mr. Engle was employed in the shops at Delano as a painter. His family was prominent in the affairs of the town and a number of his grandchildren are still among Delano's outstanding people. The children of the family were H. Clinton, Jacob, Jr., both of whom are deceased, and Calvin G., of Norwood, Pa., and Sallie, (Mrs. King), of Mahanoy City, Pa. Calvin is now employed as a sheet metal worker.

ENGLE, Clinton—came to Delano from Mahanoy City, Pa., in 1882. He resided there until his death in 1928. He was employed as a boiler inspector in the shops and was one of the shopmen who were retained at Delano following the closing of the shops in 1899. Mrs. Engle, who is a daughter of the former Michael Reynolds, and has the double distinction of being the first child born in Delano as well as having the longest continuous residence there, is still active in Delano's affairs. One child of the family, Ruth, died in Delano in 1907. The living children are: James, connected with the store at Delano; Charles, a machinist at Delano; Claude, crew dispatcher, residing in Mahanoy City, Pa., and Harry, a clerk, married and living with his mother. James Engle is married to Ruth Depew, daughter of J. A. Depew, another of Delano's prominent families. Charles is married and has one daughter. There are three children of the James Engle family: One a student in The Teacher's College at West Chester, Pa., another daughter in the schools at Delano, and a son in the Delano schools.

ENGLE, Jacob, Jr.—came to Delano with his parents in 1884 from Mahanoy City, Pa., and resided there until 1895, when he moved to Philadelphia, where he remained until his death in 1923. While at Delano he was employed as a painter in the shops. Mrs. Engle is the former Mary Hughes, of Delano, from one of the town's prominent families, and she is still residing in Philadelphia with their one child, Thomas Hughes Engle, who is an assistant city surveyor for the city of Philadelphia. Mr. Hughes, Jr., is married.

EISENBACH, Samuel J.—moved from Mount Carmel, Pa., to Delano in 1882 and had a continuous residence there until his death in 1921. He was employed as a trainman and engine hostler. Mrs. Eisenbach died in Delano in 1918 and two children are deceased: Lewis E., who died in Delano in 1886, and Mrs. Albert Gibson, at Hazleton, Pa., in 1931. The living members of the family are: George W., a mechanic in Baltimore, Md.; Walter L., railroad storekeeper at Delano, and Harry S., at Delano. Walter is at present a member of the School Board of Delano, and is a graduate of the High School there. Harry was the unfortunate victim of an accident about two years ago which had totally incapacitated him.

EVANS, Edward E.—was another of the pioneers, coming from Pottsville, Pa., to Delano in 1870. He was a machinist there until the removal of the shops in 1899, when he moved to Shamokin, Pa., and later to Elizabeth, N. J., where he remained until his death in 1917. Mrs. Evans died in Delano in 1887. The children of the family are: Bessie, (Mrs. Joseph V. Bannan), Elizabeth, N. J.; Fred, a salesman at Elizabeth, N. J., and Harry W., a barber at Newark, N. J. Harry will be remembered as conducting the barber shop at Delano for a number of years.

ECKER, William—resides in Delano at present with his family, coming from Shenandoah, Pa., in 1899. He is a trainman for the Lehigh Valley Railroad. One member of the family, Anna, died in Delano in 1920. The living children are: Mrs. Fred Evans, Harrisburg, Pa; Mrs. G. R. Stecker, Hazleton, Pa., and William, Jr., a student at Delano.

EDWARDS, Thomas—came to Delano from Mahanoy City, Pa., in 1898 and resided there until his death in 1931. He was conductor and yardmaster for the railroad during that time. Mrs. Edwards is the former Olive Clemens, a long-time Delano resident. The children are: Mrs. Paul Luckenbill, Kutztown, Pa., who taught in the Delano schools for a time, Thomas, Jr., store manager in Philadelphia, and Dorothy, a teacher in Sinking Springs, Pa.

ENGLE, James—James Engle was born in Delano and has resided there ever since, as was and has his wife, who is the former Ruth Depew.

Mr. Engle is the son of Mrs. Clinton Engle. Both Mr. and Mrs. Engle can trace their Delano ancestry to the very beginning of its history. Mr. Engle has been employed in the Delano store for many years. There are three children: Elizabeth Jane, Margaret Charlotte, and James Albert.

ENGLAND, William—resides in Delano, having come there from Park Place, Pa., in 1911. He is employed in the Lehigh Valley shops at Ashmore, Pa. Mrs. England is the former Elmira Edinger, a Delano-born girl. There is one son, Clayton, residing with his parents.

EDINGER, William—came to Delano many years ago and was an engineer during most of his residence. He remained in the town until his death there in 1916. Mrs. Edinger died in Delano in 1931. Harry, a son, resides in Delano, his wife being the former May Houser, a Delano girl. Another son, Frank, and a daughter, Mrs. England, also live in Delano.

FAUST, Charles—made Delano his home in 1882, coming from Trenton, Pa. He was transferred to Mount Carmel, Pa., in 1897, but returned to Delano in 1901, where he remained until his death in 1909. He was one of the Lehigh Valley's best engineers. The family moved to Reading following Mr. Faust's death and Mrs. Faust died there in 1928. The children are: George, machinist residing in Hazleton, Pa.; Mary, (Mrs. Roberts), Mahanoy City, Pa.; Anna, (Mrs. Ocksrider), Reading, Pa., and Elsie, a nurse now residing in Astoria, Long Island.

FAUST, Henry—moved from Park Place, Pa., (then known as Meyersville), to Delano in 1870. He was a machinist and brass worker and lived in Delano until 1889, when he moved to Scranton, Pa. He later died in New York City in 1916. Mrs. Faust died in Paterson, N. J. in 1924. All of the children of the family are living: Elizabeth, (Mrs. Fritsch), New York City; Mrs. K. Sloss, Scranton, Pa.; Clara, (Mrs. Kaeppel), Scranton, Pa; Sue, (Mrs. Ace), Buffalo, N. Y.; George, dispatcher for the I. R. T. Company, at Paterson, N. J., and Edward, maintainer for the I. R. T. Company, at Paterson, N. J. This family belongs to Delano's pioneers.

FOLWEILER, George W.—became a resident of Delano in 1886, coming from East Mahanoy Junction, Pa. He began work there in 1879. With his good wife, he still resides in the town, having been retired several years ago after a long service as an engineer. The Folweiler family has been a leading one in Delano all through the years. Mrs. Folweiler is one of the most active church workers the town ever had and was one of the prime moving spirits in the reunions held there in 1930 and 1931. Three children of the family are deceased: Annie, at Mahanoy City, Pa., in 1882; Harry, at Mahanoy City in 1884, and John at Delano, in 1896.

The children living are: Kathryn, (Mrs. Joseph Barlieb), Bethlehem, Pa., and Irene, (Mrs. Frank Wagner), Mahanoy City, Pa. It is to Mrs. Folweiler that this history has been dedicated.

FRITZ, Henry F.—located in Delano early in the 80's. He was for many years an engineer and died in Delano about 1916. Mr. Fritz was always very active in the religious life of Delano. Mrs. Fritz died at her home in Delano in 1931. The children of the family are: Annie, (Mrs. Harry Perry), living in the old homestead at Delano with one of her sons, Zillah, (Mrs. Edward Thamarus), Allentown, Pa., and Harold, Allentown, Pa. Harold is a graduate of Dickinson Law School and is one of the four lawyers who came out of Delano.

FLETCHER, David—was one of Delano's most prominent citizens and a member of one of its first families. He came to the town early in the 60's, and took the position of general foreman in the shops under Mr. A. A. Mitchell, master mechanic, a place that he held all through his residence. Besides his responsible position in the industrial life of the place, he was an outstanding leader in civic affairs. He started the first Sunday School in the town, advanced the money for equipping the first band, which was organized in his home, and always was in the lead of any movement for bettering the town's standing. Mr. Fletcher died in 1895 in Waverly, N. Y., and Mrs. Fletcher in 1913, in Philadelphia. A daughter, Carrie, (Mrs. Smink), died in Lancaster, Pa., in 1912, and Will in 1921, in Philadelphia. The members of the family still active in this world's affairs are: Edward, head of a tool supply business in Cleveland, O.; Margie, (Mrs. Ashley), Philadelphia, and Emma, (Mrs. H. F. Bickle), Plainfield, N. J.

FLEXER, Dr. Lewis A.—was a resident of Delano from 1900 to 1910, the time of his death. Mrs. Flexer now resides in Catasauqua, Pa. A full history of Dr. Flexer's life has been given in a previous chapter of this book.

FEGLEY, Jesse—was one of the first persons to locate permanently in Delano. His daughter, Mary, was the third child born there. Both Mr. and Mrs. Fegley have been deceased for many years. They resided in Delano for only a few years right in the beginning of its history, removing later to Quakake, Pa.

FEGLEY, Jefferson—resided in Delano during the 80's, and was for many years an engineer. He moved to Quakake and in later years to Philadelphia. Mrs. Fegley died while the family resided in Delano. No information is available as to the present location of the members of this family.

FEGLEY, Harry—a son of Jesse Fegley, resided in Delano for many years. He had a residence there at two different times, early in the 80's, and again returning there about 1900. Mrs. Fegley died in Delano many years ago. Mr. Fegley now resides with his son, Edgar, at Grier City, Pa. He was an engineer during his residence in Delano. The children living are: Edgar, engineer, Grier City, Pa.; Earl, Grier City, Pa.; Guy, railroader, Delano; Jesse, Nescopeck, Pa.; Laura, Berwick, Pa., and Carrie, Berwick, Pa.

FLEMING, Thomas—was employed in the blacksmith shop at Delano for many years. Mrs. Fleming is the former Mary Lynch, of one of the pioneer Delano families. Mr. Fleming was a noted ball player, catcher on the Delano team for years. He now resides in Pottsville, Pa., and is active in trade union circles.

FETTERMAN, U. G.—came to Delano in 1917 from Hazleton, Pa., and still resides there. He has been assistant trainmaster for a number of years. His family has had a prominent part in the activities of the town since its residence there, Mrs. Fetterman being a member of the reunion committee.

FOLWEILER, Michael—came to Delano many years ago and was a railroader for the Lehigh Valley Railroad until he was killed while in service in the Delano yards several years ago.

FAUST, Henry E.—came to Delano with his family from Hosensack, Pa., in 1898 and still resides there. Mr. Faust has been for many years an engineer for the Lehigh Valley Railroad. One son, Elmer, died in 1928. The other members of the family are all residents of Delano.

GERHARD, Wallace T.—moved to Delano from Mount Carmel, Pa., in 1901, and resided there until 1902, when he moved with his family to Tamanend, Pa. He was an engineer for the Lehigh Valley during his residence in the town. Later he entered the employ of the Reading Railway at Tamaqua, Pa., and was an engineer for that company until his retirement about two years ago. Mrs. Gerhard is the writer's sister, and had been a resident of Delano in her girlhood in the 80's, when the Moser family first came to town. One child of the family is deceased: Roberta, who died in Mount Carmel in 1897. The other members of the family are: Millard, bookkeeper, at Tamaqua, living at Barnesville, Pa; Eva, (Mrs. George Schaeffer), Tamaqua, Pa.; Harold, mail-carrier, Tamaqua; Ira, salesman, Barnesville; Donald, railway mail clerk, New York City; Merle, clerk, Barnesville, and Harry, student, at home.

GASSER, George—and family are of the pioneers. Mr. Gasser came to Delano in 1870 from Berks County. He resided there until 1902, when he moved to Tamanend, Pa., and later to Quakake, Pa., where he still resides with his wife and daughter, Sallie. Mr. Gasser was employed about the shops and engine houses in Delano and was well known to everyone connected with the town. The family one time resided on the Hazleton road at the place known as Bunker Hill, but in later years lived on Hazle Street. The deceased members of the family are: Cora, (Mrs. DeFrehn), at Delano in 1905; Charles, at Tamanend in 1923, and William, killed at Slatington, Pa., July, 1931. Those living are: Robert, machinist, Delano; Mrs. Fred Gerhard, Lehighton, Pa.; Frank, Quakake, Pa.; Sallie, Quakake, and George, Jr., Jacksonville, Fla.

GOULDNER, William—located in Delano in 1892, coming from Tamaqua, Pa. He was employed as a locomotive engineer during his residence there and returned to his old home in Tamaqua in 1918, where he remained until his death in 1925. Mrs. Gouldner died in Delano in 1909. The children of the family are: Irvin, engineer at Delano; Claude, a machinist, at Lebanon, Pa.; Carrie, (widow of Lewis Markle), Tamaqua, Pa., and Albert, assistant foreman, Tamaqua. Mrs. Irvin Gouldner is the former Annie Reynolds, of Delano's first family, and Claude's wife is the former Lillie Bretz, another Delano girl from an old-time family.

GOULDNER, Calvin—became a Delano resident in 1880, moving there from Tamaqua, Pa. He was a passenger conductor for the Lehigh Valley Railroad for many years and resided in Delano until 1894, when he moved to Mauch Chunk, Pa., and later to Philadelphia, where he remained until his death in 1930. His widow, who was Mary E. Depew, a daughter of Samuel Depew, is at present living in Philadelphia with her son, Benjamin Gouldner, who is in the employ of the Philadelphia Electric Company. Mrs. Depew came to Delano in 1867 with her father's family, and is one of the first family members.

GLENN, Edward—was one of Delano's prominent residents over a long period of time. He came there during the 70's and was yardmaster and trainmaster for most of the time. He also had charge of the Delano boarding house located in the old station building. This was headquarters for a great many employes whose homes were located in other towns. Mr. Glenn left Delano quite a number of years ago, but the writer has not been able to get information as to where he located. Both Mr. and Mrs. Glenn and their son, Alonzo, have been dead for a number of years. John, another son, resides in Topeka, Kan., and is employed in the shops of the Sante Fe Railroad there, while William, the other son, lives in Akron, O., according to the best information the writer has been able to get.

GRIFFITHS, William—and his wife came to Delano from Mount Carmel, Pa., sometime between 1910 and 1920, he being employed as a railroader for a number of years. They now reside in Frackville, Pa.

GICKING, John—was one of the old-timers in Delano. He came there in the 70's, and was for a long time the town's barber, the barber shop being then located in the old station building. Later he became a railroader and was a conductor in the passenger service at the time of his death in Hazleton, Pa., some years ago. Mrs. Gicking still resides in Hazleton.

GOTHIE, Joseph L.—made Delano his home in 1903, coming from Mahanoy City, Pa. He is still a resident. Mrs. Gothie is the former Katie Hartung, born in Delano. Mr. Gothie is a conductor for the Lehigh Valley Railroad. The children are: Mrs. Ivan Kopenhaver, Tamaqua, Pa.; Joseph, Jr., bookkeeper, Mahanoy City, Pa., and James L., not at present employed.

GOULDNER, Irvin—came to Delano with his parents in 1892, and has resided there ever since. He was an engineer for many years, but has been retired for some time. Mrs. Gouldner is the former Annie Reynolds, of Delano's First Family. Four children are deceased and these living are: William, clerk, at Hazleton, Pa.; Wilbur, air brake inspector; Clinton, machinist helper; Lewis, laborer, all of Delano, and Albert, stationary engine fireman, Philadelphia.

GULDNER, Lewis—became a resident of Delano in 1901, coming from Mount Carmel, Pa. He has been a conductor on the railroad for many years. Mrs. Guldner is the former Gertrude Mowery, a long-time Delano resident. One child is deceased: Charles, at Delano, in 1913. Those children living are: Gertrude A., Philadelphia; George, bookkeeper, Mahanoy City, Pa.; Mary R., and Evelyn A., students, Delano. Mrs. Guldner is a member of Delano's reunion committee.

HALDAMAN, Eli—belonged to the select class of the 60's, coming to Delano in 1867 from Tamaqua, Pa. He was a machinist in the shops until he left the town in 1892, moving to Altoona, Pa., where he worked for the Pennsylvania Railroad Company for many years. He died in that city in 1929. One son, Edgar, died in Delano in 1892. Mrs. Haldaman still resides in Altoona, as do two daughters, Gertrude, (Mrs. Bradley), and Ruth C. Haldaman.

HARTUNG, James W.—was a long-time resident of Delano, arriving there from Mahanoy City, Pa., in 1880, and continuing his residence until his death in 1910. Mrs. Hartung died in Delano in 1915. Two sons, Thomas and George, died in Delano, Thomas in 1926, and George in 1931. Both sons were married, Tom having lived at Beaver Meadows, Pa., where his family still resides, and George at Weatherly, Pa., where his family now resides. The living members of the family are: John H., employed in a hosiery mill in Philadelphia; Mamie, (Mrs. John F. Owens), Delano; Katie, (Mrs. Joseph L. Gothie), Delano, and Tillie, Schuylkill Haven, Pa.

HOEFLICH, John J.—came to Delano from Pottsville, Pa., in 1886. He was foreman of the work train for many years and left Delano in 1916, moving to Mahanoy City, Pa. One son, Casper, died in Delano in 1887. All the other members of the family are living. Mr. and Mrs. Hoeflich at present reside in Allentown, Pa., as do these children: Charles F. and Mrs. R. F. Klingler. John J. is in business in Philadelphia, and Bernard M. in business at Slatington, Pa.

HOFMANN, Charles—came to Delano from Pottsville, Pa., in 1882 and has never left it since. He began as a clerk in the Delano store and has been one of the managers there for many years past. With his family, he has occupied the residential part of the store building almost from the beginning of his connection with the town. No one ever belonging to Delano is better known than Mr. Hofmann and his brother, George. He has been one of the town's most substantial citizens for fifty years and was always deeply interested in anything that made for the advancement of its best interests. The following members constitute one of the finest families ever raised in the town: Mary E. Hofmann, the wife, and children: Mary, (Mrs. Tim Welsh), now residing in Mahanoy City, Pa.; Cyrie, clerk, in Philadelphia; Charles F., Clerk, Sterling Hotel, Wilkes-Barre, Pa.; George W., clerk, in Philadelphia; Leo V., clerk, in Philadelphia; Hubert W., clerk, in Wilkes-Barre, Pa.; Paul A., insurance, Frenchtown, N. J., and Christine, (Mrs. Louis Rufe), Doylestown, Pa.

HOFMANN, George—came to Delano from Pottsville, Pa., at the same time as his brother, Charles, in 1882, and has been a resident continuously since then. He has been associated with his brother through all the years in the operation of the store and has also served as postmaster for many years, as well as in other civic positions. He has been supervisor and treasurer of the school board for many years. Mrs. Hofmann died in Delano in 1925. A niece who was a member of his family, (now Mrs. Agatha Raab), resides in Drexel Hill, Pa. Any Delano prodigal returning to the old home town after many years' absence can recover the homelike atmosphere in no better way than to drop into the store and greet Charles and George Hofmann.

HOUSER, David—first located in Delano in 1880, coming from Tamaqua, Pa. He was for many years an engineer for the Lehigh Valley Railroad. For a time he was transferred to Mount Carmel Pa., but returned to Delano after an absence of about three years and remained there until his death in 1916. Mrs. Houser died in Delano in 1909. One child, Franklin, died in Tamaqua before the family came to Delano. The living members of the family are: Edward, shop foreman at Tamaqua, Pa.; William, a machinist at Linglestown, Pa.; Katie, (Mrs. Harry Taylor), Easton, Pa.; Irvin, mineworker, Llewellyn, Pa.; Robert, engineer, at Delano; John, foreman at Delano; May, (Mrs. Harry Edinger), Delano, and Esther, (Mrs. Pike), Flint, Mich. Edward's wife is the former Emma Markle, a Delano girl, while Will's wife is the former Miss Wallauer, daughter of William Wallauer, also a Delano girl.

HUGHES, Thomas—came to Delano in the early days, 1878, from Shenandoah, Pa. He was assistant foreman of the blacksmith shop for many years and resided in the town until his death in 1891. The family left Delano in 1896, moving to Philadelphia. Mrs. Hughes died in Philadelphia in 1922. A son, William, died in Tamaqua, Pa., in 1912. The members of the family are: Mary, (Mrs. Jacob Engle), Philadelphia, Pa., and Meriam, (Mrs. Jacob Ebling), Camden, N. J. Both Mr. Engle and Mr. Ebling were former Delano residents and are both deceased.

HEIN, Mrs. Jonas—came to Delano with her family in 1882, Mr. Hein having died in St. Clair several years previously. Mrs. Hein had been a resident of Delano many years before, coming with her parents, Mr. and Mrs. Jacob Messersmith, at the very beginning of the town's history. Mrs. Hein left Delano in 1890, going to Scranton, Pa. She later returned to Quakake, Pa., where she remained until she died in 1927. The other members of the family deceased are: Hannah, (Mrs. William West), William Hein, Mary, (Mrs. George Brown), and Augusta, (Mrs. John Eroh). The living members of the family are: Clara, (Mrs. Charles Mills), Newark, N. J.; Katherine Elizabeth, (Mrs. Ed Fischer), Clifton, N. J., and Alice, (Mrs. George Morgan), Quakake, Pa. Mrs. Clara Mills had formerly been the wife of William Taylor, who was an engineer of the Lehigh Valley Railroad at Delano and was killed in service in 1900. Will Hein was a boiler-maker while residing in Delano.

HARRIS, David—came to Delano from Quakake, Pa., in the 90's. He was an engineer and lived in the town until his death many years ago. He lost his life in a railroad collision in the Packerton yards. Mrs. Harris has been dead for many years, as also the only daughter, Edith, (Mrs. Stewart). Three sons are living: Edward, an engineer at Hazleton, Pa.; David, at Hazleton, Pa., and Joseph, at Philadelphia.

HOFFMAN, Franklin Pierce—worked at Delano early in the 80's, and was married while working there to Miss Alice Wessner, of Mahanoy City, Pa. They located in the town in 1887, and resided there until 1896, when Mr. Hoffman was transferred to Mount Carmel, Pa. He was employed by the Lehigh Valley as an engineer and lost his life in 1914, at Mauch Chunk, Pa., when his engine overturned on a sharp curve. Mrs. Hoffman is now living in Mount Carmel. Mary, the eldest daughter, formerly a member of the public school teaching corps of Mount Carmel, died several years ago, and Frank, a son, who was an engineer for the Lehigh Valley, suffered a tragic death on June 2, 1928, near Mount Carmel, when the engine which he was firing on that day, jumped the track. The children living are: Ethel, (Mrs. Harold Burmeister), Ashland, Pa.; Mildred, a teacher at Palmerton, Pa, and Warren, a student in Susquehanna University at Selinsgrove, Pa. Frank Hoffman's widow, who was Miss Phoebe Smith, of Mount Carmel, is a teacher in the public schools in that town.

HOEGG, John—came to Delano early in the 80's. One son, Augustus, was a prominent shop-worker in Delano until the removal of the shops in 1899, and has since lived in Weatherly, Pa., where he holds a responsible position as a shop foreman. Mr. and Mrs. Hoegg, Sr., have been dead for many years, but the writer has no information about other members of the family.

HANSEN, Nels—succeeded Nels Nelson as gardener for A. P. Blakslee sometime in the early 90's, and he continued in that position until the Blakslee family left the town. Mr. Hansen was married to Ella Righter, a Delano girl, and located near Allentown for a number of years. Mrs. Hansen died several years ago and Mr. Hansen now resides with his daughter in Allentown, Pa.

HEPLER, Miss Ida—taught in the Delano schools for a number of years in the 90's, and later was married to Robert Swank, Esq., since which time she has resided in Mahanoy City, Pa. Miss Hepler during her residence in Delano, was very active in the affairs of the town, particularly in church and school work, an interest that she still maintains to this day.

HECKMAN, John—came to Delano from Quakake, Pa., in 1909, and still resides there. He is a trainman in the service of the Lehigh Valley Railroad. A son, Albert, died before the family came to Delano, and one daughter, Pauline, has just completed the course at State College, and will teach in the term beginning with the fall of 1932.

HERMAN, John—is one of the old-time residents of Delano. He has been an engineer for many years and came up through the various grades of railroading at Delano. He still makes Delano his home. A son, John, Jr., is married and has his home in Delano.

HERMAN, Frank—was a resident of Delano for many years and was an engineer during his residence there. He has been dead for several years and there is no information available about the other members of his family.

HARTZEL, Frank—made his home in Delano in 1900, coming from Quakake, Pa. He was a fireman there until his death in 1913. His widow still resides there, together with those other members of her family: Cledville, an engineer; Raymond, an engineer; Mrs. Harry Redka, Mrs. Albert Levy, and Mrs. Fred Diefenderfer. Charles, another son, is a machinist helper at Hazleton, Pa., and a daughter, Mrs. Warren Nussbaum, also resides in Hazleton. Mrs. Hartzel is very active in civic and church affairs, and is a member of the reunion committee. One daughter of the family, Eliza, died in Quakake, in 1897.

HESS, David—came to Delano from Mount Carmel, Pa., about 1920, and still resides there. He is employed as an engineer on the railroad. Mrs. Hess is a former Mount Carmel resident.

JAMES, John R.—came to Delano very early in the history of the town, coming from Cressona, Pa. He was foreman in the blacksmith shop for many years and was prominent in the affairs of the town in that early day. He served for some time as Justice of the Peace. He has been deceased for many years, as is also Mrs. James. The children of the family are: John R., Erie, Pa.; William T., Worcester, Mass.; Martha, (Mrs. Bachman), Gordon, Pa.; Llewellyn, Lake Helen, Fla.; Thomas J., Pelham, N. Y., and Elizabeth, Lake Helen, Fla. A grandson, William J. James, will be remembered by all the youngsters of the 90's. He spent his vacations in Delano at the home of his maternal grandparents, Mr. and Mrs. Joshua Butler, and was looked upon as one of Delano's own. He now resides with his family in Elizabeth, N. J., and he and Mrs. James and daughter were present at the 1930 reunion in Delano.

JEFFRIES, William—made Delano his home in 1872, coming there direct from England. Mr. Jeffries was one of the best-known men in the town during his residence. He conducted the only shoemaker shop in the village and the youngsters of his day have vivid recollections of his kindly spirit and his little shop at the junction of the Hazleton and Quakake roads. He left Delano in 1905, going to Cressona, Pa., later locating at Weatherly, Pa., where he died in 1910. Mrs. Jeffries died in Weatherly in 1905. One daughter of the family, Lizzie, died in Hornell, N. Y., in 1922. The other members of the family are: Eliza, (Mrs. Lathlean), Duncannon, Pa.; Susan, (Mrs. Coover), Cressona, Pa.; Margaret, (Mrs. George Butler), Weatherly, Pa.; William, Hornell, N. Y., and Joseph, Richmond, Cal.

JAMES, Garfield—made his home in Delano in 1920, coming from Hazleton, Pa. He has been signal maintainer for the Lehigh Valley Railroad during that time. He and his family are still residents of the town. Mr. and Mrs. James are very active in civic and religious affairs in the community, and Mr. James has been chairman of the reunion committee which arranged and so successfully staged the two reunions in Delano in 1930 and 1931. A son and Mrs. Symons, the mother of Mrs. James, are the other members of the family.

KEIBER, William C.—came to Delano from Schuylkill Haven, Pa., in 1890. He was chief clerk to the division superintendent, a position which he has continued to hold to this day. He left Delano for Hazleton, Pa., in 1898, when division headquarters were moved from Delano. Since then he has been transferred to Easton, Pa., where he now resides. Mrs. Keiber is the former Emily Butler, a member of one of Delano's pioneer families. One daughter, Marietta B., died in Hazleton in 1929. The other children are: William C., Jr., and Robert Jack, both students in the schools of Easton. Mr. Keiber has rendered the writer of these chronicles very valuable service in gathering information about Delano.

KESSELRING, Lewis—became a resident of Delano in 1888, coming from Fountain Springs, Pa. He was a baggagemaster in the passenger service of the Lehigh Valley Railroad for many years. He moved to Ashland, Pa., in 1898, and later went to Hazleton, Pa., where he remained until his death in 1926. Mrs. Kesselring, who is the former Kathrine Reynolds, of Delano's first family, now resides in Lansford, Pa., as does a daughter, Mrs. B. B. Barrow. Two sons, J. H. and L. P. Kesselring, reside in Hazleton, Pa., the first a clerk for the Lehigh Valley Railroad, and the other for the Pennsylvania Power and Light Company.

KISTLER, Daniel—moved to Delano from Grier City, Pa., in 1906, and remained a resident until 1924, when he moved to Tamaqua, Pa. He was a railroad conductor while in Delano. Mr. and Mrs. Kistler now reside in Tamaqua. Two children are deceased: Wilman, at Delano in 1920, and Alton, in Tamaqua in 1927. These children are living: Pauline, a nurse at Mahanoy City, Pa., and Laura, (Mrs. Patterson), at Delano.

KLECKNER, Oscar—began his railroading experience in Delano in 1881, coming from Tamaqua, Pa. He was successively, laborer, brakeman, fireman, and engineer. He remained in Delano until 1895, when he was transferred to Hazleton, Pa., where he still lives. He operated a passenger train between Hazleton and Slatington, by way of Pottsville. He has just been retired from the service in February, 1932.

KIMBEL, Peter F.—took up his residence in Delano in 1882, and his family was prominent in the affairs of the town for many years. He came from Barnesville, Pa., and was an employee of the shops. He moved to Buffalo, N. Y., in 1898, and later came to Barnesville, where he died in 1901. Mrs. Kimbel died in Tamaqua, Pa., in 1916. The other deceased members of the family are: Curtis, who died in Roselle, N. J., in 1931;

Arthur, at Roselle, N. J., in 1925. Those living are: Cora, (Mrs. James MacClure), Hershey, Pa.; Clara, (Mrs. Perrin Camp), Tamaqua, Pa.; Kathryn, (Mrs. P. H. Bosworth), Jenkintown, Pa.; G. B. Kimbel, Union, N. J., and R. W. Kimbel, Reading, Pa.

KOCH, Frank—located in Delano early in the 80's. He was for many years a passenger conductor on the Lehigh Valley. He moved to Mount Carmel, Pa., about 1910 and resided there until his death from a fall some years ago. Mrs. Koch also died in Mount Carmel some years ago. A son, Robert, died in Delano in the 90's. The children living are: Elmer, a railroader, Quakake, Pa.; Harry, mineworker, Mount Carmel, Pa., and Bessie, (Mrs. John Daugherty), Hazleton, Pa.

KLINGER, Francis—came to Delano from Quakake, Pa., in 1896, and was an engineer there for a number of years, when he was transferred to Lehighton, Pa., in 1910, and later to Mount Carmel, Pa., where he still resides and is still employed as an engineer on the road. He and his family were Mount Carmel people before going to Delano. Besides Mrs. Klinger, the family consists of: Mrs. Earl Camp and Mrs. John Estock, daughters, both of Mount Carmel, Pa.; Reuben, a fireman at Lehighton, Pa., and Elwood, a brakeman, at Lehighton.

LINDEMUTH, Edward—moved from Shenandoah, Pa., to Delano in 1886. He has been for many years an engineer, and was transferred to Hazleton, Pa., in 1898, where he still remains with his family. One son, Roy Claire, died in Delano, in 1894. The other members of the family are: Mrs. George Wancoe, Edward, Jr., both of Hazleton, Pa.; Mrs. John Smith, Drums, Pa.; Mrs. Lawrence Murray, of Weatherly, Pa., and Harold Lindemuth, of Newberry, Pa. The father of Mr. Lindemuth, Jonathan Lindemuth, worked at Delano for many years, but never lived there. A sister, Mrs. Kathryn Overholt, now residing at Mauch Chunk, Pa., also spent much time in Delano years ago. Another sister, Annie, wife of Gottlieb Miller, lived in Delano for a number of years, and died in Weatherly, Pa., in 1927.

LINDEMUTH, David—became a resident of Delano in 1888, coming from Raven Run, Pa. He has been a trainman for the Lehigh Valley for many years. He moved to Mount Carmel, Pa., in 1898, and at present resides at Shenandoah Heights, Pa. The first Mrs. Lindemuth died in Mount Carmel in 1908. One son, Irvin A., was killed in the World War in France. His body was brought to America two years later and interred at Mount Carmel. These sons still are living: Oliver, a machinist; Elmer R., foreman; Reuben, automobile mechanic, all of Mount Carmel; Oscar, Fullerton, Pa.; Clarence, Allentown, Pa., and John, Ardmore, Pa.

LUTZ, Mahlon—came from Quakake, Pa., to Delano in 1899, and resided there until 1902, when he was transferred to Lehighton, Pa. He was a freight conductor until his death in 1927. Mrs. Lutz died in 1917. The children of the family are: Effie, (Mrs. George Hill), Chester, Pa.; Miriam, (Mrs. William Marsden), Nesquehoning, Pa.; Myra, (Mrs. William Busocker), Lehighton, Pa., and Alfred, a conductor still residing at Delano.

LYNCH, Dennis—belonged to the elect first family group, coming to Delano from Philadelphia in 1865. He was employed in the machine shops until 1900, when he was transferred to Weatherly, Pa., where he remained until his death in 1915. Mrs. Lynch died in Pottsville, Pa., in 1926. The children of the family are: Andrew, air brake foreman, Hazleton, Pa.; Mary, (Mrs. Thomas Fleming), Pottsville, Pa.; Thomas, machinist, Altoona, Pa., and Margaret Lynch, Pottsville. The Lynch family was always prominent in Delano affairs. Andrew was an active member of the Delano band.

LONG, John—came to Delano early in the 80's. He was a prominent engineer for many years. He was transferred to Mount Carmel, Pa., about 1899, and still resides there with his family. He left the employ of the Lehigh Valley Railroad some years ago and has been employed since then as a colliery worker. The members of the family are: Mr. and Mrs. Long and daughter, Ella, and son, Victor, all residing in Mount Carmel; John, an engineer for the Pennsylvania Railroad, at Sunbury, Pa.; Edward, in the service of the Interstate Commerce Commission at Washington, D. C.; Marcellus, employed at Washington, D. C.; Aloysius, a railroad man at Delano; Ignatius, at Mahanoy City, Pa., and Leon, at Collinsgswood, N. J.

LAMB, John—was a railroad man at Delano for many years, coming there some time in the 80's. He was transferred to Mount Carmel, Pa., about 1900, and remained there until his death some years ago. Mrs. Lamb also died in Mount Carmel several years ago. A son, Joseph, is in the employ of the Pennsylvania Power and Light Company at Mount Carmel. A son of the family lost his life by drowning while skating at Delano, many years ago.

LOFTUS, Anthony—took up his residence in Delano in the 80's. He was an employee of the shops and died in Delano early in the 90's. His family resided there until some time in the 90's, when they moved to Berwick, Pa. The writer has not been able to locate any member of the family, but was told that Charles, the son, had lived in Philadelphia a few years ago, and Mrs. Loftus and Bessie were in Berwick. He could not verify this.

LUTZ, Alfred F.—has been a resident of Delano since 1911, coming from Lehighton, Pa. He and his wife are active in affairs in Delano. Mrs. Lutz is the former Winifred Neifert, daughter of Charles Neifert, and Mr. Lutz is a son of Mahlon Lutz, and is a conductor for the Lehigh Valley Railroad. A son, Alvin, is an automobile mechanic at Easton, Pa., and a daughter, Jacqueline, lives at home.

MACK, John J.—was one of the early residents of Delano, coming there in 1878 from Quakake, Pa. His family was one of the prominent ones in the town and Mr. Mack was always actively interested in public affairs. He was an engineer for many years, leaving Delano in 1910 and returning to Quakake, where he died, in 1911. Mrs. Mack died in Delano, in 1887. All of the children of the family but one are living. Mary, (Mrs. George Rohrer), Orwigsburg, Pa., died just a few weeks before these lines were written. The other children are: Angie, (Mrs. Robert Moyer); Elizabeth, Fred S., in the employ of the Bethlehem Steel Company, and George F., in the employ of the Bethlehem Steel Company, all residing in Bethlehem, Pa., and Sue, (Mrs. Charles Martz), New York City.

MASON, Isaac—came to Delano from Mahanoy City, Pa., in 1881. He was employed in the shops there until his death some time in the 90's. Mrs. Mason was a sister of Charles and Jonathan Bretz and died in Delano in the 90's. Mr. Mason's connection with the town began quite a time before he became a resident. He drove a stage coach over the old turnpike between Tamaqua, Pa., and Catawissa, Pa., before Delano was founded, passing within a mile of the site of the town. He also hauled supplies to the town during the development and worked at a saw mill operating near Nigger Hollow, just north of the town. There was one son, J. O., or Ollie, Mason, who was an engineer on the road for a number of years and left the town in 1893, lived at Tamanend and Freeland, Pa., for several years, and then went south, where he has been residing for the past thirty years. He has been an engineer on a southern railroad all these years and now resides in Montgomery, Alabama. Mr. Mason has never lost his interest in Delano and was present at the two reunions held there in 1930 and 1931.

McCARROLL, John—became a Delano resident in 1865. He was one of the early engineers for the Lehigh Valley Railroad. He lived in Delano until his death in the 90's. His was one of the first families, and William McCarroll, his eldest son, has achieved distinction in the industrial and business world, as the foreign representative for the Baldwin Locomotive Works for many years. He visited practically every country of the world in his work for this great company and just recently relinquished his service with it. He is now living retired in Melrose Park, Philadelphia, Pa. His contribution to this history has been most valuable, as the reader will have seen. His sister, Linda, (widow of Augustus

Read), resides with him. Harry, for many years connected with the store at Delano, and later owning a farm near Berwick, Pa., has been dead for a number of years, as has also the younger daughter, Bertha. John resides in Selinsgrove, Pa.

McCARROLL, Samuel—came to Delano in 1882 from Lovelton, Pa. He was a car inspector for the railroad for many years, or until he left the town in 1899, when he moved to Bethlehem, Pa. He continued his residence in Bethlehem until his death in 1930. Mrs. McCarroll died in Bethlehem in 1911. Other members of the family deceased are: Lena, (Mrs. Nathan Singley), in 1913, at Carbondale, Pa.; Blanche, (Mrs. Robert Hauser), in 1911, at Wilkes-Barre, Pa.; James, in 1898, at Delano. Those living are: Walter, fireman, residing at Quakake, Pa.; Annie, (Mrs. Frank Bretz), Delano; Mabel, (Mrs. W. P. Gray), Bethlehem, Pa.; Mida, (Mrs. William Waters), Wilkes-Barre, Pa.; Howard, a machinist, Bethlehem, Pa., and Lewis, in the employ of the United States Rubber Company, at Detroit, Mich.

MARKLE—The Markle family located in Delano early in the 80's. No information has been furnished as to the place from which they came or when or where the various members of the family who are deceased, died. Mr. Markle died in Delano many years ago, as did also Mrs. Markle, to the writer's best information. One of the daughters was the wife of William Rhoades, and still resides in Delano. Emma is the wife of Edward Houser and now resides in Tamaqua, Pa. Elizabeth, (Mrs. Kline), resides in Tamaqua; Lewis died in Tamaqua about four years ago, and Winfield, the youngest, is in the employ of the Lehigh Valley Railroad Company, and resides in Mount Carmel, Pa. Reuben, until recently, worked in the C. R. R. of N. J. shops at Elizabeth, N. J.

McMULLEN, John—came to Delano with the pioneers, in 1868, from Mauch Chunk, Pa. He had a very prominent place in the railroad service, having served many years as a passenger engineer, after which he was made road foreman of engines, which position he held until he left Delano in 1901. He moved to Bethlehem, Pa., and for many years held an executive position with the Lehigh and New England Railroad. He died there just last year, June 22, 1931. His family was prominent in the civic and social life of Delano during its residence. Mrs. McMullen is still residing in Bethlehem, with her daughter, Mrs. William Frederick Brodnax. Mrs. Brodnax, as Miss Hattie McMullen, shared with Leon Bailey the distinction of being in the first class to graduate from the Delano High Schools in 1893. Her husband, Mr. Brodnax, died in New York City, April 17, 1931. Mitchell Derr McMullen, the son, is now located in Scranton, Pa., where he is sales manager for the Russell Motor Car Company.

MERRICK, George, Sr.—came to Delano late in the 80's. He conducted the confectionery and cigar store in the old station building and which was known to all Delano people as the Pefferwasser Shop. His grandson and granddaughter, George and Sadie Merrick, were residents of Delano for a number of years. Miss Merrick later was married to John Butler, a sketch of their family being given elsewhere. George Merrick is now an attorney-at-law, practicing in Los Angeles, Cal.

MILLS, Charles—is another of the original Delano families, coming to the town direct from England in 1867. He was an employee of the shops and left Delano in 1891 for Mahanoy City, Pa., where he resided until his death in 1905. A son, William, died in Allentown, Pa., in 1930. The other sons are: Daniel, a machinist in Huntingdon, W. Va., and Joseph, a painter in Scranton, Pa. William left Delano in 1880 for Wilkes-Barre, Pa.; Daniel in 1890 for Selma, Ala. Joseph, the youngest son, was born in Delano in 1869.

MOORE, John S.—made his home in Delano in 1879, coming from Sugar Notch, Pa. He was a master car builder and had charge of the work of car construction in the shops, when passenger, baggage, and other cars were built there. His family was very prominent in the life of the town. Mr. Moore left Delano in 1899, going to Allentown, Pa., where he continued his residence until his death in 1928. Mrs. Moore died in Allentown in 1910. The children of the family are: Carolin, (Mrs. L. J. H. Grossart), Allentown, Pa.; Ria, (Mrs. Pursell), Allentown, Pa., and Elizabeth, (Mrs. Rosenberger), Doylestown, Pa.

MOSER, Millard F.—and family were the first of this name to locate in Delano, coming from Quakake, Pa., in 1882. His service record for the Lehigh Valley Railroad Company began at the age of fifteen years, when he worked under his father as a section hand, later starting as a brakeman, which position he held when he moved his family to Delano. The family left Delano in 1887, moving to the country, returning again in 1893, to remain until 1897, when it moved to Mount Carmel, Pa., where it has since resided. Mr. Moser became a fireman and later an engineer, which position he held until 1928, when he was seriously injured in an automobile accident, as a result of which he was compelled to relinquish his railroad work, after a continuous employment of fifty-five years. He was a passenger engineer for seventeen years and had been tendered the position of road foreman of engines, which he declined. Mr. and Mrs. Moser are at present living in Mount Carmel, as are these others of the family: Carrie, at home; Oliver, (the writer), a lawyer; Ida, (Mrs. J. N. Smith), and Bess, (Mrs. Alfred Gaetz). A daughter, Lillie, (Mrs. W. T. Gerhard), lives in Tamaqua, Pa., and another daughter, Florence, is a supervisor in the Bellevue Hospital in New York City. M. F. Moser is one of five brothers who have been engineers on the Lehigh Valley Railroad, three still being actively so employed.

MOSER, Jacob—came to Delano in the 80's and resided there for several years, moving to the country and later to Weatherly, where he still resides. He was a fireman and engineer for the Lehigh Valley for many years and is still employed at Ashmore for the company. Mrs. Moser died in Weatherly about two years ago. All of the children are still living, most of them in Weatherly.

MOSER, Ephraim—made his home in Delano in 1894, coming from Quakake, Pa. He had been in the employ of the Lehigh Valley Railroad for many years before this. He remained in the town until 1901, when he was transferred to Buffalo, N. Y., where he now lives. He has been an engineer for many years and for a long time has been pulling the Lehigh's crack train, the Black Diamond, between Buffalo and Sayre. Mrs. Moser died in Buffalo, in 1924, as did two daughters: Maude, in 1918, and Grace, in 1918. Mr. Moser has since remarried. The other children are: Anna, (Mrs. John McCall); Henrietta, (Mrs. Frank Krueger); Ruth, (Mrs. George Moseler), and Warren, all of Buffalo.

MOLL, William—located in Delano in 1885, coming from Trenton, Pa. He was a machinist during his residence in the town. He moved to Tamaqua, Pa., in 1899, and has resided there ever since with his family. Mr. Moll was noted as a very fluent and entertaining speaker and humorist, and was often called upon in Delano on public occasions to entertain. All of the family are still living: Mr. and Mrs. Moll, with Harry, Charles, and Esther, (Mrs. Cooper), residing in Tamaqua, Pa., and Hattie, (Mrs. Miller), in Mauch Chunk, Pa.

McAVOY, John—became a resident of Delano many years ago, sometime in the 70's, and was for many years a passenger conductor. His family was very active in the social and civic life of the town during its residence there. The writer has no definite knowledge as to when they left Delano, but it was probably early in the decade 1900-1910. Mr. McAvoy has been dead for many years. Mrs. McAvoy now resides with her son, Eugene, a physician, at Catasauqua, Pa. Another son, Jerry,, who was a practicing physician in Catasauqua, died there in 1930. Bertram died quite a number of years ago. The other children are: Nellie, (Mrs. F. A. Willette), East Orange, N. J., and Edward, an engineer for the Lehigh Valley at Manchester, N. Y.

MILLER, Charles—resided in Delano for many years, coming there early in the 80's. The writer is not able to give much information about them, but one son, Gottlieb, who was a skilled machinist at Delano, has resided in Weatherly for many years, and Fred and Charles, according to the best information available, are also located there. A daughter, Hannah, was a member of the family, but the writer has no record of her present address. Gottlieb has a responsible position as a shop foreman.

MATZ—The Matz family came to Delano from Quakake, Pa., some time in the late 90's. The only members of which the writer has any knowledge at this time are Milton, boilermaker at Delano, now residing in Grier City, Pa., and Robert, residing in Delano. Mrs. Milton Matz is a daughter of Oliver Walbert, a Delano family of long residence.

MINNICH, Edward—made his home in Delano early in the 80's. He married the widow of Fred Payne, a sketch of which family is given later. The Minnich family left Delano about 1892, going to St. Clair, Pa., where they resided until the deaths of Mr. and Mrs. Minnich. Mrs. Minnich has been dead for about ten years, and Mr. Minnich lost his life in an automobile accident in 1926. A son, Roy, who was born in Delano, resides in St. Clair. Mr. Minnich was in the employ of the shops at Delano.

MICHAEL, Harry—moved to Delano from Quakake, Pa., in 1927. He is engaged as a yardmaster for the Lehigh Valley Railroad, and has been in that service for many years. He still lives at Delano with his family. One child, Dorothy, died in Quakake, in 1914, and those still living: Mrs. Eva Phillips, and Mrs. John Weeks, of Quakake, Pa.; Charles P., a clerk, and Margaret M., both of Delano.

NEEB, Martin—was one of the early arrivals in Delano, coming there in 1879. He was at first employed in the home of A. P. Blakslee and in 1880 entered the machine shop as an apprentice and continued to work there as a machinist until 1899, when he moved to Bethlehem, Pa., where he entered the employ of the Bethlehem Steel Company. He remained there until 1903, when he moved to Easton, Pa., where he now resides Mr. Neeb was married in 1886 to Elizabeth Flexer, of Tamaqua, and began housekeeping in the little house that once stood next to the old station. He was always very active in the affairs of the town, especially in church and fraternal circles. He had an active part in enlarging old Union Hall, and was president of the Sunday School Board when he left Delano. The children of the family are: Elvin, merchant in Easton, Pa.; Robert, residing in Easton, and William, in Paterson, N. J. A son, Oscar, died in Delano in 1880.

NEIFERT, Edward—came to Delano early in the 80's, and was in the employ of the Lehigh Valley Railroad as a passenger conductor for many years. He left the town some time early in the 90's, and has been deceased for quite a number of years. He moved to Pottsville, Pa., from Delano, where his widow now resides. Mr. Neifert was one of a family that has had a very active part in the life of Delano, and the operation of the Lehigh Valley Railroad Company.

NEIFERT, Milton—came to Delano in 1879 and worked there in various branches of railroading until 1896, when he moved to Pottsville,

Pa. He was a passenger conductor at the time of his departure. Mrs. Neifert died in Lehighton, Pa., in 1925, at which place Mr. Neifert is now residing. These are the children of the family: Floyd, railroading at Lehighton, Pa.; Bessie, (Mrs. Davis), Bethlehem, Pa., and Marion, (Mrs. Diehl), Allentown, Pa.

NEIFERT, John J.—moved from Quakake to Delano in 1884 and entered the employ of the Lehigh Valley Railroad as a telegrapher and later was advanced to train dispatcher and trainmaster. With the various changes in division headquarters, the nature of his work has changed through the years and he now occupies the position of chief dispatcher at Hazleton, Pa., where he has lived since 1898, when headquarters for the division were moved there. Mrs. Neifert died early in this year, 1932. The children of the family are: Grace, (Mrs. Giles), Orient, Ill.; Blanche, Philadelphia; Pearl, (Mrs. Pollock), Hazleton, Pa., and Dorothea, student at State Teachers' College, West Chester, Pa. The first three daughters were born in Delano. Mr. Neifert was always very active in civic affairs in Delano and the writer is indebted to him for valuable information concerning the early railroad history of the town.

NEIFERT, Albert—has been for many years an engineer for the Lehigh Valley Railroad and came to Delano from Quakake, Pa., in 1897, and still resides in the town. One child, Morrel, died in Delano, in 1905, and the other children are: Wilbur, machinist at Delano; Verda, (Mrs. Bartholomew), Milton, Pa.; Beatrice, secretary, Milton, Pa.

NEIFERT, Charles—came from Quakake, Pa., to Delano in 1899, and resided there until 1912, when he returned to Quakake. He was a section foreman for the Lehigh Valley Railroad for many years. He died in Quakake in 1930, his wife preceding him in death in 1927. The children are: Bertha, (Mrs. John Derr), Delano; Pauline, (Mrs. Edward Applegate), North Hills, Pa.; Joseph, Quakake, Pa., and Winifred, (Mrs. Alfred Lutz), Delano.

NEIFERT, Joseph—is another member of this family that has had a long and honorable record of service with the Lehigh Valley Railroad Company. He has been for many years an engineer. He came from Quakake, Pa., in 1900, and still lives in the town with his family. The writer has no information available as to the various members of the family, their present locations and occupations.

NELSON, Nels—was for many years one of Delano's best-known residents. He had charge of the gardens of the Blakslee family and the beautiful result of his handiwork gave him an outstanding reputation throughout the region. The magnificent gardens created by him made one of Delano's chief attractions and their fame was widespread. Mr. Nelson left Delano early in the 90's and located in Tamaqua, Pa., where he now resides. He has been in the florist business since leaving Delano.

NOONE, Michael—came to Delano from Lost Creek, Pa., July 14, 1917, and still resides in the town. He is employed as a brakeman on the road. Mrs. Noone and two children, Kitty and John, both school children, comprise the rest of the family.

NEARY, Michael—was the head of one of Delano's best-known families. He came to the town from Ireland in the very beginning and his family joined him a little later. He and his family belong to the first family group. He resided in Delano until his death, the exact date of which the writer was not able to ascertain. Mr. Neary was employed in the shops and for a long time had charge of the shop storehouse, in which position he won the respect of men and his employers alike for his strict honesty and efficiency. He assisted in the erection of the shops in 1864. The deceased members of his family are: Patrick, at Delano; John, at New York City; Thomas, at Chicago, Ill., and Bridget, (Mrs. James Connell), at Hazleton, in 1923. Miss Kate, a daughter, is the only one still living, now residing in Scranton, Pa.

OLPP, Charles—became a resident of Delano in 1880, coming from Mahanoy City, Pa. He was employed in the shops as a blacksmith and left Delano in 1891, moving to Barnesville, Pa. Mr. Olpp died in Tamaqua, Pa., in 1923, and three children of the family died in Delano: Elmer, Roy, and William, all in 1884. The other members of the family are: Mrs. Olpp, residing in Lebanon, Pa.; Katie, (Mrs. John Faust), Buffalo, N. Y.; Mrs. Harry Metzger, and Lester Olpp, a machinist, Lebanon, Pa.

OPP, William—was the head of one of Delano's pioneer families, coming to the town in 1866 from Bellville, Ill. He was one of the Lehigh's outstanding engineers during his residence in the town. He died in Delano in 1927, Mrs. Opp having preceded him in death at Delano in 1906. William, Jr., died in Hazleton, Pa., in 1922, and Harry, at Allentown, Pa., in 1919. William, Jr., was also an engineer at Delano, and Harry was a machinist. The children still living are: George E., now an engineer at Delano, having spent his whole life in the town, and Anna, (Mrs. Mahlon Whitebread), Chicago, Ill. Mr. Whitebread is a former Delano boy. George Opp is at present president of the Delano Township School Board.

OWENS, John F.—came to Delano from Ashland, Pa., in 1902. He is an engineer in the service of the Lehigh Valley Railroad and had for a time been road foreman of firemen. His wife is the former Mamie Hartung, who was born in Delano. Two children of the family are deceased: Elmer and James, both dying in Delano, in January, 1911.

PAYNE, Fred—was never a resident of Delano proper, but resided in Park Place and was employed by the Lehigh Valley Railroad as a baggagemaster. He was killed while on duty near Penn Haven early in the 80's, and his family moved to Delano shortly thereafter. Later Mrs. Payne was married to Edward Minnich, a record of whose family is given early in this record. The family left Delano about 1892, moving to St. Clair, where both Mr. and Mrs. Minnich died several years ago. The members of the family are: Walter, a machinist at Wilkes-Barre, Pa.; William Frederick, a machinist at Elizabeth, N. J.; Daniel, a machinist at St. Clair, Pa.; Annie, (Mrs. Thomas Pierce), Milford, Mass. One daughter, Lucia, who was the wife of John Clay, a former Delano boy, has been dead for a number of years.

PACKER, Frank—became a resident of Delano in the early 80's. He was attached to the engineering force of the division offices during his stay in Delano and left the town when the offices were moved in 1898. Mr. Packer at present resides in Allentown, Pa. One son, Ward, is located in Canada, but no information has been furnished as to the present locations of the daughter, Mabel, (Mrs. Turnbach), or the son, Worthington.

PATTERSON, Walter, Sr.—came from Shenandoah, Pa., to Delano in 1890, and has been for many years a conductor on the railroad. He still resides with his family in the old town. Mr. Patterson has always been active in civic and religious life in Delano and has been superintendent of the Sunday School there for a long time. One daughter of the family is deceased: Ethel Patterson, at Delano in 1919. The other members of the family are: Ruth Patterson, Delano; Joanna, (Mrs. Liddicoat), Delano; Mrs. Henry Long, Allentown, Pa.; Warren Patterson, signalman, Delano; Joseph Patterson, towerman, Delano; David Patterson, operator, Delano; James Patterson, student, Delano, and Walter Patterson, cement worker, Amityville, L. I.

PERRY, Henry V.—came to Delano in 1885 from East Mahanoy Junction, Pa., beginning work as a telegrapher and being advanced to trainmaster. He resided in Delano until 1899, when he moved with his family to Tariffville, Conn., where he entered the employ of the New York, New Haven, and Hartford Railroad. He was in the service of this road until his retirement about a year ago, and now resides in Griffins, Conn. Mrs. Perry died in Griffins in 1922. The members of the family are: Bessie, Nellie, Leon, and Leighton, all of whom reside with the father at Griffins, where they operate a farm; George, insurance clerk, Tariffville, Conn.; Herbert, insurance clerk, Hartford, Conn.; Charles, insurance clerk, Simsbury, Conn., and Fred, bank teller, Seattle, Wash. The Perry family was one of the most prominent in Delano during its residence there. Mr. Perry, as noted elsewhere, was leader of the Delano band and the three older sons were members of it—all of them musicians-born. Mrs. Perry was a member of the Kleckner family, of Grier City, where several of her sisters still reside.

PERRY, James—became a resident of Delano early in the 80's, and lived there until some time between 1900 and 1910, when he moved to Hazleton, Pa. He was an engineer on the railroad and still resides in Hazleton. The children of the family are: William, clerk, Hazleton, and Clayton, insurance superintendent, Philadelphia. Harry, another son, lost his life while at work as a car inspector at Delano many years ago. He was married to Annie Fritz, who still lives with her sons in Delano.

PHILLIPS, Edwin—belonged to the old-time families, coming to Delano in 1872 from Wilkes-Barre, Pa. He resided in the town until his death there in 1897. He managed the store at Delano for several years and then was a bookkeeper in the shop office until his death. His family left Delano in 1898, moving to Philadelphia. Mrs. Phillips died there in 1931, as did also two children: Sarah, (Mrs. Howard Bowman), and Fred, who was a business man in the city for many years. Martha, (Mrs. Startman), died in Oglesby, Ill., in 1926. Another daughter, Mary, died in Delano in 1879. These members of the family are living: William, inspector; John, foreman, and Samuel, foreman, all of Philadelphia; Edwin, machinist, Norwood, Pa., and Leroy, foreman, Glenolden, Pa.

PRICE, Charles—was among the early residents of Delano, coming late in the 70's. He was an engineer for many years, or up to the time of his death. The family left Delano some time between 1900 and 1910. Both Mr. and Mrs. Price have been dead for many years, as are also George and Charles. Charles practiced medicine in Philadelphia for many years and was a prominent physician of that city. His widow, who is the former Lizzie Butler, lives in the city with her children. Dr. Price died in 1931. Ivan, the eldest of the family, resides in Tamaqua, Pa., where for many years he was an engineer for the Lehigh and New England Railroad. He has been retired for several years because of ill health. No information has been furnished as to the present location of the daughter, Audrey.

PURCELL, Edward, John and Joseph—three brothers who came to Delano in the 90's and were all employed on the railroad. Edward still resides in Delano, while John, who lived in Frackville for a number of years, died in 1931. His widow is the former Lizzie Reynolds, a daughter of the First Family. The writer has been informed that Joseph Purcell is also deceased, but has no information as to when and where he died.

RAEDER, Fred—came to Delano from Mount Carmel late in the 90's and lived there for several years, employed as a trainman. He later returned to Mount Carmel, where he now resides. His children are all married, one daughter residing in Mount Carmel, and two sons in West Virginia. Mr. Raeder came from a family of musicians in Mount Carmel, and while in Delano had a prominent part in the activities of the Delano band. He was severely injured in the railroad service some years ago, and has not yet been able to follow that work since.

READ, Alvin A.—came from Mahanoy City, Pa., to Delano in 1881. He was roadmaster for the Lehigh Valley Railroad during his residence in Delano and held that position until his death in the town in 1905. Mrs. Read died in Delano in 1887. Augustus, the elder son, who was married to Miss Linda McCarrol, a Delano girl, has been deceased for a number of years, while Alvin A., Jr., married to Miss Katie Becker, also a Delano girl, is now President of the Duquesne Slag Company, of Pittsburgh, Pa., and resides in that city.

RIEGEL, John—made Delano his home in 1900, coming from Grier City, Pa. He was an engineer for the Lehigh Valley Railroad and moved to Weatherly, Pa., in 1911, where he resides at present, still engaged in the same occupation. The members of the family are: Mrs. Riegel, Mrs. Maurice Young, Clara, a bookkeeper, all of Weatherly; Victor, foreman of the gas company at Kearny, N. J.; Ray, a mechanic, Allentown, Pa., and Ruth, a nurse in Philadelphia.

REYNOLDS, Michael—was the head of the first family to settle in Delano permanently. He had charge of the construction of the railroad from Quakake to Delano and westward and first came to the town in 1860. He was superintendent of the construction of the railroad under the contractors, Peter and James Collins. In 1861, he brought his family to Delano and occupied the first permanent residence built there. He continued his connection with the Lehigh Valley Railroad Company as assistant road foreman until 1881, when he was the unfortunate victim of a railroad wreck which occurred on the Mahanoy Branch, between Park Place and Shoemaker's. His family continued its residence in Delano and three of the daughters still make it their home. The eldest daughter, Mrs. Mame Walters, and the eldest son, Thomas, were born before the family came to Delano, but all the rest of the children are Delano-born. Margaret, (Mrs. Clinton Engle), was the first child born in Delano and still lives there, as has been noted elsewhere; Kathryn, (Mrs. Lewis Kesselring), lives in Lansford, Pa.; Annie, (Mrs. Irvin Gouldner), still lives in Delano, while Elizabeth, (Mrs. John Purcell), now resides in Frackville, Pa. Michael and Thomas, the sons, have been dead for many years, also another son, Charles.

RICHARDSON, Thomas—moved from Quakake, Pa., to Delano in 1898, and was employed as a trainman and conductor on the railroad until his death in 1931 in Delano. Mrs. Richardson moved to Philadelphia upon the death of her husband and resides there with a daughter. These children of the family are deceased: Mary, at Delano, in 1918; Ethel, at Delano, in 1913, and Kathryn, at Delano, in 1911. The other children are: Myles, a telegrapher for the Reading Railway at Danville, Pa.; Myra, (Mrs. Fisher), Fountain Springs, Pa.; Gwendolyn, (Mrs. Driver), and Marcella, (Mrs. Davis), both of Philadelphia.

RICHARDSON, John—came to Delano early in the 70's and belonged to one of Delano's old families. He and Mrs. Richardson were known to all Delano people of that period as "Uncle John and Aunt Mary." An excellent likeness of Mrs. Richardson is shown in this book on a group of the J. A. Depew family. Mr. Richardson was employed as an engineer and later engine hostler. Both Mr. and Mrs. Richardson have been dead for some years, Mr. Richardson dying in Delano in 1908, and Mrs. Richardson in Philadelphia, in 1929.

RUNKLE, Charles—came to Delano from Port Carbon early in the 80's, and worked in the shops for many years. He returned to Port Carbon after the shops were closed and still resides there.

RUNKEL, John W.—became a resident of Delano in 1885, coming from Mahanoy City, Pa. He was employed in the carpenter shop and remained in Delano until 1899, when he moved to Port Carbon, Pa., where he died in 1913. Mrs. Runkel lived in Port Carbon, until her death in 1926. The children are: Annie, (widow of H. C. Kimbel), Roselle, N. J., and Edward, a machinist, at Elizabeth, N. J.

RICHARDS, Miss Florence—was a teacher in the public schools of Delano from 1889 until 1902, coming from Minersville, Pa., and returning to her home thereupon resigning from her position in Delano. Miss Richards is at present a resident of Minersville. More extended mention of the important part she had in the religious and educational life of Delano has been made in previous chapters of this book.

REESE, Thomas—has resided in Delano since 1911, when he moved from Trenton, Pa. He is a trainman for the Lehigh Valley Railroad, and is a member of the school board, being vice president at this time. He has been active in the affairs of the town since his residence there. The children of the family are: Mary, graduated from the Delano High School in 1931; Julia, a sophomore in the same school, and Betty, a student, all of Delano.

RIDDLE, Matthew—moved to Delano in 1897, coming from England. He has been in the train service of the railroad for many years. Mrs. Riddle died in Delano in 1926, and the rest of the family still live there, including these children: Ruth, (Mrs. Folweiler); Sarah, (Mrs.

Noone), and Dorothy. Annie, (Mrs. Garber), another daughter, resides in Tamanend, Pa. Mr. Riddle has been a member of the school board for a long time and is at present its secretary.

RYAN, Jerry—was among Delano's first settlers. He lived with his grandmother, Mrs. Cushing, and was one of the eight pupils who attended the first school opened in the town in 1865. He was for many years an engineer and left the town for the West late in the 90's, dying in Chicago in February, 1915. Mrs. Ryan died in Delano in March, 1915. Three children: Julia, Thomas and Vincent, died in Delano in infancy. Two sons are still living in Delano: John, an engineer for the Lehigh Valley, and Jerry, occupying the same kind of position with the company. They are both married.

SHAFER, Josiah—came to Delano from Mauch Chunk in 1872, making his family one of the pioneers. He started work as a trainman and was advanced to engineer, which position he held until his death in 1888, in Delano. Mrs. Shafer died in Delano in 1910, and a daughter, Katie, died there in 1879. The other members of the family are: Samuel, a machinist at Delano, residing in Grier City, Pa.; Harry, retired, Trenton, Pa.; Harriet, (Mrs. C. E. Depew), Schuylkill Haven, Pa.; Josiah, Jr., clerk, Hazleton, Pa., and Robert, machinist, Bethlehem, Pa. This family always had a prominent place in the affairs of the community. Harry was for many years Justice of the Peace and a member of the school board, and still retains his old interest in the town.

SHAFER, John—was one of the old-time residents of Delano, coming from West Penn Township. His connection with the town goes back to the early 70's. He at one time resided in the building that was Delano's first school house. No definite information is available as to when Mr. Shafer moved from Delano.

SHAUP, Jonas—became a resident of Delano in 1874, another pioneer. He was a railroad man all during his residence in the town, having been a passenger engineer for many years until his tragic death near Pottsville, Pa., in 1897, when his train collided with some cars that had run from a siding onto the main track. Mrs. Shaup died in Scranton, Pa., in 1900, as did a daughter, May. Lloyd died in Delano in 1907, and Annie in Pine Grove, Pa., in 1908. The other members of the family are: Clara, (Mrs. Lewis Brill), Delano; Harry, an engineer, Delano; Lewis, fireman, Delano, and Edward, California. Mrs. Brill, the eldest daughter, resides in the home formerly occupied by her parents, and has had a continuous residence in that house of over fifty years.

SCHROPE, James M.—took charge of the Delano schools as principal in 1892, coming from Tower City, Pa. He was one of the most prominent citizens of the town during his residence there and left an influence for good that has not lost its force to this day. He organized the first High School and placed the school system on a modern foundation. He and Mrs. Schrope were very active in the religious life of the community. He resigned his position in 1906, and went to Pottsville, where his work is located at present. He has been assistant county superintendent of schools of Schuylkill County for many years. His home is in Hegins, Pa., the town of his birth, where he and Mrs. Schrope occupy a beautiful modern home. During their residence in Delano, a brother of Mr. Schrope, William, lived in his home, coming there in 1894, and graduating from the high school in 1897. William later graduated from the West Chester Normal School and taught school for several years, later locating in Anderson, Ind., where he lives at this time, employed as a draftsman in an automobile factory there. He married Miss Mann, of Bangor, Pa., and has a fine family of five children and a charming wife. His eldest son is preparing for the Lutheran ministry, and all of the children are receiving advanced educational training. Miss Blanche Yohe, a relative of Mrs. Schrope, was also a member of the household for several years, graduating from the Delano High School in 1904. Miss Yohe, (now Mrs. Lewis), resides in Port Carbon, Pa.

SCHULER, John and Elizabeth—were among Delano's first families, coming to the town in 1869. Mr. Schuler worked at Delano for many years, finally moving to Quakake, Pa., where he died in 1928. Elizabeth Schuler Walton continued her residence in Delano until her death there in 1918. A son, James R. Walton, left Delano in 1903, and moved to Lofty, Pa. He was employed for a number of years as section foreman for the Lehigh Valley Railroad and became interested in county politics, in which field he has achieved much success, having at different times held most of the county offices in Schuylkill County. He was warden of the prison for several terms, prothonotary, county commissioner, and had several clerkships in the various offices before aspiring to office himself. He has been located in Pottsville, Pa., for many years. He has several sons, one a dentist in Pottsville. A brother, George, who lived all his life in Delano, was killed on the railroad several years ago. A sister, Kathryn, (Mrs. Ramsey), has resided in Reading, Pa., since 1903. Mrs. Elizabeth Schuler Walton was known to every resident in Delano over a period of many years as one of the most kind-hearted women in the town. No case of sickness or distress in the place ever occurred without an offer of help from her and countless were the times she gave this needed help.

SINGLEY, Maurice—began his connection with the Delano school system as assistant principal in 1905, being made principal a few years later, a position that he still holds. He came from Zion's Grove, Pa. The Delano schools under Mr. Singley's capable supervision have steadily advanced through the years to their present high place in the very front rank of Pennsylvania schools. During his service, the capacity of the building was doubled and the grading of the schools brought to the highest level. Elsewhere is a detailed account of the high place occupied by these schools and the part Mr. Singley had in developing them. Mr. and Mrs. Singley are both very active in the civic and religious life of Delano. One son, Donald, died in Delano in 1917, another son, Eugene, is associated with the Proctor and Gamble Company, at Staten Island, N. Y., as a chemical engineer, and the other children of the family are students. Mrs. Singley is a member of the Delano reunion committee, and Mr. Singley was a member of the building committee in charge of the erection of the new church building.

STROHL, William—made his home in Delano early in the 90's. He was for many years an engineer, moving to Hazleton, Pa., in 1900. He has been incapacitated for work for a number of years because of illness. The family is still living in Hazleton. Mrs. Strohl is the former Mary Wagner, a daughter of one of the old-time Delano families. There are two children: Clarence, painter, and Russell, miner, both of Hazleton, Pa.

SWANK, Josiah—established one of Delano's first families. He came to the town from Mauch Chunk, Pa., in April, 1867, and in October of the same year brought his bride, Anne Jane Porter, from Mauch Chunk to the new town in the wilderness. Mr. Swank during all his residence in Delano had a most prominent place in its industrial, civic and religious life. He was a foreman in the machine shops, the first superintendent of the Sunday School organized in the 60's, an interest that he never relinquished during all his life there, and in all other activities for the betterment of the town, he was always in the forefront. In 1899 the family left Delano for Downingtown, Pa., where Mr. Swank resided until his death in 1928. A public meeting of the people of Delano to express the town's esteem for Mr. and Mrs. Swank and their children, was held before their departure and a Morris chair and Bible were presented to him, with resolutions of respect that were adopted at the meeting. In Downingtown, Mr. Swank engaged in the coal and ice business and was one of the most successful business men of the community for many years. He was active in the work of the Presbyterian church in that town, and was an elder for twenty-four years. Mrs. Swank died there in 1922. Two members of the family, Leroy, and Anna, (Mrs. Leon Bailey), still have their homes in Downingtown, while Robert has been one of Schuylkill County's outstanding lawyers for many years, being located at Mahanoy City, Pa. Mrs. Robert Swank is the former Miss Ida Hepler, an instructor in the Delano schools in the 90's. The writer is particularly indebted to Mrs. Bailey and to Mr. and Mrs. Robert Swank for much assistance in compiling these records.

SCHLIER, Daniel—and family were residents of Delano for many years, coming early in the 80's and residing there until some time after 1900, when they moved to Lehighton, Pa., where they still reside. Mr. Schlier has been a freight conductor for the Lehigh Valley Railroad for many years. No information as to the present locations of the children is furnished, but several of the sons reside in Lehighton, Pa.

SCHLIER, John—was one of Delano's pioneers. He was for a long time supervisor of the township and it was the writer's privilege to work under him for a short time. He died many years ago. His family was prominent in the affairs of the town. Two grandchildren, Albert and Bertha, were members of his household.

SCHLIER, Pierce—was another of the Schlier family who had a long and prominent residence in Delano. He was a passenger conductor and moved to Hazleton, Pa., sometime after 1900, where he remained until his death several years ago. Mrs. Schlier has been deceased for a number of years. The children of the family are: Roy, Blanche M., Mary, (Mrs. Boomer), and George, all residing in Hazleton, Pa., and Dr. Earle, a physician at Bethlehem, Pa.

SCHLIER, Frank—was another member of this family that made his home in Delano for several years during the 90's. He is at present a resident of Sayre, Pa., where he is a foreman in the shops of the Lehigh Valley Railroad.

SCHLIER, Albert—is a native of Delano and, with his cousin, Bertha Schlier, (Mrs. Robert Shafer), also born in Delano, lived with their grandfather, John Schlier. Mr. Schlier left Delano quite a number of years ago for Hazleton, Pa., where he is now located, and he runs an engine for the Lehigh Valley Railroad. Mrs. Shafer has resided in Bethlehem, Pa., for many years.

STEWART, Claude—came to Delano from Quakake, Pa., in 1900, and resided there for a number of years, later moving to Hazleton, Pa., where he now resides, an employee of the Lehigh Valley Railroad. His wife, who was Emma Schultz, was for many years housekeeper in the family of A. A. Read.

STIEGERWALT, William—worked in the Delano shops early in the 90's, and resided there for a number of years. He is now located in Frackville, Pa., and is a machinist in the Reading shops in Mahanoy Plane, Pa.

SLYKER, Charles—came to Delano from Quakake, Pa., late in the 90's, and was an engineer for the Lehigh Valley Railroad there for many years, later moving to Hazleton, Pa., where he now resides, still an engineer for the Lehigh. A daughter, Henrietta, (Mrs. James Shafer), resides in Rochester, N. Y. No information has been furnished about the other members of the family.

SCOTT—The Scott family was a prominent one in Delano in the 80's, and left there some time early in the 90's. The only member of the family of which the writer has knowledge is William, who now resides in Pottsville, Pa., and is employed as a machinist for the Reading Railway at Mahanoy Plane, Pa.

SYMONS, George—was a long-time resident of Delano, coming there some time early in the 80's and remaining until about 1910, when he moved with his family to Pottsville, Pa. Mrs. Symons and a son died there several years ago, but the writer has no information as to Mr. Symon's present location. He was a machinist in the shops at Delano.

SMITH, John Wesley—and family were among the prominent people of Delano over a long period. Mr. Smith came there some time early in the 80's, and was a foreman in the machine shop department. The family left the town some time after the shops were closed and Mr. Smith has been deceased for many years. A daughter, Lizzie, who taught music in Delano and vicinity for a long time, died in Hazleton, Pa., several years ago. Millie, (Mrs. Will Perry), who taught in the schools of Delano for a number of years, now resides in Hazleton, where she was on the teaching corps in the schools for a long time. Mary also resides in Hazleton, as does Kate, (Mrs. Alex Sterling). The sons are: John, a machinist, at Bethlehem, Pa.; George, at Palmerton, Pa.; Will, a machinist, Altoona, Pa. Mrs. John Smith, who was the former Ida Kistler, a teacher in the Delano schools, died in Bethlehem several years ago.

SMITH, Richard—resided in Delano for a number of years in the 90's. He was employed as a railroader. His wife was a daughter of John Schaffer, a resident of Delano at that time. Mr. Smith left Delano for Mount Carmel, Pa., late in the 90's, and has been deceased for several years. His widow now resides on a farm near Mount Carmel, and a son, Leonard, is a mine foreman at Mount Carmel. Information about the other members of the family is not available.

SCHAFFER, John—came to Delano early in the 80's and was employed in the shops for many years. He resided on Hazle Street, and the writer believes he died while a resident of Delano. A daughter, Mrs. Richard Smith, resides near Mount Carmel, Pa.

SHILEY, Hiram—and family were pioneer residents of Delano. Mr. Shiley came from Mount Carmel, Pa., early in the 80's, and was employed on the railroad. He lost his life on the railroad many years ago. His family later moved from town, Mrs. Shiley and two daughters: Lottie,

(Mrs. Katzenmoyer), and Edna, (Mrs. Miller), now residing in Reading, Pa., and the son, John, being a yardmaster for the Lehigh and New England Railroad at Pen Argyl, Pa.

STURTEVANT, Benjamin—made his home in Delano for a number of years in the late 90's. He was a foreman of the shop forces during his residence there. He moved to Bethlehem, Pa., where he and his family now reside.

SPRAGUE, William—came to Delano from the West during the middle 90's and was employed on the railroad for several years. He later moved to Allentown, Pa. The writer does not have information as to whether he is still living, but Mrs. Sprague now resides in Allentown, Pa. A son, William Long, is a conductor on the railroad at Hazleton, Pa.

SWANK, William—lived in Delano in the 90's and was an engineer for the Lehigh Valley Railroad. His wife was Frances Whitebread, of Delano. The family moved to Hazleton, Pa., in 1904, and in 1905 Mr. Swank was killed when his train ran away on the Weatherly hill and jumped the track at Black Creek Junction. Mrs. Swank now resides in Newark, N. J., with the following children: Leonard, Myrtle, and Romaine.

SHAUP, Harry—is a native of Delano, being born there fifty years ago. He is a son of Jonas Shaup, one of Delano's old-time engineers. Harry followed family tradition and has been an engineer for many years. He married Bertha Depew, daughter of William Depew, who is also a lifelong resident of the town. The children of the family are: James, owner of the drug store at Delano, Stanley, signalman, and Ruth, sophomore in Delano High School, all residing at home.

SHAUP, Lewis—is another son of Jonas Shaup who was born in Delano and has made it his home ever since. He also is a railroad man. His wife is the daughter of Oliver Walbert, and has resided in Delano for most of her life. There are several children, all at home.

SHEA, Daniel—came to Delano from Weatherly, Pa., in 1915. He was employed as a trainman and died in Delano in 1919. His wife is the former May Walters, daughter of Mr. and Mrs. Ben Walters. One son is deceased, Eugene, at Delano, in 1917. The widow and these children still reside in Delano: Claire, Dorothy, and Charles.

History of Delano

STAUFFER, Silas—moved from Audenried, Pa., to Delano in 1905, and has resided there ever since. He is an engineer on the railroad.

STRAUB, William, Sr.—has lived in Delano since 1913, coming from Quakake, Pa. He is an engineer. The children of the family are: William, Jr., brakeman; Melvin, miner; Florence, all of Delano, and Helen, (Mrs. Smith), Tamaqua, Pa.

SHARKEY, William—has been a resident of Delano for many years and has been prominent in the civic and other activities of the town. He has been a railroad man all the years of his residence in the town.

TAYLOR, William—was for many years a resident of Delano. He was an engineer for the Lehigh Valley, and lost his life in a railroad wreck while so employed. His wife is the former Clara Hein, (now Mrs. Mills), a resident of Delano many years ago.

TAYLOR, Harry—was a railroad conductor in Delano for many years. He came to Delano from Tamaqua, Pa., in 1890. He moved to Easton, Pa., in 1916. Until shortly before his death he was conductor on the Easton-Pittsburgh Express, between Easton and Mount Carmel. His widow is the former Katie Houser, who still resides in Easton with her family. One son, Harry, Jr., died in Easton in 1930. The children living are: Dorothy, (Mrs. Kiefer); Marian, (Mrs. Scott), and E. Lawrence Taylor, all of Easton.

THAMARUS, Philip—was the head of one of Delano's pioneer families, coming there from Tamaqua, Pa., in 1877. He was an engineer for the Lehigh Valley Railroad for many years, being in passenger service for a long time. He moved to Lehighton, Pa., in 1899, and remained there until his death in 1906. The family later moved to Allentown, Pa., where Mrs. Thamarus died in 1924. The children: Katie, (Mrs. Llewellyn Bannan), and Edward, who is a machinist, both reside in Allentown, Pa. Edward's wife is the former Zillah Fritz, a native of Delano.

TROUT, William, Sr.—came to Delano from Quakake, Pa., late in the 90's. He was an engineer for many years and up to the time of his death at Delano some years ago. Mrs. Trout has been deceased for a number of years. A son, William, is a resident of Delano and employed on the railroad. A daughter, Annie, (widow of Milton Beltz), also resides there. Alfred, another son, is a railroad man at Weatherly, Pa.

THOMPSON, James—moved from Hazleton to Delano in 1929, and still resides there. He is a signal maintainer for the railroad company. Besides Mrs. Thompson, the family includes a son, James, Jr., who resides at home.

VAN SANT, Homer—came from Pottgrove, Pa., to Delano in 1910, where he was employed until 1924 as a fireman on the railroad. He moved to Hazleton, Pa., at that time, where he has since resided. He now holds an executive position with the Brotherhood of Locomotive Firemen and Engineers and his office in that capacity is located in St. Louis, Mo.

WAGNER, George William—came from New Market, N. J., to Delano in 1879, another of the pioneers. He was employed in the paint shops during his residence, which continued until 1900, when he moved to Hampton, Va., where he remained until his death in 1911. Mrs. Wagner died in Delano in 1885. The children of the family are: The Rev. Dr. Frederick R. Wagner, now pastor of St. John's Lutheran Church at Martinsburg, W. Va.; Wallace Wagner, division chief accountant for the Lehigh Valley Railroad, located at Easton, Pa., and Mary, (Mrs. William Strohl), residing at Hazleton, Pa.

WALLAUER, William—belongs to the pioneers, coming to Delano in 1878 from Tamaqua, Pa. He was a railroad man during his residence in the town, which terminated in 1909, when he moved to Harrisburg, Pa., with his family. He still resides there. Mrs. Wallauer died in Delano in 1905, as did three others of the household in the same place: Samuel in 1887; Clara, in 1888, and Mrs. Mary Mace in 1888. These children are still living: Mrs. John Zerbe, Harrisburg, Pa.; Mrs. William Houser, Linglestown, Pa., and Charles, a trainman for the Reading Railway, Catawissa, Pa. William Houser is a former Delano resident.

WEAVER, Charles—first made his home in Delano in 1880, coming from Port Carbon, Pa. He was a machinist and resided in the town until 1898, when he moved to Grier City, Pa., where he remained until his death in 1902. Mrs. Weaver died in Grier City in 1906. Three children are deceased: Ada, (Mrs. A. E. Bachert), at Tyrone, Pa., in 1921; Elmer, at Connellsville, Pa., in 1922, and John, at Buffalo, N. Y., in 1924. One daughter, Mary, (Mrs. J. W. Raudman), is now living at Connellsville, Pa.

WENTZ, William—was a resident of Delano for many years, coming there late in the 70's. He was an engineer and his family was one of the prominent ones of the community. Mr. Wentz died in Delano several years ago and Mrs. Wentz has been dead for a number of years. A

History of Delano

daughter, Susie, has been dead for many years, and another daughter, Ella Righter, (Mrs. Nels Hansen), died several years ago. There are no members of this Wentz family surviving.

WENTZ, Frank—was another prominent resident of Delano for years. He came there in the 70's, and for a long time was a passenger conductor. He left the town sometime subsequent to 1900, and moved to Allenwood, Pa., where he remained until his death about five years ago. Mrs. Wentz died in Allenwood some time later. The only other member of this family, a niece, Emma Faust, (widow of Harry Zimmerman), who lived with them at Delano, died in Allenwood in 1931. She had one daughter, Grace, (Mrs. Gleason Fullmer), who resides in Milton, Pa.

WENTZ, Elmer—came to Delano from Mahanoy City, Pa., in 1913, and lived in the town until 1930, when he moved to Norristown, Pa., where he now resides. He was a trainman while residing in Delano. One son, Elmer, Jr., died in Delano in 1919. The other members of the family are: Mrs. Wentz, Charles H., Betty J., Marie and Lydia, all of whom reside at home.

WERNER, A. L.—has been one of the best-known men in Delano since he arrived there in 1887, coming from Lansford, Pa. He is still prominent in the affairs of the town, his regular occupation being towerman for the Lehigh Valley Railroad, and his avocation being that of Justice of the Peace, an office that he has held with distinction for the past twelve years. He attained a reputation as an amateur photographer of note, a sample of his work being shown in a previous chapter—the photograph of the family of John Mack, taken in 1887. Mr. and Mrs. Werner and one daughter, Marian, reside on Hazle Street, in the old town, and a daughter, Sara, (Mrs. Walker), lives in Allentown, Pa., and another, Helene, (Mrs. Blew), in Brooklyn, N. Y. Mr. Werner is descended from distinguished German ancestry, his great-grandfather having been a world-famous mineralogist in Alsace-Lorraine years ago.

WHITEBREAD, Mrs. Lucinda—moved to Delano from Upper Lehigh, Pa., in 1884, being then the widow of Mahlon Whitebread. She was a housekeeper for George W. Wagner for several years and was later married to William Scheckler, after which she moved to Quakake, Pa., returning to Delano again in 1886, where she resided until her death in 1890. Mr. Scheckler was later killed on the railroad in 1891, just east of Delano. The Scheckler children are: Esther, (Mrs. Thomas Carr), Waynesville, O., and Ralph, of Philadelphia. The members of the Whitebread family are: Frances, (widow of William Swank), now living in Newark, N. J.; Mary Ann, (Mrs. Winebert Flexer), Quakake, Pa.; David, machinist, Hazleton, Pa.; William Edgar, railroader, Chicago;

Mahlon, a railroader in Chicago, Ill. One son, Philip, was killed on the railroad near Shenandoah, Pa., in 1894. He was yardmaster for the Lehigh Valley Railroad at the time. Mrs. Swank's husband was also killed on the railroad in 1905. Mahlon's wife is the former Annie Opp, a Delano-born girl.

WHITEBREAD, Mahlon—came to Delano from Hazleton, Pa., in 1900, and was a railroad conductor there until 1906, when he moved to Pottsville, Pa. He later moved with his family to Chicago, where he now resides, still in the railroad business. Mrs. Whitebread, formerly Annie Opp, was born in Delano. The children are: Elwood, an accountant; Emily, (Mrs. John Winks), and Evelyn, (Mrs. Earl Bringe), all of Chicago.

WITMAN, Charles—came from Barnesville, Pa., to Delano in 1883, being employed in the blacksmith shop there until he left Delano in 1899. He moved to New Ringgold, Pa., where he has resided since. Mrs. Witman died in New Ringgold in 1910. Mr. Witman is now in the milling business. One son, Edgar F., has been an accountant in Philadelphia for many years.

WYNN, George—belonged to one of Delano's first families. He settled in the town in 1867, coming from Minersville, Pa. He remained a resident of the town until 1899, when he moved with his family to Ashley, Pa., where he remained until his death in 1907. He was foreman of the blacksmith shop for the greater part of his Delano residence. Mrs. Wynn died in Ashley in 1910. One daughter, Bessie, (Mrs. William Rupp), died in Hazleton, Pa., in 1919. The other children are: Rachel, (Mrs. Harris), Bethlehem, Pa.; George, Jr., blacksmith, Undilla, N. Y.; William, machinist, Ashley, Pa., and Lydia, (Mrs. Everett), Wilkes-Barre, Pa. This family had a very prominent part in the activities of Delano over a period of many years. Will, one of the sons, was a noted bicycle racer in the 90's.

WANAMAKER, Jacob—was a passenger conductor on the Lehigh Valley Railroad in Delano during the 80's. He came to the town some time during that decade. He died while the family resided in Delano and his widow later married a man named Henry and moved to Mount Carmel, Pa. Mrs. Henry has been dead for several years. The daughters are: Carrie, (Mrs. C. Wesley Rowe), Bayside, L. I., and Emily, (Mrs. Ralph Weaver), Sunbury, Pa.

WHITEHEAD, Charles—is another of the first family group. He came to Delano early in its history and was for many years a foreman in the machine shops. He moved to Altoona, Pa., and after several years returned to Delano and remained there until the removal of the shops, in

1899, when he moved to Weatherly, Pa., where he later died. Mrs. Whitehead has been dead for many years. Two sons, Harry and Edward, are residents of Altoona, Pa., both employed in the Pennsylvania Railroad shops at that place.

WATKINS, Lee—has been a resident of Delano since 1915, coming there from Pottsville, Pa. He is employed as a boilermaker.

WALBERT, Oliver—has resided in Delano for more than thirty years. He is employed as a towerman for the Lehigh Valley Railroad. His children are all married and, with two exceptions, are residents of Delano. One daughter, Helen, (Mrs. Charles Collings), is a member of the Delano reunion committee. The members of the family have been prominent in Delano affairs for many years.

ZIMMERMAN, D. W.—is entitled to a place among Delano's first families, as is also Mrs. Zimmerman. He came to Delano late in the 60's, while his wife, then Miss McCarroll, located there about 1867. Mr. Zimmerman was a machinist during his residence in Delano and he and his family left Delano when the shops were closed and moved to a farm near Shickshinny, Pa., where they lived until recently, when Mr. and Mrs. Zimmerman and their son, Al, moved to a location near Berwick, and resided with a daughter, Linda, (Mrs. Frank Robbins), at which place Mr. Zimmerman died in 1931, shortly after the reunion in Delano. Mrs. Zimmerman and Al still reside with the daughter. The children of the family deceased are: Harry, who was killed at Quakake, Pa., on the railroad while at his work as a car inspector, and two children who died in infancy in Delano. The other members of the family are: Al, Berwick, Pa.; Robert, Wilkes-Barre, Pa.; Bertha, (Mrs. Albert Cadwalader), Larksville, Pa.; Evan, Archbald, Pa.; Linda, (Mrs. Frank Robbins), Berwick, Pa. Mr. and Mrs. Zimmerman were married in Delano in 1874, and the family was always prominent in the social life of the town.

ZIMMERMAN, Washington—was a resident of Delano for many years in the early 80's. He was a railroader, but no information is available as to when he left Delano or where he or his family may now be located.

ZIMMERMAN, Isaac—resided in Delano for many years, being a railroad man. He now lives in Lehighton, Pa., being still in the employ of the Lehigh Valley Railroad.

ZIMMERMAN, Harry E.—moved from Quakake, Pa., to Delano in 1919, and still resides there. He is a conductor for the Lehigh Valley Railroad. The other members of his family, in addition to Mrs. Zimmerman, are: Harry and Jane, a school teacher, both at Delano, Pa.

HISTORY OF DELANO

The following supplemental list is made up of the names of the present residents of Delano. The writer feels that such a list will be interesting to former residents of the town and, also, that it should be included in this book for its historical value.

No biographical facts are given here, as all family information, so far as furnished the historian, was set out in the record preceding this. It will undoubtedly be a matter of much interest to former residents of Delano to note the many familiar names still to be found in the present-day Delano roster. Some of these folks are children of the old-timers and many of them grand-children. Only the names of the heads of families are stated.

Robert Anthony
Robert Applegate
Ralph Applegate
Mrs. Milton Beltz
Lewis Brill
Mrs. Lucetta Bretz
Frank Bretz
Oscar Bretz
Adolph Bones
Mrs. Sallie Boughner
Clarence Bachert
Harry Boughner
John Becker
Joseph Bowman
George Beers
Arthur Blew
Mrs. Verna Blackwell
Mrs. William Cauley
Edward Cauley
Joseph Cauley
Frank Carl
John Collins
Mrs. Cowley
Charles Collings
Metro Garfchak
John Derr
Samuel Deeble
Charles Donat

James Doyle
Michael DeJohn
Thomas DeFrehn
Ephraim Davis
Fred Diefenderfer
Mrs. Elizabeth Depew
Frank Daughterty
Raymond Dietz
Elmer Dietrick
John Dirgis
Samuel Dudra
Metro Dotsko
Mrs. Sophia Dudra
Harry Edinger
August Edinger
Mrs. Clinton Engle
James Engle
Charles Engle
Harry Engle
Mrs. Olive Edwards
Frank Edinger
William England
William Ecker
Walter Eisenbach
Harry Eisenbach
George Folweiler
Harold Folweiler
Henry Faust

U. G. Fetterman
Charles Fetterman
Harry Folweiler
Thomas Folweiler
Joseph Gothie
Irvin Gouldner
Wilbur Gouldner
Lewis Guldner
Arthur Gregor
Robert Gasser
John Houser
Robert Houser
John Herman, Sr.
John Herman, Jr.
George Hofmann
Charles Hofmann
William Hinkle
David Hess
Mrs. Sarah Hartzel
John Heckman
William Hess
Jacob Hess
John Hentosh
Mike Hentosh
Garfield James
William Jones
Henry Klock
O. D. Kistler

Louis Kistler
Robert Kahley
John Korinchock
Steve Kotch
Matthew Kichula
John Kureychack
Wassil Korinchock
Metro Kruka
Albert Levey
Alfred Lutz
John Lawczak
Michael McCarron
John McAndrew
John Morgans
William Maurey
A. Merriam
Harry Michael
John McAndrew, Jr.
Robert Matz
Carl Maurey
Mike Mogish
Paul Morba
Harry Mocknick
John Mogish
Joseph Neifert
Albert Neifert
Wilbur Neifert
Michael Noone

John Owens
George Opp
Harry Osenbach
Mrs. Annie Perry
Ronald Perry
Walter Patterson
Edward Purcell
Harry Perry
Warren Patterson
John Ryan
Jerry Ryan
William Rhoads
Samuel Rhoads
Henry Reinmiller
Thomas Reeves
Mrs. William Reeves
Ronald Reese
Harvey Redka
Matthew Riddle
John Rysack
Paul Radick
Reuben Steiner
William Sharkey
Clark Schuman
Mrs. May Shea
Mrs. Sophia Schuler
Mrs. Emma Spencer
Harry Shaup

Lewis Shaup
William Straub, Sr.
William Straub, Jr.
John Spaar
Maurice Singley
Silas Stauffer
Peter Stahl
Joseph Schilling
Melvin Straub
Harry Spaar
Reuben Steiner, Jr.
William Trout
Joseph Tarn
James Thompson
Pius Trently
Daniel Thomas
James Taylor
James Wetzel
Lee Watkins
James Warntz
Oliver Walbert
Albert Werner
Mrs. Emma Wistler
Joseph Wazno
Anthony Yarnall
Harry Zimmerman
William Zimmerman
Marvin Zimmerman

www.ingramcontent.com/pod-product-compliance
Lightning Source LLC
Chambersburg PA
CBHW062002220426
43662CB00010B/1199